But You Don't Look Arab

But You Don't Look Arab

And

OTHER TALES

of

UNBELONGING

HALA GORANI

hachette
BOOKS

NEW YORK

Hachette Books
Hachette Book Group
1290 Avenue of the Americas
New York, NY 10104
HachetteBooks.com
Twitter.com/HachetteBooks
Instagram.com/HachetteBooks

First Edition: February 2024

Published by Hachette Books, an imprint of Hachette Book Group, Inc. The Hachette Books name and logo is a trademark of the Hachette Book Group.

The Hachette Speakers Bureau provides a wide range of authors for speaking events. To find out more, go to hachettespeakersbureau.com or email HachetteSpeakers@hbgusa.com.

Books by Hachette Books may be purchased in bulk for business, educational, or promotional use. For information, please contact your local bookseller or Hachette Book Group Special Markets Department at: special.markets@hbgusa.com.

The publisher is not responsible for websites (or their content) that are not owned by the publisher.

Print book interior design by Sheryl Kober.

Library of Congress Control Number: 2023948307

ISBNs: 978-0-306-83164-5 (hardcover); 978-0-306-83166-9 (ebook)

Printed in the United States of America
LSC-C
Printing 1, 2023

For my mother

Contents

Contents

Contents

Author's Note

This book is the result of independent research and historian interviews. It is also the fruit of many hours of conversations with members of the Gorani family, on the maternal side of my family tree. My mother, Nour, has been an invaluable asset throughout the process, as she helped translate my grandfather Assad Gorani's autobiography from Arabic and possesses a precise and detailed memory of Aleppo during the 1950s and 1960s, providing me with firsthand accounts of that era. I am also fortunate that her three siblings—two older sisters and a younger brother—were able to contribute their own recollections.

The parts of the book that cover modern-day events are based on my own childhood memories, hundreds of pages of notes taken during my years working as a journalist for CNN, and, when possible, are fact-checked by cross-referencing my recollection of events with the people involved.

Though all the stories in this book are based in fact, some names and details have been changed to protect the privacy and/or identity of certain individuals.

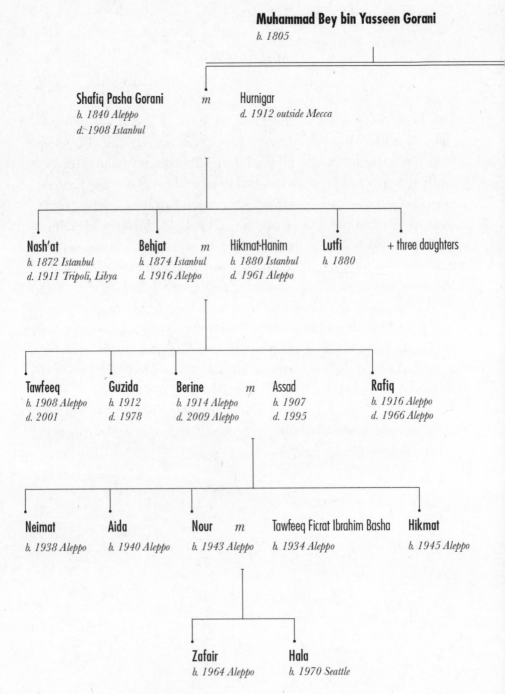

Muhammad Bey bin Yasseen Gorani
b. 1805

Shafiq Pasha Gorani   *m*   Hurnigar
b. 1840 Aleppo   *d. 1912 outside Mecca*
d. 1908 Istanbul

Nash'at   **Behjat**   *m*   **Hikmat-Hanim**   **Lutfi**   + three daughters
b. 1872 Istanbul   *b. 1874 Istanbul*   *b. 1880 Istanbul*   *b. 1880*
d. 1911 Tripoli, Libya   *d. 1916 Aleppo*   *d. 1961 Aleppo*

Tawfeeq   **Guzida**   **Berine**   *m*   **Assad**   **Rafiq**
b. 1908 Aleppo   *b. 1912*   *b. 1914 Aleppo*   *b. 1907*   *b. 1916 Aleppo*
d. 2001   *d. 1978*   *d. 2009 Aleppo*   *d. 1995*   *d. 1966 Aleppo*

Neimat   **Aida**   **Nour**   *m*   Tawfeeq Ficrat Ibrahim Basha   **Hikmat**
b. 1938 Aleppo   *b. 1940 Aleppo*   *b. 1943 Aleppo*   *b. 1934 Aleppo*   *b. 1945 Aleppo*

Zafair   **Hala**
b. 1964 Aleppo   *b. 1970 Seattle*

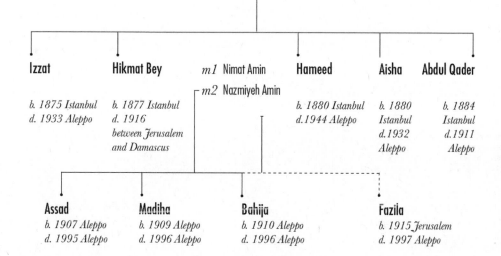

Husni Bey Gorani
b. 1845 Aleppo
d. 1920 Aleppo

m   **Abrutar**

Izzat

b. 1875 Istanbul
d. 1933 Aleppo

Hikmat Bey

b. 1877 Istanbul
d. 1916
between Jerusalem
and Damascus

m1 Nimat Amin
m2 Nazmiyeh Amin

Hameed

b. 1880 Istanbul
d.1944 Aleppo

Aisha

b. 1880
Istanbul
d.1932
Aleppo

Abdul Qader

b. 1884
Istanbul
d.1911
Aleppo

Assad
b. 1907 Aleppo
d. 1995 Aleppo

Madiha
b. 1909 Aleppo
d. 1996 Aleppo

Bahija
b. 1910 Aleppo
d. 1996 Aleppo

Fazila
b. 1915 Jerusalem
d. 1997 Aleppo

Time Line of Key Events

1909	Sultan Abdul Hamid II deposed
1923	French mandate for Syria and Lebanon comes into effect
1925–1927	Great Syrian Revolt against French mandate
1946	Syria gains independence
1948	State of Israel declared, First Arab-Israeli War
1949	The first of several coups that destabilize Syria
1952	Revolution in Egypt; monarchy overthrown
1956	Suez Canal Crisis
1958	Creation of United Arab Republic formed by the union of Syria and Egypt
1961	United Arab Republic dissolved following coup in Syria
1967	Third Arab-Israeli War
1970	Hafez al-Assad assumes power in Syria
1991	First Gulf War
2000	Bashar al-Assad assumes power in Syria
2000	George W. Bush elected US president
2001	9/11 attacks, US invades Afghanistan

2003	US invades Iraq, Second Gulf War
2005	Syrian occupation troops withdraw from Lebanon
2006	Israel-Hezbollah War
2008	Barack Obama elected US president
2011	Arab Spring uprisings in Egypt, Syria, Bahrain, and Yemen
2011	End of US combat operations in Iraq
2013	Suspected chemical attack on civilians in Ghouta, a Damascus suburb
2014	ISIS proclaims caliphate in parts of Syria and Iraq
2014	Abdel Fattah el-Sisi assumes power in Egypt
2015	Russia launches first air strikes in Syria
2015	More than a million refugees, most of them Syrians, arrive on European shores
2016	Donald Trump elected US president
2020	Beirut port explosion
2023	Turkey-Syria earthquake
2023	Syria readmitted into the Arab League

But You Don't Look Arab

Part 1

"You Don't Even Look Arab"

The crowd of journalists and onlookers gathered around the ruins of the Napoli Inn hotel spoke in hushed tones. We had been told to be quiet so that rescuers could hear the tapping coming from within the building's wreckage. News of the operation's progress was whispered, traveling from mouths to expectant ears like a secret, a precious message that only a select few were chosen to hear. "They're saying they'll pull him out in five minutes," my producer told me. I was on assignment for CNN covering the January 2010 earthquake in Haiti, and I would soon break the news on air that a survivor had been found. The rescue team had sent a woman into a narrow gap in the collapsed hotel because she was the smallest member of their team and could easily fit into the tiny opening. With every passing minute, the sense of optimism swelled. After eleven days trapped under rubble and corrugated iron, the young man buried under the Napoli Inn was alive and conscious and on the verge of being pulled to safety. "He's moved his extremities," one of the French firefighters on the scene told me, elated, breathing heavily. He said that was a good sign. It meant the survivor was less likely to die of crush injury. When a body pinned down for a long time is suddenly freed, muscle swelling can release toxins into the bloodstream, causing kidney failure, even death. I imagined being stuck under concrete blocks for almost two weeks but dying just as I was squeezed out of a small hole, into the light, like a stillborn child.

Wismond Exantus Jean-Pierre's second birth was recorded at 4:53 p.m. local time on January 23, 2010. The twenty-four-year-old had survived by diving under a table in the hotel grocery store where he worked when the earthquake struck and by eating cookies and drinking beer and Coca-Cola from the Napoli Inn bar. How did you keep the faith? How did you not lose hope? "Every night, I thought about the revelation that I would survive," he told reporters while recovering in the hospital after he was saved. We all wanted to know how he had been able to keep going when so many others would have let go. As a journalist, I record the time, the place, the facts. As a human being, I want to know why some people don't break.

The dead hadn't quite died yet in Haiti in the days following the earthquake, like ghosts that hadn't crossed over into the afterlife. Their bodies had frozen in the poses they were in when the earth broke open: sitting on a stool, straddling an overturned bicycle, curled up on the ground. Limbs stuck out from under mounds of blasted rock as if pointing us in a multitude of directions at the same time. Look up! No, look here! It's down here! I couldn't stop to think of who they had once been. I needed to rush, to get the story out. "Look," a man told me the day Wismond was pulled out. I was sitting on a pile of rocks on the side of the street, exhausted, after our report on the rescue. "*Regardez*," he had said in French, pointing at something to my right. I turned my head: the bloated body of a woman, half-protruding from the rubble, stunned me. She was probably middle-aged, though it was hard to tell, so advanced was her state of decomposition, and I felt suddenly like a voyeur, as if I had walked in on someone in bed, still sleeping.

We'd been hearing the crackle of gunshots in the distance throughout the day, but it sounded like they were getting closer to us as we started packing up the car to leave the scene. Carefully, we drove toward some sort of commotion a few blocks away. The streets looked like bombed-out war zones. There was no way to describe where we were to someone who knew the city before. The shops, the apartment blocks, the hotels, the sidewalk fruit stands—everything was obliterated. Every once in a while, a building was left standing, for no other reason than because its precise location, to the millimeter, somehow spared it from annihilation.

"I think we should check it out," I said. As we got nearer, on a side street a few hundred meters from the Napoli Inn, we saw men loading crates into a truck. They had formed a tight line from the back of a half-destroyed liquor store to the waiting vehicle, passing boxes of booze from one person to the next. Johnnie Walker, Absolut vodka, a case of Valdivieso Chilean wine. More shots in the background. Our satellite phone rang: "Come back now," I was ordered by the producer running operations at our hotel in Port-au-Prince. "I'm telling you, it's too dangerous." I was never really a risk-taker and I promised to leave if the shooting got uncomfortably close. Large parts of the city were being looted, and whoever owned this store wasn't waiting for the thieves to pay him a visit.

I noticed a fair-skinned man behind a shop counter, his head down, studying a ledger. Was he in charge? I asked. Yes, he told me. "I paid them with bags of rice to help me load the truck. Not taking any chances," he said sternly. We filmed the men, some young, some older, in an orderly queue, carrying heavy wooden crates, bottles rattling inside, working as quickly as they could so they could collect their rice payment and leave. The owner said he would later drive the truck to the relative safety of a warehouse on the outskirts of the city.

A short burst of shots from a semiautomatic rifle, this one a bit nearer. I was starting to feel uncomfortable. This wasn't a war zone, so we weren't wearing bulletproof vests. The white man didn't flinch, as if he'd been through ten of these apocalyptic earthquakes before. Though I transcribed our conversation in my notebook, I can't recall if the liquor store owner and I spoke in French or English, but I do remember that his accent sounded familiar. "Where are you from?"

I asked. He looked confused. "Why would you want to know?" The answer was that I always wanted to know where someone who looks out of place is from because I'd felt that way my entire life. Born in one country, raised in another, with parents from somewhere else entirely. "I'm from Syria," he finally answered. In the middle of death, destruction, and chaos, I suddenly felt a spark of something resembling joy. "Me too!" I nearly shouted back, this time in Arabic. Well, not really, I explained, my parents were from Aleppo and I was born in America. "Aleppo?" he said smiling broadly. "Me too!"

We had nothing else in common and would never meet again. I didn't even write his name down, as he didn't want to appear on camera. For a moment, though, there was a connection: two uprooted vagabonds with Syrian roots meeting in the most unlikely of places, surrounded by misery, seeing a speck of themselves in the other. A rare occurrence. Citizens of everywhere and nowhere belong to tribes of one. We sometimes spend a lifetime looking for a sense of belonging and a place to call home.

There wasn't time to waste. The absurdity of exchanging social niceties in Arabic with a Syrian immigrant in Port-au-Prince as looters were closing in on us was almost comical. He needed to leave, and so did we. Before saying our goodbyes, he looked at me more closely. "I would never have guessed you were Syrian," he said. "You don't even look Arab."

My great-great-grandmother Hurnigar Gorani was likely not able to see much of the Bosphorus from inside the harem of Sultan Abdulaziz's Dolmabahçe Palace. She was five, perhaps six, years old when she was kidnapped by a man in the hills outside her village somewhere in Abkhazia, an Ottoman protectorate on the Black Sea, and forcibly brought to Istanbul sometime in the mid-nineteenth century. The Russians and Turks had been fighting for influence over Abkhazia, a small principality within the Kingdom of Georgia, for so long that it's impossible to know where exactly Hurnigar's family were from, where they had settled in the region, or whether they were ethnic Abkhaz or Georgian. In her old age, she would tell the story of how her abductor, a one-eyed man, had one day snatched her and delivered her to her new living quarters in the sultan's palace. She never saw her family again.

Dolmabahçe, completed in 1856, was the empire's new, Western-style palace overlooking the Bosphorus Strait. Built over thirteen years, marrying neoclassical and baroque architectural styles and surrounded by gardens looking out on the water, Dolmabahçe Palace featured almost three hundred rooms dripping in gold leaf and crystal. The largest Bohemian crystal chandelier in the world, sold to the sultan by Britain's Queen Victoria, still hangs in the main ceremonial hall. The older Topkapi Sarayi was being left behind. Its traditional Turkish tiled walls and Ottoman architecture were considered passé. It had served as the seat of imperial power for four centuries but was largely deserted by the time Hurnigar was brought to Istanbul, with only the wives and concubines of Sultan Abdulaziz's predecessor, Abdulmejid, housed in the Topkapi's private wing.

In Ottoman palaces, the harem was a separate, private family area for the sultan, his consorts and children, his immediate male relatives, and hundreds of other women who held various ranks in the palace's ruthlessly competitive hierarchy. The pecking order there was clear and could not be appealed. The woman at the top was the sultan's mother, the *valide sultan*, who ruled over the others and even chose the leader's consorts. Just below this queen mother were the sultan's wives and the consorts he maintained relationships with, and whose importance grew with every male heir they bore. The other women and girls were either married off to family members of the sultan or to his ministers and pashas throughout the caliphate.

Only a small number of girls in the harem were chosen to become the sultan's concubines, most often by the ruler's own mother. Once selected, they became *ikbals*, or favorites, and were given privileges the others did not have: a private apartment and slaves of their own. Many more, however, would never even meet the leader.

The private quarters within Ottoman palaces looked nothing like the nineteenth-century orientalist depictions of harem life with half-naked bejeweled odalisques draped in expensive fabrics, lazily lounging on daybeds, being fanned by eunuchs. Rather, the harem was a ruthlessly hierarchical world where women competed for attention and favorable treatment. The women lived a life of contradictions: they were both slaves and members of the Ottoman elite, both servants and wives, both sisters and competitors. And like all women during that time and in almost every culture around the world, they had no control over their own destinies. The women of the harem were enslaved in a world that had thrown them together as a result of the desires and ambitions of men, then made to compete for the affections of men and forced to rely on men for freedom from their palace prison.

The harem was a fortress within a fortress that included its own mosque, a school for the Ottoman princes, an infirmary, baths for the *valide sultan*, separate baths for the sultan himself, and quarters for the midwives, among many other distinct areas. Topkapi, for instance, "had almost 400 rooms centered around the courtyard of the *valide sultana*, containing the apartments and dormitories of other women," wrote Alev Lytle Croutier in the book *Harem: The World Behind the Veil*, about the harem in Topkapi Palace.

Hurnigar Gorani had the fair skin and pale eyes typical of Circassian women and prized by nineteenth-century Ottoman high society. In Sultan Abdulaziz's harem, she was one of hundreds of girls either selected by the leader or brought up to become the wives of aristocratic men or functionaries of the empire. They were educated in the arts of music, dancing, and painting, or taught skills like sewing or coffee making. They were trained to observe the rules of etiquette and given Turkish writing and reading courses. For centuries, women from Ottoman provinces as far from Istanbul as present-day Georgia and Bulgaria were either brought to the palace by their families or taken from their villages and homes against their will. The promise of a life of luxury helped the parents of the Circassian, Georgian, and Abkhazian girls overcome any guilt they may have felt in turning over their daughters to the palace. Some Circassians even took their own children to slave markets. A customs declaration from 1790 cited in Croutier's book gives an idea of the girls' monetary worth: "Circassian girl, about eight years old; Abyssinian virgin, about ten; Circassian woman, fifteen or sixteen years old; about twelve-year-old Georgian maiden; medium tall negro slave; seventeen-year-old negro slave. Costs about 1000–2000 kurush." During that time, she writes, a horse sold for about 5,000 kurush.

In the palace, Hurnigar Gorani was placed in the harem's musical troop and taught to play an instrument, though no one in the Gorani family remembers which one, and no story passed down to my mother includes that detail. Female musicians and dancers performed for the sultan in the Hunkar Sofrasi, his private hall, perhaps hoping to be noticed by him, or perhaps, on the contrary, praying that they would not catch his eye. Accompanied by eunuchs and girls of service, Hurnigar would have attended weekly lessons in designated rooms on Dolmabahçe's ground floor. If she had been a member of the Western music orchestra, she would have been expected to practice twice a week in the palace's ornate music rooms, under crystal chandeliers and carved and frescoed ceilings.

Hurnigar would not have known before her wedding who her chosen husband would be or that he was an Arab from Aleppo who served as a functionary of the empire and who would later become Sultan Abdul Hamid's minister of security. She would not have known then that she would marry my great-great-grandfather Shafiq Pasha Gorani.

Hurnigar was a child when she was taken and either couldn't remember or did not speak much about her abduction. Images, like snapshots, might have come back to her: perhaps the strong hand that grabbed her or the feel of the kidnapper's clothing on her skin as he lifted her into a horse-drawn carriage. Hurnigar's blond hair and bright blue eyes would have attracted the attention of the men who roamed the empire's distant provinces in search of fair and bright-eyed girls. Few attributes were more prized in women in Ottoman culture than white skin. Pallor, in women and girls particularly, can still be associated with beauty in Middle Eastern culture today. A vestige of centuries of obsessive infatuation with fairness as a mark of purity and physical desirability. What the historian Keith David Watenpaugh once told me was a "hyper-sexualization" of the pale woman. Ottoman harems might be ancient history, but the effects of this colorism can be traced centuries later to the faces of the women in my family—and to my own.

I can only wonder which of my facial features came from my great-great-grandmother: perhaps her blue eyes, her fair skin, or her high cheekbones and square jaw, those very physical traits that make me look foreign to Arabs and that people from Slavic countries sometimes recognize as closer to their own. "You're Polish? We have Halas here," I am often asked. "Russian, then? Georgian?" In some ways I am at least partly Slavic, though I will never know exactly from where. There are no doubt distant cousins in mountain villages somewhere in Abkhazia or in Bulgaria whose lives are as far removed from my world as mine is from the women of the Ottoman palace harems.

At what point did the memories Hurnigar have of her mother and father and her village in Abkhazia fade to the point of becoming hazy shadows in her mind, losing definition year after year until, as an adult, she had become only the product of the harem, educated and skilled in the art of being an Ottoman wife whose sole purpose was to produce heirs and run a household? Harem girls were often non-Muslims who came from provinces where Islam was not always the dominant religion. Once at the palace, they were converted to Islam, and Hurnigar clung to her adopted faith until the day she died, just outside of Mecca, in 1912. If Allah willed it, she must have thought, then it must be so: her kidnapping, her life in the harem, her marriage to Shafiq Pasha Gorani, her six children, and the death of her firstborn, Nash'at Gorani, who fought for the Ottomans in Libya and perished on the battlefield in Tripoli in 1911, far from his beloved mother.

There are no known pictures of Hurnigar. Women in the region rarely posed for photographs back then. Though the faces of their husbands and sons are familiar to us, the women of that time and place have remained invisible, almost ghostly, present only in the memories of those who knew them and who passed their stories down through the generations. As time passes, and with each retelling, those stories are gradually losing some of their color and definition. "I can't remember more than that," an aunt would tell me. "Too bad your nana isn't here to fill us in," another relative would say.

We do know that Hurnigar was never quite the same after leaving Istanbul in 1909 following the death of her husband, Shafiq Pasha. The fall of Sultan Abdulaziz's successor, Abdul Hamid, deposed by the Young Turks that year, prompted a mini exodus among the members of my mother's side of the family back to Aleppo, where the Gorani men were originally from. For reasons that would soon become clear, Hurnigar was told she needed to follow them to a city as foreign to her as Tokyo or Marseille might have been. She had only ever heard of the Syrian province. The name, Halab—*Aleppo* in Arabic—was just an image in her mind, not a physical place. Once there, she never adjusted to life in the family house by the citadel. It was, perhaps, one displacement too many. The little girl from the mountains of Abkhazia had traveled too far from home.

Part 2

Aleppo

Beit Kbeer

Hikmat-Hanim, who had recently married Hurnigar's son Behjat Gorani, placed the brass carriage clock she had transported from Istanbul to Aleppo on her bedside table. The piece, about five inches high, with an enameled face featuring roman numerals, was designed for travel. It had lived in her bedroom in Istanbul, and she would place it in a roughly equivalent spot in her new living quarters in one of the Ottoman Empire's Syrian provinces. When she forgot to wind it up and it stopped ticking, she would sometimes allow it to sit idle. Its function wasn't solely to tell the time; it was also a visual anchor to another world.

Hikmat-Hanim, my maternal great-grandmother, must have known when she walked into the vast stone courtyard of the house that would soon become her new home that nothing would ever be the same again. Her old life as the wife of a high-ranking officer in the sultan's military would soon only be a memory.

On that day, in 1909, Hikmat-Hanim was eighteen years old. And like for all women then, essential decisions were never hers to make. Marriage, children, when and how to spend money, and, in this case, relocating entire families across one of the largest empires in the world: men took care of all that. Women, if they had any luck, followed them with the resigned surrender of those who know nothing they do or say will make a difference either way.

On that first day, Hikmat-Hanim began to assess the livability of a house that was, she thought, nothing like the more refined palaces and villas she was accustomed to in Istanbul. It had been built in haste in 1850 by Muhammed Bey bin Yasseen Gorani, who'd wanted it finished in time for his son Shafiq Gorani's wedding. The Beit Kbeer, in that sense, was really the family home of her husband's ancestors—a house that belonged to someone else, in which she worried she would always feel like a visitor.

Though it was constructed with the finest stone and marble, workers had not been given the time to add carvings around windows, and the wrought iron balustrades leading up to the second floor lacked some of the decorative scrolls and finials found in other prominent Aleppine homes.

What the house lacked in embellishments, it made up for in sheer square footage. It featured a dozen separate living quarters arranged around a central courtyard, where fruit trees bore several varieties of oranges and lemons during the cooler months. The structure was so vast that it became known as the Beit Kbeer—Arabic for *big house*—at a time when homes were traditionally identified by the family name of their inhabitants rather than their size.

A large fountain in the middle of the tiled patio produced a consistent flow of water that echoed throughout the house. A tippity-tap of water droplets trickling, trickling, trickling, like a second hand, marking time during those rare moments of silence when the family napped after lunch or at dawn, before the servants started their work for the day. On summer days, the scent of jasmine from flowering trees climbing up the inner walls of the compound traveled in and out of windows and doors with every breeze, following the wind's random lead.

In the last few miles leading up to Hikmat-Hanim's final destination, the horse-drawn carriage transporting her and her husband, my great-grandfather Behjat Gorani, would have kicked up considerable dirt on its way around the city's citadel, past the covered souks and the Mamluk-era hammam, as it finally inched down a narrow alleyway leading to a thick wooden door on a small cobblestone side street. The single-door entryway did not hint at the immenseness of the compound on the other side, a huge multigenerational family building on a triangular plot northeast of the citadel. The structure included at its southwestern tip a smaller home with its own courtyard that was used, over the years, either by caretakers or members of the extended family.

Though Hikmat-Hanim did not embrace this forced relocation, it was of no use to protest. Neither she nor any of the other members of the Gorani family had been given much choice in the matter. Two brothers from Aleppo, Shafiq and Husni Bey Gorani, who'd moved to Istanbul as young men in the mid-nineteenth century and risen to high ranks within the Ottoman Empire, had decided to move their families back to their ancestral home after the fall of Sultan Abdul Hamid II in 1909.

In the decades before the sultan was deposed by the Young Turks, some Syrian Arabs had been given top posts in the sultan's palace, and their loyalty to him was viewed with suspicion by the ascendent leaders. Shafiq Pasha Gorani had been named one of Sultan Abdul Hamid's powerful interior ministers, and Husni Bey worked across the empire as an influential judge. They had left Aleppo as students decades earlier, married, and raised families in Istanbul, but worried that the new leaders, who had forced the sultan to step aside and removed high functionaries from their posts, would come for them too. Though there was a brief period of patriotic unity following the Young Turk rebellion that forced a return to constitutional rule in 1908 and 1909, there were also acts of retaliation against those suspected of belonging to Abdul Hamid's regime. The life of privilege and power they had become accustomed to was disappearing. Returning to the house that Muhammed Bey bin Yasseen Gorani had built in Aleppo, where the family still had land and influence, taking their wives and children with them, seemed like the most reasonable course of action.

One of the brothers, Shafiq Pasha, died in 1908 before the family's return to Aleppo, so it was Husni Bey, a stern man with an affinity for harsh words and Black Label whisky, who ordered and oversaw the family's repatriation back to the Beit Kbeer. About half of them heeded Husni Gorani's call and packed crates, children, and servants and left the most important city in the empire for a provincial capital they knew almost nothing about.

With every breath, Hikmat-Hanim took in Aleppo's dry air, laced with the smells of a foreign culture, beating to the rhythm of an alien tongue, Arabic, so different from her native Turkish.

That first day, there were wooden crates to unload, pry open, and empty. But of the dozen or so boxes sent from Istanbul, only two or three made it to their destination, the rest lost or stolen along the one-thousand-mile train and carriage journey to the Gorani compound. The doorman and other house workers took down the trunks and crates from the carriages as the horses stomped and brayed.

My grandmother Berine Gorani's parents had set off from Istanbul's Haydarpasa train station a few weeks earlier on a line operated by a German contractor for the Ottoman government. A Deutsche Bank subsidiary called the Société du Chemin de Fer Ottoman d'Anatolie started construction on the railway line in 1889 with the aim of extending the network all the way to Baghdad. By 1896, it had reached Konya, halfway between Istanbul and Aleppo. There, Hikmat-Hanim and Behjat changed trains and boarded a steam locomotive on the partially completed Baghdad Railway, with stops in the Taurus Mountains, the Cilician Gates, Adana, the small town of Rajo, and, finally, Aleppo.

Perhaps more than the other residents of the Beit Kbeer, Hikmat-Hanim was finding the move distressing. The crates that had been stolen contained precious silverware and bibelots from her Turkish residence. The area around the citadel hadn't been paved yet, and carriages circling the fort dislodged dirt and debris that wafted into the courtyard, something she found profoundly exasperating. The Bedouins and passersby selling dates and bric-a-brac in the walled city inspired in Hikmat-Hanim only condescension. Her house may have been in Aleppo, but her home was in Istanbul. "If the Prophet Muhammad was an Arab, then God is Turkish," she'd often say.

Hikmat-Hanim, Behjat, and their baby son, Tawfeeq, were joining a large, extended family that occupied other wings of the sprawling house. They would have to share socializing areas, a large common kitchen, and a hammam. Through marriage and forced displacement, some fifteen people were thrown together like travelers pitching tent in a caravanserai for the night, but without the option of leaving the following day. This wasn't a happy homecoming; the Gorani family had been brought together by forces beyond its control, the kind that shape history and redraw borders.

In 1914, my grandmother Berine was born, but in the few years that followed, the house lost several of its residents: her father, Behjat Gorani, died of typhoid; the family patriarch, Husni Bey, slipped and broke his hip on the tiled patio and was found the next day, hypothermic and near death. Husni's children, Izzat, Hikmat Bey, Hameed, Aisha, and Abdul Qader, would either leave the house for the newer, more modern neighborhoods west of the old city or fail to make it back from one of the Ottoman Empire's provinces before illness cut their return journeys short.

The deaths, in close succession, of the men who'd returned from Istanbul a decade before marked the beginning of a shift, imperceptible in the beginning, that would lead to profound changes for the family. The house, at first, remained unaffected. The black and sand-colored Aleppo stone walls, some half a meter thick, continued to absorb the summer heat and protect against the cold in the winter months. The climbing jasmine bloomed every spring, and the fruit trees produced oranges and clementines in the autumn. The heavy wooden front door, fixed with steel nails and reinforced with lead plates, kept the city at bay. The *mashrabiyas*, enclosed latticed and carved balconies overlooking the street below, provided some protection against the dusty city air that drifted into the Haramlek and the private apartments. The Beit Kbeer was an inward-looking cocoon, built to last. But it would not survive the changes that were taking place outside its walls for long.

❦

A few years after the family's return to Syria in 1909, Aleppo was convulsing. Already weakened by centuries of land wars and internal revolts, the empire's decision to side with Germany in World War I precipitated its collapse. It lost territory to the Allied powers across the Arab world in battles between 1914 and 1918. After it was over, the Ottoman Empire was on its knees. The United Kingdom and France had secretly agreed on a zone-of-influence map during the war, and France was "given" much of the Ottoman Syrian province, which included present-day Lebanon and extended to the southeastern Mediterranean port city of Alexandretta. Following what became known as the Sykes-Picot agreement, the French took control of Syria and changed Aleppo's status and identity almost overnight. New borders were drawn, creating new countries. The Arabs felt betrayed: those who'd revolted against the Ottoman army had been promised large swaths of territory in exchange for their help. Instead, the French and the British divided up the land and created new nations with government institutions modeled on their own. In the process, Aleppo lost its direct connection to Istanbul as an Ottoman province and was, instead, roped into a newly created state with Damascus as its capital.

One of the other Beit Kbeer residents, the patriarch Husni Bey's grandson, Assad Gorani, then thirteen years old, witnessed French troops entering Aleppo in July 1920 and taking up posts in the citadel. They played loud military music on their way into the city. Tunisian soldiers recruited by the French army led the advance. The spectacle was designed to be seen and heard.

As a high school student during the early years of the French mandate, my grandfather Assad took part in small anti-French protests. "We removed our fez and wore the keffiyeh and went down to the souks," he later wrote in his memoir. The keffiyeh, the traditional Arab headdress, was a visible symbol of identity, unlike the Turkish fez, worn throughout the empire before the region fell into the hands of Western powers.

Though the French mandate was meant to be some sort of benevolent occupation intended to prepare Syria for independence and self-rule, revolts by the locals were never welcome. When a small group of nationalists gathered in Aleppo's Al-Sabil Park to protest the French presence, a single mortar fired from French positions scattered the crowd. The demonstrators got the message. This was France's empire now.

There were other forces destabilizing Aleppo during that time. Damascus had become the politically influential capital of Mandate Syria, and Egypt under the British mandate was surpassing Aleppo in commercial importance. In fact, Egypt had started chipping away at the city's status as a central trading hub several decades prior to the fall of the Ottoman Empire with the opening of the Suez Canal in 1869. Goods from the Far East needn't pass through Aleppo and its caravanserais and souks anymore; they could circumvent that stretch of land altogether and instead sail seamlessly through a new man-made canal. The rich merchant class, especially from notable Aleppine Christian and Jewish families, sent their sons to Egypt to take advantage of its booming economy, further cementing Aleppo's commercial decline. Goods traded over traditional land routes for centuries could, instead, be transported on cargo ships. Cities like Aleppo paid the price in lost business.

France and the United Kingdom had defeated the Turkish Ottoman Empire, and they were going to make the most of that victory.

The lines they drew on maps didn't just create new countries, they cut through tribal, ethnic, and religious communities. Entire regions were reshaped and remolded, cut and pasted with no regard for culture, history, or the local populations' desire for self-rule.

Within Syria itself, the French initially divided the country into the states of Aleppo, Damascus, and an autonomous Alawite territory, giving outsize power and autonomy to minorities to weaken the Arab nationalist movements threatening their supremacy. It was a period of identity crisis and extreme anxiety. Aleppo was neither Ottoman nor Syrian in the way the word carries meaning today. It was Muslim, but with a sizable Christian population that had grown larger with the influx of Armenian refugees fleeing the 1915 genocide.

The French put down rebellions across Syria, and in the countryside outside Aleppo in particular, before they established full formal control in 1923, when the League of Nations, the predecessor of the United Nations, granted France a mandate over the country. It was meant to be a temporary arrangement—looser than a colony—in theory in place until the country's inhabitants could govern themselves. Instead, the occupying power would actively work to suppress independent political activity. For Arab nationalists after World War I, this was a profound betrayal they would not soon forget.

Inside the walls of the Beit Kbeer, the family felt that they had been displaced without moving an inch. It sometimes felt like borders were not just shifting around them but were slicing right through the house's central courtyard. The Beit Kbeer occupants stood still while the countries around them shifted, like earth spinning on a slightly off-center axis.

What did it really mean to be Syrian, anyway? One was Aleppine, Homsi, Damascene, Hamwi. People were Sunni, Christian, or Alawite, and many other things in between. For Hikmat-Hanim and most members of the family who'd returned from Istanbul, no single description really fit. She had only ever learned rudimentary Arabic, enough to communicate in basic ways, but that meant that she could never fully integrate into a culture that was still foreign to her. She had continued to long for Istanbul her entire life, where she had left siblings and cousins behind. The Goranis were a patchwork of Arabs, Bulgarians, Circassians, and Turks brought together by the Ottoman Empire, which had tentacles that reached deep into Europe, Asia, and northern Africa, and which, in the end, disintegrated so rapidly, it's easy to forget it lasted over six hundred years.

Independence

1946–1963

By the 1930s, the French colonial influence was having a profound impact on all aspects of life for the Gorani family inside the Beit Kbeer and outside of the house's thick perimeter walls. Schools, government institutions, roads: the brand-new Syrian state was being molded in France's image. During that time, Hikmat-Hanim's two daughters—my grandmother Berine Gorani and her older sister, Guzida—would walk on school days from their home to the École Saint-Joseph, an all-girls' Catholic institution in Jamalia, one of the newer neighborhoods, west of the old walled city, up the narrow cobblestoned streets around the citadel, through the old Jewish quarter, across Bab al-Faraj square, and down the newly named Boulevard de France. On their way, they passed the Great Synagogue, located in the Farafra District, a few hundred yards from the grand Umayyad Mosque and its eleventh-century minaret. They would then walk through Clock Tower Square, built at the end of the nineteenth century by Sultan Abdul Hamid II and surrounded by newer Western-inspired architecture.

Generational, historic changes were taking place: Muslim women of Berine's generation started appearing in public without a headscarf and socially mixing with men. All the while, the French put down revolts, including the one that my grandfather Assad Gorani took part in in the fall of 1925. In his memoir, he remembered French forces firing live rounds into a crowd gathered at the Aleppo governate. Soldiers killed ninety people and injured hundreds more that day. "Some of them were my friends," he later wrote.

In the 1930s, when my grandparents Assad and Berine married, the Goranis had left the Beit Kbeer for modern, European-style homes west of the old city. They had one son and three daughters, including my mother, Nour, and for the first time in several generations, settled in Aleppo with no expectation that they or their children would ever leave their home city.

Assad, who had studied law, became justice minister in the 1940s. Photos of him in his ministry in Damascus show a young, studious man wearing round-rimmed glasses, usually holding a pen, as if caught mid-writing. He had started work on a new civil code, which, like the judicial system the Ottomans had tried to reform decades earlier, was a messy collection of sometimes contradictory religious, civil, and common laws.

These were years of extreme political instability. Syria had gained independence in 1945, but the political situation remained chaotic. Governments lasted sometimes only a few months before being overthrown in a coup. Syrian democracy was new and fragile. Too many forces were vying for control in a nation-state so young that it had not found its identity as a country yet.

⚜

ALEPPO, SEPTEMBER 28, 1961

There were loud knocks on the door. When no one answered, there was the continuous sound of the front door buzzer. It was two in the morning and, one by one, members of the Gorani household woke up in a panic. Berine ran down the hallway of the Hay al-Sabil apartment and burst into my mother and uncle Hikmat's bedroom. "Don't leave the room. Under any circumstance. You stay here. You keep the door closed," she told them. There were loud voices in the entrance followed by the marching sound of boots on the ground. A group of men made their way to my grandfather's study.

Assad Gorani was a heavy sleeper. It had taken him a few minutes to fully wake up and join the late-night visitors. Two officers in military uniform were waiting for him, including George Mhassel, a northern Syrian military commander and a Christian. He'd been sent by revolutionaries who'd just overthrown the government that was collaborating with Egypt in an entity called the United Arab Republic. The coup plotters were unhappy that Syria had formed an alliance with Egypt. They felt like the UAR treated Syrians as junior partners.

The rebels wanted Assad to go straight to Damascus to form a new government. "The car is outside," they told him. The coup plotters needed a civilian figurehead to legitimize the rebellion. My grandfather sent them away with the message that there can be no legitimacy without elections.

Though new Syrian rulers eventually appointed a civilian head of government, no one was fooled: the real power remained in the hands of the armed men in charge. A year after the rebels had burst into his Aleppo home, Assad Gorani decided to join the government after all, as justice minister and interim prime minister, at the insistence of the civilian president. It was a risk that he wrote later was worth taking. Leaving the country to the military alone was even more potentially perilous than remaining on the sidelines. He must have known even then that it would be futile. Chaos, infighting, and a lack of real civilian oversight of the armed forces would eventually pave the path toward the government's downfall. The creeping rot that would not go away. The divorce with Egypt, which continued to meddle in Syrian affairs, had caused additional tumult. All of this laid the groundwork for the Ba'ath Party, a socialist anti-imperialist political movement, to take over. This time, the coup would have lasting effects. The Ba'athists, inspired by a successful regime overthrow in neighboring Iraq, took over with confidence in 1963. They ousted the president and purged the military and government, progressively installing members of the minority Alawite sect in high-ranking positions. Syria's modern-day dictatorship was born. There were still Ba'athist dreams of a socialist utopia among its civilian party members, but they would soon be sidelined too. It was the Ba'ath Party's country now.

Elvis Is Dead

T he day Elvis Presley died, my older brother, Zaf, and I were on a visit to Aleppo from America, and Hafez al-Assad had been president of Syria for more than six years.

Zaf was making a stove-top grilled cheese sandwich when our grandmother Berine Gorani appeared in the kitchen of the Hay al-Sabil apartment. It was midafternoon the day after. She stopped just beyond the threshold, her slim silhouette outlined by the light coming from the hallway behind her and broke the news in Arabic: *"Elvis mat."* Elvis Presley, forty-two years of age at the time of his premature death, had succumbed to a drug-induced heart attack. His demise sent shock waves throughout the world, the stunning announcement landing at my brother's feet as he was making an afternoon snack.

Those were the two worlds my brother and I straddled: the culture of Elvis Presley, McDonald's, Disney, and Coke and the isolating, repressive regime of totalitarian Syria. We traveled from one to the other as if passing through a portal into another dimension. We lived in the US, where my father and mother had emigrated in the '60s and

29

where I was born but continued to visit our parents' home country on school holidays every few years. Elvis to Hafez and Hafez to Elvis.

"I don't remember anything else," Zaf told me. "I was twelve. Elvis music wasn't popular with kids my age back then. I just remember her standing there and announcing it."

My grandparents Berine and Assad lived northwest of the Beit Kbeer then, on the first floor of an apartment building near Al-Sabil Park, where Nana Berine would take us on walks in the early evenings when temperatures dropped. Al-Sabil was a relatively new neighborhood developed in the 1950s beyond the initial expansion out of the old city in Aziziyah and Jamilia. Notable families—both Christian and Muslim—built European-style apartment blocks with modern amenities like central heating, large family bathrooms, and outward-looking terraces. There was great sectarian entente during those years. Religion mattered, of course, but less than wealth and status did on the Aleppo social scene. Christians and Muslims went to the same clubs, sent their children to the same schools, traveled to the same Western vacation destinations. Families from all religious backgrounds formed lasting friendships, though there was almost no intermarriage—the boundaries of sectarian mixing remained clearly defined.

The floor plan of the Hay al-Sabil apartment looked nothing like the inward-looking Beit Kbeer. It was all corridor: a central spine, with the kitchen at one end, Assad Gorani's study at the other, and the living rooms and bedrooms in between on either side of a long hallway. It was the kind of house that had a "formal sitting room" only used to entertain guests, where wall sconces and chandeliers glittered in the penumbra. The furniture in Syrian bourgeois homes of the time was often French inspired—replica Louis XVI armchairs and tables, nineteenth-century gilt mirrors, copies of Louis XV love seats with rigid backs upholstered in damasked silk—usually arranged over handmade Persian rugs. The crystal vases and bibelots, often imported to the Middle East from Czechoslovakia in the 1800s, were made specifically for the Arab market in bright colors like ruby red, pistachio green, and turquoise blue. The interiors of notable Levantine families' homes now mimicked the design aesthetics of the European bourgeoisie. The traditional Arab houses like Beit Kbeer had been left behind, and so had their cultural authenticity and style.

In Assad's study, there were bookshelves lining every wall with leather-bound legal tomes organized by size and color. As a child, I would sometimes peek in, tiptoeing silently into this intimidating room if the door was open and it was empty. The room smelled of book leather and gravitas. There was a weight to the air in my grandfather's study, as if the atmosphere in that one room was somehow different from the rest of the apartment. The heavy desk in the center, the oversize club chairs, the dark wooden shelving: the furniture matched the man. Imposing, serious, studious, and organized.

On the desk, an old-school inkwell, a leather writing pad, and a black marble penholder. On one of the low tables in a corner of the room, Hikmat-Hanim's brass travel clock. It had stopped at 3:06 p.m., what was said to be her time of death on March 5, 1961. In truth, no one knew for sure if she had indeed died at 3:06 p.m., or 3:06 a.m., or even what exact time my great-grandmother had passed away. But the fact that the clock had perhaps stopped ticking around the time of her death imbued her passing with a supernatural power; to stop time, to break mechanisms. The timepiece that had traveled with Hikmat-Hanim and her husband, Behjat, from Istanbul in 1909 and landed in my grandfather's study no longer served a practical function. It was, solely, a remnant of an era long gone.

Syria during that time was still adjusting to the 1970 Ba'ath Party power grab that brought Hafez al-Assad to the presidency the next year. The new president had worked his way up after the Ba'ath coup in 1963 from commander of the Syrian Air Force to defense minister, to prime minister, and, ultimately, to the top position. Al-Assad and his close circle were now in charge of every institution in the country.

Their brand of authoritarian rule meant no real dissent was tolerated. Every aspect of life was controlled by the regime and its cronies. Criticizing the government could land you in prison. Speaking up could mean never being heard from again.

Hafez al-Assad, from the minority Alawi community—an offshoot of Shia Islam—ruled over a majority-Sunni country. The Ba'ath Party he belonged to, founded in 1947, officially advocated socialism and Pan-Arabism. In reality, the coup plotters hijacked its ideology to rob their people. Top jobs were given to family members, other Alawites, and loyalist Sunnis and Christians. Islamist rebellions were put down with brute force in the early 1980s in Hama and Aleppo. Hafez al-Assad consolidated his country's alignment with the Soviet Union during the Cold War, which cut off the Syrian economy from most trade with Western nations. The Soviet influence was everywhere: Ladas rather than Volkswagens on the streets, Soviet-made appliances and utensils, a corrupt economic system, a state-controlled media. For my brother and me, raised on American supermarket produce and French croissants, Syria was a grim and depressing consumer wasteland. It wasn't all bad, though: the caviar was cheap.

It wasn't just the culture shock that made me feel out of my element. I was a foreigner there, too, and reminded of it often. Since my first visit to Aleppo with my mother as a toddler, my aunts and uncles and some of my cousins enjoyed teasing me by calling me "Hala the American," which I loathed. What was amusing to them was, to me, another reminder of the fact that I was just a visitor. But if I didn't belong in my own family, why wasn't I able to feel at home anywhere else?

The Not-So-Secret Police

Over the years, I felt both happy and stifled during my visits to Aleppo. I loved family reunions and the overwhelming beauty of the city, but it was also a place where the social scene was small and where privacy was a luxury. And then there was the secret police—the *mukhabarat*—always potentially watching. Even if its agents were not physically there, lurking, reporting back up the chain of command, they *could* be. That was the point. That is how the system worked: you *could* be watched at all times. It keeps people on their toes, vigilant, worried. A neighbor might tell on you. A traffic cop. The fear of being reported, summoned, imprisoned was a constant companion. Once I started working in journalism in my twenties, the possibility—the near certainty, really—that I would become more interesting to the regime was always on my mind.

I'd only been in Aleppo a few days in the summer of 1996 when I spotted a black sedan with tinted windows behind the car I was in. It was clearly following us, because every time we stopped, it would stop behind us, maybe three car lengths away. It was around 2:00 a.m., perhaps later. I don't remember the exact time. Very late, anyway.

Were we being trailed? "Don't worry," Emile said, looking worried. "I think it's the *mukhabarat*," he added, trying to minimize the
incident with a timid smile. "They're following us," I said more defini-
tively. We had been kissing in his car after sneaking out of my cousin's
wedding at the Meridien Hotel a few blocks from Aleppo University in
the western part of the city. I was in Syria that summer for the wedding
and had made a new group of friends; many were the descendants of
the elite Christian and Muslim families Hikmat-Hanim and, later, my
grandparents socialized with in the early days of Syrian independence.
Some worked abroad; others had returned to Aleppo after studying
in America or Europe to work in family businesses, often in textiles or
manufacturing. Emile split his time between Beirut and Aleppo, where
his family owned a textile business. About ten of us became close very
quickly that summer, in the way young and unattached people can.
Emile, who was Christian, wasn't the only one I flirted with. There was
also Rasheed, who was Muslim, and one of the most beautiful men I'd
ever seen. While sitting in the back of a car on our way home from a
trip to the desert with my new friends, his hand brushed against mine
and came to rest on his knee so that it touched my thigh, quite inten-
tionally, and I let him keep it there. For a brief moment, an invisible
charge connected us.

Emile had the delicate hands and nails of someone who took care
of himself. Tall and slim, he carried himself with the confidence of
a man who did not have to work too hard to land a date. He was also
much more forward than Rasheed. The night we were followed, he'd
called Nana Berine's house directly and had asked for me. "I'll take
you to the wedding. We can go together," he'd said. There was nothing unusual about Emile knowing my grandmother's phone number.
Aleppo families had socialized together for decades. Hikmat-Hanim
might have had coffee with Emile's great-grandmother when Muslim women started mixing in public places more openly in the 1930s.
Notable Christian and Muslim families had mingled and coexisted

for generations; Aleppo's upper crust was a small village within a sprawling city.

"He just turned his headlights off. Maybe he's parking," Emile said.

We had stopped kissing. He leaned toward me, holding the car's steering wheel with one hand and reaching for my cheek with the other. I froze. It felt unsafe. "Would you rather we go back to the wedding?" he said. "What if it's the *mukhabarat*?" I asked. I whispered the word *mukhabarat*—which literally translates as "intelligence"—as if the car itself was bugged. After the 1963 Ba'athist coup and especially since Hafez al-Assad came to power in 1971, people in Syria became used to whispering when talking about anything other than mundane subjects. By the mid-1990s, al-Assad had been president for a quarter century. Most Syrians had never known another regime. Al-Assad's pictures were everywhere: giant posters on government buildings, photos of the leader smiling and waving, arm outstretched in the window display of every storefront, stickers on the back windshields of cars. The leader was there at all times. He smiled and waved, but he could reach out of the picture, snatch you, throw you in a cell without warning, and no one would ever hear from you again.

Even at home, even around the dinner table, even when exchanging a few words with a spouse in the bathroom before going to work, conversations about politics or the regime took place in hushed tones, furtively, as if getting the words out quickly was safer than lingering on a topic for too long. "Remember where I am," my mother, who was visiting Aleppo, once told me when I called her from London. I had carelessly brought up politics, and, because it was always assumed that phones were tapped, it could have been dangerous to speak too freely. They are everywhere, these agents of the regime; and they could be anyone: the cherry juice seller in the springtime, the garbage collector, the travel agency employee, the taxi driver, even a family member. That is the police state's power: you never know who is keeping tabs and reporting back.

Emile started the car. "Let's go, then," he said disappointedly. The headlights behind us came back on. We were followed until we drove back to the Meridien, where the party was still in full swing and where nobody had seemed to notice our short absence.

When my mother and I were driven back to Nana Berine's house later that night, someone was also following us. How could anyone truly feel at home in a country where the regime's agents are always prowling, watching every move, spying? They may not have been colonizers, but they had stolen the country just the same.

We Are Watching You

A small wall-mounted television broadcasting Syrian state pro-gramming flickered in the waiting room of the Syrian Ministry of Information, Department of International Press Visas. We had been waiting almost an hour for our appointment, seated on plastic chairs placed in a row against a plain white wall. An assistant called us in: Dr. Wassim is ready for you.

A large, smiling man with slicked-back hair greeted us.

Sit, please. Yes, make yourselves comfortable.

My producer, Schams Elwazer, and I were asked about our assignment.

Will you be fair? Will CNN tell the world the true story of Syria? Yes, of course, of course. We are journalists, and that is our job.

Dr. Wassim stopped talking. He stopped asking questions. He sat back in his office chair and looked at us like a principal would look at pupils sent in for bad behavior. An uncomfortable silence developed between us. It lingered, slowly expanding into an almost palpable entity. We waited for him to speak again. The silence made me particularly nervous; I was secretly recording our conversation on a 2004 model Nokia phone, which included new features like an integrated video camera. The quality was poor, but it was a useful and novel tool for journalists in the field. At that moment, I was furious with myself for taking the risk. The cell phone, in my jacket pocket, felt heavy and cumbersome. Would it click or beep or vibrate, exposing my stratagem? Dr. Wassim leaned forward.

"Remember that you are our guests," he said. "And we are responsible for your safety. If you report something that is wrong, I can't guarantee that we will be able to keep you safe."

Yes, of course. Thank you, Dr. Wassim. We will report the truth.

It is how these meetings went. We already had a press visa, without which travel to the country for journalists wouldn't be allowed. This was an additional, informal step. One designed to intimidate and muzzle. We had a license to film with the permission of the police state but were warned that expulsion was a constant threat. Perhaps worse. Don't stray. Don't test us.

"Remember that you are our guests."

We took the elevator down to the ground floor of the imposing building in the Mezze District in Damascus and climbed back into a waiting van Schams had reserved for our trip. We were going to drive cross-country, starting in Damascus and then continuing north to Homs and Hama, ending our journey in Aleppo. The plan was to shoot a long-form story on Syrian youth. Over the past few years, the country had been slowly modernizing and opening its borders to tourists and foreign investment after decades of isolation under former president Hafez al-Assad. We wanted to document some of these changes through the eyes of young people living in three major cities. Hafez's son Bashar, in power since 2000, with a glamorous wife raised in London at his side, initially seemed to embody a new era of freedom and opportunity. In interviews, he spoke with a lisp, in a soft, whispery voice. His receding chin and young age when anointed president made him appear more benign than his father and, in some ways, more approachable. He promised to liberalize the economy, to allow independent political parties, and to loosen the state's grip on the media, though always in vague and noncommittal terms. The young eye doctor was untested, but Syrians were so starved for change that they chose to believe that a new generation of leaders, who'd lived and studied abroad, would be likelier to set them free because they had tasted freedom themselves. In some ways, the decision to believe in a new leader felt like blind religious faith: even without evidence, there is sometimes comfort in the act of trust itself, however briefly the moment lasts.

"Did it record?" Schams asked. I pressed Play. We could only make out every other word, so we immediately hit Record again, repeating what we had been told in our own voices, filling in the blanks while we still remembered what Dr. Wassim had said almost word for word. We felt triumphant. We had a record of something that came across as a threat. We couldn't use it in a news report, but it gave us a sense of having achieved something. The regime spied on its people. It disappeared dissidents. When Syrians spoke about politics, they whispered, even in their own homes. There was always a possible microphone hidden somewhere in a telephone receiver. The garbage collectors sometimes followed people when they moved. "Didn't you work in our old neighborhood?" a novelist friend of mine once asked a street sweeper who appeared outside her new address. "They moved me," he answered. Who moved him was not a mystery, though it needed to remain unsaid.

Aleppo was our last stop. Schams and I had driven eighty miles from Hama on the Damascus-Aleppo Highway, merging from the north with the Idlib-Aleppo Highway. There, greeting drivers on their way in, at the center of a huge ten-exit roundabout, was a rotating globe inscribed with the words *The World's Oldest City*. It's a boast many other Middle Eastern settlements have made, including Jericho in the West Bank, Byblos in Lebanon, Kirkuk in Iraq, and Crocodilopolis on the river Nile (now known as Faiyum in Egypt). Like them, Aleppo claims to be the oldest *continuously inhabited* city in the world, dating back eight thousand years, ruled by the Kingdom of Armi, the Akkadian Empire, and the Hittites, all before most human settlements had even laid their first foundational stone.

From there, cars would either go straight to the central neighborhoods and the old city and its covered souks, or veer left toward the newer Hay al-Sabil District, part of Aleppo's development outside the medieval walled city in the early twentieth century.

The constant honking, the warm, dust-laced air, the sidewalks crowded with passersby, dodging street sellers crouched on the ground offering trinkets and baked goods and unshelled green pistachios: Aleppo had always felt at once familiar and foreign to me. Like a childhood friend I felt too awkward to fully embrace. The sounds of simultaneous calls to prayer from hundreds of mosques, broadcast over loudspeakers, in some cases competing with church bells in the Armenian district or the mainly Christian Aziziyah and Jdaydeh neighborhoods: Aleppo envelops and overwhelms. The covered souk, the largest in the world before it became a front line in the war between government forces and rebels in 2012, could take an entire day to navigate, from beginning to end. The journey through its alleyways was slow and winding through the gold market, the textile quarter, and to the stalls selling cheap plastic toys and racy women's lingerie. Turn a corner and there are butchers hanging meat next to a baklava shop, turn right, turn left, go straight, get lost, even, in what was the city's nerve center.

"Stop here," I told our van driver. I'd noticed rows of men standing at the edge of a busy road with tools piled at their feet, apparently offering their services to anyone who would hire them. First, I only spotted a few workers, then dozens more. I addressed one man and was immediately surrounded. "If there's no work, how can there be a future?" a young man named Fawaz Mohammed told me. Farhi Abdallah, twenty-two: "I've been here since dawn." Hamid al-Ali: "I'm married and I have three children. I have no money for them."

Most of the workers I spoke to that day had left Lebanon after Syrian troops, occupying the country for three decades, were forced to leave. The Syrian military had entered Lebanon at the start of that country's civil war in 1976 but had overstayed its welcome after the end of hostilities. On Valentine's Day 2005, a bomb in a parked van exploded as the convoy of the former Lebanese prime minister Rafik Hariri drove past. The impact of the blast was so powerful that windows shattered several streets away and killed twenty-one people in addition to Hariri. His assassination was immediately blamed on the Shiite group Hezbollah and on its allies in the Syrian intelligence services. Hariri had publicly spoken against Syria's presence in Lebanon and so, many Lebanese believed, the Syrian regime made sure he could never speak again. The day workers in Aleppo told me they'd been attacked in Beirut because they were Syrian. They said they had no choice but to leave even if they only made a dollar or two a day back home in Syria. How many of these men were among those who later chanted, "The Syrian people will not be humiliated," during the 2011 Arab Spring protests against the regime? How many were mowed down as they demonstrated?

That afternoon, in May 2005, after my work was done, I visited my grandmother Berine Gorani. After Hay al-Sabil, Berine and Assad had moved farther west to Shahba, an even newer part of the city where more affluent residents built villas and low-rise residential buildings starting in the 1980s. Two aunts, a cousin, an uncle, and my grandmother all lived on the same street in Shahba District after moving to the area in the early '90s. Berine Gorani had been a widow almost ten years, since my grandfather Assad's death in 1995, but was surrounded by family and visitors every day, as well as by a live-in housekeeper. She greeted me at the front door wearing a belted robe cinched at the waist over her tiny frame. In my conversational but unsophisticated Arabic, I told her about the story we were filming and about my job at CNN. It was rare for us to be alone, without other members of the family. I was so exhausted from my road trip that I could not stay awake. "May I just close my eyes for a few minutes?" I asked her. "Just here, on the sofa?" I don't remember how long I was asleep, but it was dark out when I woke up with a blanket on me, still wearing my shoes. Nana Berine sat on an armchair opposite me. "I just wanted to make sure you were warm enough," she said.

Issam, Rima, Randa, Lutfi. The names in my reporter's notebook from that 2005 Syria trip come back to me like handwritten letters from another time. They are sent from a place that no longer exists. The country itself is gone, broken into pieces, emptied of half its inhabitants after a war so brutal that entire neighborhoods were blasted into fine dust. In 2005, though, there was still life: on the campus of Damascus University, Rima told me she was an English literature major who also studied at the High Institute of Music; Lutfi was a medical student; Randa, twenty-one, was thinking of applying for a Fulbright scholarship. "If things don't move the right way economically, we're going to again be an isolated country, sitting in the middle of this world that's moving forward while we are standing still," said Issam.

I reread the notes. Little details about each student scribbled in the margin:

Mom teacher.

Wants to work in banking.

Loves music.

Wants to get master's degree in America.

In my hurried handwriting, I can see the seeds of the 2011 revolution, when a young, mobile, ambitious generation of Syrians witnessed the Arab Spring uprisings in Tunisia and Egypt and believed they, too, could ask for more freedom and opportunity. More dignity, as well. I am surprised by a quote from a twenty-four-year-old Damascus University student named Jomana Abdo: "The young people deserve a change of this political system. It shouldn't be like a royal system." The public expressions of discontent had grown louder, just above the murmur of their parents' generation. "Are you okay for me to put this on television? Everyone will see it," I always confirmed. It was important that I heard them say it back to me. "Yes, I understand that this will be seen." I did not want there to be any confusion. If the regime came after him, I wanted to absolve myself of any responsibility. After filming was over, I always returned to my home with the uncomfortable feeling of having left the people I spoke to behind to face any possible consequences alone. This aspect of my job infused me with guilt I carried with me at all times. I pass by, I witness, I report. They experience. Sometimes, they endure.

What the university students I interviewed didn't know was that, through them, I was privately searching for clues about myself; for answers to questions that I wasn't yet able to formulate. I was the daughter of Syrian parents from Aleppo, born in the United States, raised mainly in France after a divorce, and based, later in life, in London and Atlanta. I had spent a lifetime trying to feel like I belonged somewhere. Was I Syrian? Was I Arab American? Was I, instead, French because I had grown up in Paris? If even a part of me felt Syrian, surely, I should see myself reflected in the people I met on that 2005 cross-country road trip: a sort of kinship through place of origin and ethnicity? After each interview, I realized that none of those labels felt right. I still felt stateless.

In my notebook, I wrote down the age, the number of siblings, the parents' professions, the plans and dreams of each person I spoke to. Today, as I read my notes, I feel a quasi-physical pain knowing that the hopes of the university students I interviewed that day were likely never realized. The country's youth would later be betrayed, shot, imprisoned, or exiled. They were sacrificed.

Syria's president, Bashar al-Assad, was then five years into the inherited presidential term of his dictator father, who'd ruled the country like a crime syndicate for nearly thirty years. Hafez al-Assad took over as president in 1971 after a Ba'athist coup consolidated power in the hands of a few military officers from the Alawite religious minority. Though the country is majority Sunni Muslim, the Alawite sect, which had held outsize influence in the Syrian military before the coup, would place its allies at the top of a power structure that controlled what you could say, when you could say it, and what the consequences were if you overstepped the mark. After Hafez al-Assad's death in 2000, his son Bashar—then thirty-four years old—briefly allowed civil society to enjoy relatively more freedom. There were new political forums, public discussions about politics and the economy. Bashar, the young man who'd studied ophthalmology in Britain, who'd married an attractive JP Morgan banker from a bourgeois Sunni family: Would he be the country's newest hero?

But dictators never truly soften for long. Their power is either absolute or it collapses. The strongman, like an abusive father, sometimes offers short respites, but only to crack the whip again. When every organ of the state is controlled by a single family, letting go in even one area means that the entire power structure will eventually crumble. Perhaps their existential fears aren't entirely baseless. We have seen since what oppressed people do to their leaders, those who'd sat in gilded chairs, presiding over mock cabinet meetings, sending dissidents to their deaths. They were hunted down, pulled out of hiding places and into the harsh light, beaten, insulted, spat on, and killed without mercy.

A year into his reign, Bashar al-Assad started jailing human rights activists, journalists, and dissidents again. There was speculation that the regime nomenklatura had told the new president they could not guarantee that he would remain in power if he continued on this path of even limited reforms. Whatever the reason, the "Damascus Spring," a short-lived period of open political debate and public demands of greater freedom, which had infused the intellectual elite with the romantic hope that their abusers had changed, was over.

"It's All Gone"

I check my phone and open the messages I've been waiting weeks for: pictures of the area where the Beit Kbeer once stood in the old city. A friend who still lives in Aleppo connected me with someone who agreed to photograph what is left of the triangular plot where the Gorani house once stood. It was sold in the 1960s when most of the family moved out of the old city to neighborhoods with newer, more modern homes. After the sale, developers had erected several mid-rise apartment buildings over the Beit Kbeer's original footprint, preserving only the original caretaker house at its tip and one side of the perimeter wall. I had used several historic maps to pinpoint the exact modern-day address using the known shape of the courtyard and its confirmed historic location in the city's Bayyada neighborhood across from the citadel.

The pictures are in the palm of my hand. Muhammed Bey bin Yasseen Gorani built the family compound in 1850, and photos of what the war that followed the 2011 uprisings did to the area landed in my cell phone in 2022. One hundred seventy-two years separate these two moments. In between: the collapse of the Ottoman Empire, two world wars, the French mandate, successive coups, the Ba'ath regime, the 2011 Arab Spring, the Battle of Aleppo, and, finally in 2016, the al-Assad regime back in control after a brutal campaign against civilian areas in rebel-held territory.

I tap on the first photo: the only remaining part of the old structure, the caretaker house at the tip of the triangular plot, was riddled with the pockmarks of ricocheting bullets. I swipe again. The second photo shows another view of the same house. It is still standing, but its windows are blown out and its nineteenth-century wooden *mashrabiya* balconies are hanging on to the outer wall as if defying the pull of gravity, the structure's façade peppered with bullet holes. The house is empty, clearly unlivable. The fighting in the old city between 2012 and 2014, concentrated on the western side of the citadel, in the cobblestoned alleyways of the market and in and around the mosques and hammams, had obviously also reached the other side of the massive fort.

I swipe. The third photo is of a sign for Haret al-Dulab, or Wheel Street, so called because a waterwheel imported from Egypt once provided power to the house. The street sign for Haret al-Dulab, a small alleyway that formed one side of the triangular parcel of land where the Beit Kbeer once stood, has taken exactly three bullets. The stone wall it is bolted to is also nicked. These were likely stray bullets, flying through the air without aim, scarring centuries-old walls, their casings sometimes still scattered blocks away. I swipe again. The streets are empty; the metal roller shutters in a couple of nearby shops are pulled down. Life hasn't fully returned here yet, even though it has been six years since the worst of the fighting in 2016.

Neither my mother nor most of my Aleppo-based relatives have returned to the city since the start of the war. A couple of family members returned briefly to retrieve jewelry or cash that looters missed when they ransacked the house, but most have decided to walk away forever. My mother says there is no point in going back: "There is nothing left there, anyway."

The city, of course, isn't dead, and there are things left to see amid the desolation. The market stalls have returned in parts of the souk, and the streets in downtown Aleppo are again busy with pedestrians, yellow taxis, and buses. But a city isn't just a physical entity. It occupies emotional space in the minds of its inhabitants—an intangible, sentimental attachment—that has been so badly wounded that a vital part of what breathed life into the city has vanished. For now, at least, it seems that no amount of reconstruction will heal the wounds of those who've decided to leave Aleppo in the past.

Today, the area around the Beit Kbeer has come back to life, but with the scars of a city still traumatized. There are UNHCR tarps covering holes in the domed roofs above the market stalls in the souk, and miles of the cobblestoned souk alleyways are still blackened from the fires that raged during the fighting in 2013 and 2014 during the Battle of Aleppo.

Just outside the souk, however, there is no going back to the time before. There lie the graves of Aleppo's real architectural treasures, today completely obliterated. They would almost look banal, these mountains of blasted rock, whitening in the sun, were it not for what they once embodied when they were whole: a mighty minaret, completed in 1090, that towered for nine hundred years over the Umayyad Mosque; a medieval citadel that withstood Mongol attacks and foreign invasions; a public bath, built by Mamluk slaves, where half-naked bodies had been scrubbed and lathered, lying limp in thick steam, since 1491.

Before the 2011 uprising, my mother and I would go on visits to the old city, and, every few years, we would walk past Gorani Street. She would point to the new buildings erected where the Beit Kbeer once stood and say, "Look, this is how big the Gorani house was; it took up the footprint of all these buildings put together." I remember the day she pointed at the street sign that read *Shara' Gorani*. There was pride in her voice, but also a sense of a having lost something that belonged to us, at a time when the Arabs of the Levant—the Syrians, Lebanese, Palestinians, and Jordanians—hadn't scattered around the world looking for opportunity, freedom, or both. I looked at the street signs, the perimeter wall, the old caretaker house and tried to imagine what life was like in that very spot a century earlier. It was like trying to examine a faded picture, but in real life, as if my mother and I were both inside an old snapshot for a brief moment, anachronisms, foreigners from another world, even though we were standing on our own ancestral land.

Part 3

Neuilly-sur-Seine

My First Big Lie

S tanding in the center of a tree-lined courtyard, surrounded by build-ings overlooking a large, paved stone plot, like a photo slowly develop-ing in a darkroom, forty years in the making, the image of a six-year-old girl in a strange land, frightened and alone, comes into focus.

Tall, mature oak trees arranged in a rectangular pattern around a wide-open space had started shedding their leaves. It was a September morning in 1976 and my first day of primary school in an unfamiliar country.

Four thousand kilometers and three generations away from the Beit Kbeer in old Aleppo, the École de la Saussaye, in the leafy Paris suburb of Neuilly-sur-Seine, was a government-funded institution whose pupils came from mainly middle-class backgrounds. It was located in a part of the city where property prices where high and most children were sent to class scrubbed clean and neatly dressed.

The little girls from well-off bourgeois families wore round-toed Mary Janes and pleated skirts. They had fruit-inspired names like Prune and Clementine. The boys wore patterned knit sweaters and leather lace-up shoes. The clothing suggested not just money but *old* money. These were outfits inspired by what their parents had worn before them and their parents before them. They came in classic shapes, like round-necked navy-blue cardigans and raglan coats, and in natural fabrics like cotton and wool. Though there were certainly children who did not adhere to this dress code, my memory has chosen over the years to mainly retain the images of those I felt most alien to: the kind of kids a clothing company would cast to advertise its back-to-school outfits in a mail-order catalog.

I'm not sure 1976 was the exact year of my parents' divorce, but it was definitely the year that my mind registered the fact that we were no longer a family unit. My father had stayed in America, where I was born, and my mother moved with my older brother, Zaf, and me to France, where her older sister Neimat had already settled. I was only six years old but had already lived in three countries and changed residences five times. I felt that I looked nothing like the children of Neuilly-sur-Seine and could barely speak French. I was embarrassed by everything from my name and language skills to my clothes. When, during recess one day, the school principal held up an anorak with a printed flower pattern I'd forgotten on a bench and asked for its owner to claim it, I chose to shiver in a corner of the playground rather than admit it was mine.

This feeling of otherness sank its claws right through my clothing and deep into me. Underneath what I wore, I resented my body. I didn't have the genetic skinniness of French girls my age. I didn't have the straight hair, the swagger, the sense of belonging. I didn't have grandparents who lived in some other part of the country or ancestors who'd spoken the same language. There were no registries of birth in a village church for a great-uncle I'd never met or relatives with familiar and easy-to-pronounce names. Everything had to be explained—how do you say your name, what is Syria, are you Arab, why are you blond, it must be cold in Siberia. I had been parachuted into another world, a visitor in my own home. The feeling of otherness is one that embeds itself deep into a child's core and radiates out.

"Ala" was what my classmates called me because the letter *H* isn't pronounced in French. "Hala" became "Ala" and, as a joke, became "Allah," or *God* in Arabic. "*Hala/Allah est grande* (Allah is great, or Allahuakbar)" the joke went or "*Au nom d'Allah/Hala* (In the name of Allah)." I dreamed of being called anything else. I remember looking at myself in the mirrored door of our bathroom in the small apartment I shared with my mother and brother on rue Perronet in Neuilly-sur-Seine and tried on French names for size.

Stephanie, Caroline, Diane, I would say out loud.

Cecile, Marie, Blandine.

They wouldn't mock me with one of those names, I thought.

The fact that my name and cultural background isolated me from other pupils was baggage I carried with me at all times, even as I grew older. Being a minority means that what we call identity—a foreign name, a different skin color, the otherness of one's ancestors' culture of origin—is a facet of our personhood that occupies more of our self-awareness than members of the majority tribe realize. For children of first-generation immigrants, who come from one world but are born into another, it is a struggle that shapes their inner beings in ways adults likely can't comprehend or imagine.

"So, are you Christian—or not?"

The question came from a boy from Madame Cerisier's third-grade class.

I remember, to this day, the "or not?" ("*ou pas?*") as if there'd been a conversation about it beforehand and the question was posed to settle some sort of debate.

It happened during recess, just as waves of children were spilling out onto the playground after morning classes. The buildings surrounding the courtyard, grand and administrative, were built in 1908 using new construction methods that were less expensive and more modern than the limestone Haussmannian structures of the previous century. The yellow brick façades featured decorative architraves over the windows with redbrick trim and black iron railings.

Though the exteriors were attractive, these were still the days of dull and austere school interiors. In each classroom, rows of two-seater desks made of wood and held up by a gunmetal-gray frame and legs faced a moss-green slate chalkboard. There were no play corners or colorful stickers. Teachers, even the benevolent ones, were there to drill knowledge into skulls, not to cajole. It was the French way of teaching kids, and, for what it lacked in sentimentality, it achieved in efficiency.

On that morning, to the question of whether I was Christian, I responded without hesitation: "*Oui*." I scoffed, even, implying that the act of asking alone was silly. Offensive, even.

Except, it was a lie. It was, in fact, the first fundamental lie I ever remember telling. I realize today that a nine-year-old would not necessarily know the difference between Christianity and any other religion unless they had heard the topic discussed at home. Had a parent asked for the names of this boy's classmates and, when he landed on mine, asked where I came from?

Now, to understand why I lied then, and continued to lie—by omission—about my identity for many years after that, it is important to set the scene.

In my class photos from those years in that particular school, there wasn't a single brown or Black face among the students. I even googled "photos de classe Neuilly-sur-Seine annees 70" (1970s class photos in Neuilly-sur-Seine) just to be sure my memory wasn't betraying me.

There was so little diversity that it was assumed by the school authorities that all pupils were Christian, and Catholic in particular. The school *cantine* served only fish on Fridays, since practicing Catholics didn't eat meat on that day of the week. Many of the children I grew up with would talk of weekend catechism classes, which I imagined as some sort of elite Catholic club I could never belong to. Easter, Christmas, Pentecost, Ascension, and other Christian holidays were marked in school while no other religion was ever truly acknowledged or talked about.

Regardless, I embraced almost every one of those key religious days, especially the cultural dimension of important Christian dates like Easter and Christmas. By the 1970s, those moments, for children in particular, had lost almost all religious meaning, anyway, and had become opportunities for retailers to make gift exchanges the central pillar of many Christian holiday rituals. Mass-produced and cheap *things*, the most visible feature of late-stage capitalism, had started devouring Christmas. And I, the child of a Muslim family from Syria, was there for it.

Part of the reason we came to follow Christian rituals on important dates like Christmas is because we barely marked any of Islam's holiest days. When Eid, the Muslim holiday that celebrates the end of the holy month of Ramadan, came around, my mother would remind us of the day as if she'd suddenly remembered an important appointment she'd neglected to jot down in her diary. "I almost forgot! Tomorrow is Eid. If we were in Syria, we'd do something," she'd remind us. When my mother one year tried decorating a ficus houseplant with baubles and garlands to avoid buying a proper Christmas tree, I exploded in tears. "It's not the same. It's not *tradition*," I wailed.

Sometimes, we'd get cash envelopes from an aunt or visit relatives if we were in Syria during one of the two Eid days, which fall on different days each year, but those events never matched the festive excitement that accompanied Christmas. We were an immigrant, not particularly observant family that played footsie with whatever holiday provided the most entertaining rituals. I even learned Christmas carols by heart.

"Amazing Grace—How sweet the sound—That saved a wrench like me," was how I learned to sing one of the most popular hymns.

"It's not a wrench," my friend Deborah Bordeaux, the more gregarious of a pair of identical twins from fourth grade corrected me one day. "It's a wench, not a wrench. The sweet sound. It saved a *wench*."

I didn't know what either word meant.

It wasn't until rather late into adulthood that I learned the correct lyrics. It was a "wretch" that was saved by the sweet sound and not a hand tool—or a prostitute.

The American Dream

At this stage, I must backtrack and explain why my feelings of otherness were so overwhelming in Neuilly-sur-Seine on that first day of school in 1976. It wasn't just about being an Arab in France—or a Muslim in a Catholic country—it was because I had spent the first few years of my life in what could be described as the polar-opposite environment to 1970s Paris.

My father, Tawfeeq Ficrat Ibrahim Basha, who went by Ficrat, had traveled to America to study engineering in the late '50s. He and my mother, Nour Gorani, married in the mid-'60s in Aleppo, where she gave birth to my brother, Zaf. Soon after, Nour joined Ficrat in Seattle, Washington, where he was working as a civil engineer and where she would give birth to me in March 1970.

A few months later, my father joined a firm in Saint Louis, Missouri, where he bought a suburban starter home in the Catalina subdivision in the city of Crestwood, a suburb thirteen miles southwest of the city.

Mail from Syria came regularly but infrequently in early-'70s America. Long, dense, handwritten letters to my mother from her father, Assad Gorani, the little boy who grew up in the house across the citadel in pre–World War I Aleppo, crossed seas and oceans and, eventually, with the flick of a wrist, landed in the tinny mailbox of our home on Tahiti Drive. Fat envelopes with exotic stamps and postmarks contained something more valuable than anything money could buy: reassurance that the family they had left behind was still there. Was healthy. Was alive. The life my parents left; it was still there. They may have drifted far from home, to unfamiliar American suburbs, but their anchor had not moved. They could hold on to it when they felt lost, alone, abandoned. Those they left behind were still there.

My parents had joined the 1960s wave of young, educated professionals in the Middle East who had found opportunity for professional advancement and education in the West. The Levant, rich and diverse in people and land, was disenfranchising its own youth. The political instability, the corruption, the cronyism: what had started as the promise of a new era after Western colonial powers were pushed out after World War II had morphed into dysfunctional and crooked autocracies—and the worst was yet to come.

As immigration policies in Western countries became less restrictive in the 1960s, many of the children of well-to-do families in Syria packed up and left, if they could. They hoped, like all those for whom immigration is a passage to a better life, that their children would be born in a country that gave them opportunities that their own birthplace would not.

The Syrian exodus started first with a trickle among the privileged classes, but soon, most of those who could leave to study or work abroad followed. Bankers, architects, engineers, doctors, Christians, and Muslims alike. They went where there was work: the US, Saudi Arabia, Africa, Latin America. The country whose postcolonial future at one time seemed so full of promise became hostage to a military dictatorship that cared only about maintaining its grip on power. The

Goranis, like so many Syrian families, were scattered around the world with only letters and long-distance telephone calls to maintain contact. Syria was pushing its own people away.

This displacement came at a heavy price. My mother had been raised in Aleppo with cooks, nannies, and house staff. They had a chauffeur. In Crestwood, Missouri, my parents moved into an unremarkable suburban house, one of millions of starter homes built around inexpensive timber frames to accommodate the still expanding American middle class. A 1960s Realtor ad for Crestwood's Catalina subdivision featured a drawing of a brand-new mid-century home. The headline read "Modern! Unique! Distinctive!" for "Homes UNDER $17,000." It promised "Professional Landscaping!" and "Furniture Finish Birch Cabinets!" among other amenities. "The houses were new, and we weren't going to stay there long," my father told me when I asked him later why he chose Crestwood.

The ad's many exclamation marks also communicated a sense of optimism for a neighborhood that catered to young professionals who could expect job security and upward mobility. It was a time when a husband could still support an entire family on a single salary. In the Catalina subdivision, perhaps to compensate for the dull ranch-style homes, streets were given exotic names of places America's middle class would probably never visit: Capri Drive, Aloha Drive, Samoa Drive.

"I was trapped," my mother would tell me. "I didn't have a car." She blamed my father. "He would leave me all day in the house and go off to work."

Nour settled into a social life that revolved around weekend barbecues and children's birthday parties that would have come as a powerful culture shock for someone fresh out of 1960s Aleppo high society. But these were years she has always recalled with affection and gratitude for neighbors who said they'd never heard of Syria before, but who welcomed the only Arab family into their community with open arms.

There were the Howes, the Priests, and other families whose kids were all about the same age as my brother and I. My kindergarten teacher, Mrs. Dolan, was our next-door neighbor. They came to cook-outs with trays of freshly baked brownies and Tupperware containers filled with potato salad. They exchanged recipes and kept spare front door keys for one another.

"She's forgetting the darker stuff," my brother, Zaf, who's five years older than I am, told me years later about my mother's recollections.

"Darker?" I asked. We were trying to remember the names of the kids we played with.

"Well, the Hannigans down Tahiti Drive," Zaf said. "The dad had a stack of *Hustler*s and *Playboy*s eight feet high in his basement. One day, the two older kids dressed the younger one up like a centerfold. The mom went ballistic."

"Well, it was the seventies," I replied. Life behind the façade of suburban America.

"Okay. How about: Why did Mike Dabrowski's mom and the Baldersons' mom on Capri share breast milk? There was some weird cult crap going on."

"That is odd," I conceded. The sheen was coming off.

"And don't get me started on when I got hauled into the principal's office for refusing to recite the Pledge of Allegiance. Thank goodness I was white. And our mom was superhot, so when she came to pick me up, he suddenly softened."

That aspect of our identity was always tricky. We certainly *looked* white—in the sense that our skin color was fair—and I described myself in that way for many years, but we were also Middle Eastern and Arab. What should we have called ourselves? On US Census forms, there was no separate box for the tiny "Arab American" population, and people from Arab countries were considered "White," even if they did not identify with what was, in the end, an administrative classification. Respondents in government forms back then could identify as Caucasian, African American, Hispanic, or Asian, but Arabs were lumped into a group that did not recognize their differences. It was also not possible to tick more than one box until many decades later.

From Aleppo to Crestwood in the early 1970s, one could fit into and be shaped by several worlds. For my mother, the cost of moving across continents was measured not just in significant cultural readjustments but in long periods of overwhelming homesickness and anxiety. "If I didn't receive a letter from my parents at least once a month, I imagined the worst. I thought they were dead," she would later tell me. "I could only start breathing again when the letter arrived. And then I would wait for the next one."

Telephone calls from America or France to Syria could sometimes take an entire day. My mother would lie in bed or stretch out on the sofa with a rotary telephone on her lap and dial the number to my grandparents' house dozens and dozens of times. Would the call go through on the fifty-third try? Would it go through on the sixty-seventh try? Suddenly, a click and an "Allo?" on the other end of the line. The pitch of my mother's voice would rise. "Allo? Mama? Baba?" I remember her almost crying in relief that they'd picked up the phone.

In the '60s, when my father, Ficrat, traveled back to America to work as an engineer, fewer than five thousand Syrians had been allowed into the country. Even then, a green card was one of the most desirable commodities for Arab immigrant families and Syrians in particular. Living and having children in America infused the document with a powerful aura: they could not be forced to return to a country that had long ago stopped serving its own citizens.

The America they came to wasn't the country my mother had seen in Hollywood movies before she made the journey alone to join my father. Crestwood bore no resemblance to the world portrayed in films starring Ava Gardner or Cary Grant. This was a country where her son climbed trees wearing a bath towel as a cape while singing the *Batman* theme song. Her daughter, barely three, would cry tears of genuine despair if turkey wasn't served for Thanksgiving because, I would sob, "that's what it says we should eat on TV."

Zaf and I became second-generation immigrants, the children of those who have traveled far from their country of origin, with a family history interrupted by displacement, transplanted into an environment so foreign that their own ancestors would not have been able to point to it on a map.

The Middle East of Paris

In 1970s Neuilly-sur-Seine, we settled into a satisfying wider family life. Crestwood, Missouri, and even the two years we spent in Algeria, where my father worked for an American firm, felt like a lifetime away. My mother's sister, my aunt Neimat, lived in Neuilly as well. She had three sons, one of whom, Nabil, was exactly my age.

I had no friends as a fresh-off-the-plane six-year-old, and so Nabil became my best friend and de facto sibling, in large part because my own brother was almost six years older than I. Nabil's two older brothers, Samer and Mouss, were constant presences in our lives. The wider family—aunts, uncles, cousins—banded together like drifting castaways, holding on to each other like buoys. We were a family of immigrants in a new land. But we had each other.

During that time, many other Syrian families, mainly from Aleppo and Damascus, but also from Homs and Hama, settled in Paris too.

My mother's family and friends all came from similar backgrounds. They had received university educations, were multilingual (in addition to Arabic, they often spoke French and English fluently). They were also, by and large, secular. My parents' generation of Syrian immigrants spoke French because they had attended private Catholic institutions in Syria, many of them relics of the French mandate era. They were sent to those schools because the education standards there far exceeded those of state schools. The fact that nuns and priests taught Muslim children was seen not as a problem but a badge of honor. The higher a family's status, the more likely its children would attend Jesuit schools, regardless of religion.

And so, Paris slowly became the natural refuge for Levantine families with means. There was a natural kinship among Arab elites—Muslims and Christians alike—with French culture and customs. They'd studied at their schools and learned their language. Sixty years separated my ancestors' return to Aleppo from Istanbul and my mother's move to Paris, but the notion that Arabs were trailing behind more dominant cultures was the same.

The high-society Levantines gradually transposed social circles and social lives to Paris and, in the summer, to the South of France.

Though my immediate family never had the type of money that would buy you mega-villas in the South of France or diamond necklaces, through marriage and because the wider Levantine community abroad socialized a great deal together, that was the milieu we frequented regularly.

What used to be a soirée at the Aleppo social club in Aziziyah now took place at the Palm Beach in Cannes or the Salle des Etoiles in Monte Carlo. The weddings at the Sheraton Damascus became weddings at Le Pré Catelan in the Bois de Boulogne, a lush, wooded park on the western edge of Paris.

There were lavish buffets and live bands (for those who could afford it, big stars were flown in; in 1986, Egyptian-Italian megastar singer Dalida headlined a wedding in Cap D'Antibes—rumored fee: $1 million). Fine china and tables festooned with cascades of flowers and ice sculptures were de rigueur.

During those great migratory waves, the older generation stayed behind, and a sizable portion of the younger generation did too. In that sense, we were all still connected to Syria. We would go back for regular holidays or the occasional wedding. Aleppo was still an emotional home for kids of my generation, even though we had never lived there. Aleppo was where a scattered family would reunite for a few brief weeks every two or three years before heading back to their permanent homes around the world.

The vast majority of Arab immigrants to France after World War II came from North Africa. Ex–French colonies provided much of the manual labor force that France needed for reconstruction after the war. By 2000, there were three million Arabs from the Maghreb in the country, more than half of them born in France.

For the French, the word *Arab*, in common parlance, came to almost exclusively mean people from Algeria and, to a lesser extent, immigrants from Morocco and Tunisia. *Muslim* became synonymous with the practice of very visible rituals and customs, like Friday prayers, the hijab, or halal food.

Growing up, if I did confess to being from a Muslim family, it was not uncommon to be told that I was not considered a "real" Muslim. I knew that it meant that I wasn't like the "other" Arabs, those who lived in high-rise public housing and were identifiably physically and culturally different from me. I was fair-skinned, for one thing, and my family lived in an affluent part of the city. My agnosticism would also, on the whole, shield me from Islamophobia: not only did I not practice, but I didn't believe; and so, I was safe from judgment.

I have many times wondered that if I, the privileged blond-and-blue-eyed girl from Neuilly-sur-Seine, felt concern about being seen as different because of my name and background, how did the Fatimas and the Mohammeds from the rough public-housing ghettos manage to get through a single day?

Around the time I was worried about fitting into my new school in Neuilly-sur-Seine, France was starting to hem in millions of people from its former colonies, both Arabs and Africans, in the banlieues, those deprived and isolated suburbs on the outskirts of the big cities. "Already poor, Paris sends its impoverished to the Courneuve," wrote the newspaper *Le Monde* in 1980. They were sent to the end of the train line, away from view, to the stations people who lived more centrally only knew from seeing them on subway maps.

That first summer in France in 1976, a brutal heat wave gripped the country for almost a month. It was as baking hot as it was long: weeks of uninterrupted cloudless and windless days with a sun so ferocious that the air remained boiling even overnight. No respite. It was all anyone talked about. Extreme weather trumps everything. There could be a war or a revolution consuming a nation, the crackle of small-arms fire in the distance, the faraway thud of mortars hitting the ground, yet some form of "My God, it's hot" will almost always be the first thing out of people's mouths. Crazy weather brings people together, even when they are engulfed in much more sinister disasters.

In the discomfort of the almost paralyzing heat, my family melted further into the wider community of relatively recent Syrian and Lebanese immigrants. Beyond the weddings and parties, they spent time as a community in ways that today strike me as an attempt to replicate some of what was lost in their countries of origin. The summer of 1976, hot and sticky, slowly breathed life into a partially reconstituted family, composed of pieces brought back together from a variety of places around the world.

The story of the Gorani family, like so many others from that part of the world, was one of being dispersed and then made whole again, in seasonal ebbs and flows. We had become a constantly moving tide circling the globe, made of people traveling to wherever they needed to be to reunite with family, find jobs, or go to school—and then back again. The to and fro of immigrant families. A form of perpetual motion.

On the hottest nights that first summer, I remember my mother and her sisters and their husbands complaining about the heat, fanning themselves with newspapers, sitting on balconies into the night.

They drank tea; they smoked cigarettes. Sometimes, they'd open a cold beer. There would be several servings of Turkish coffee throughout the day.

"Two sweet, one plain, two medium?" Whoever was making the coffee would ask a variation of this, depending on who was present, trying to remember everyone's orders. Turkish coffee is sweetened on the stove top, directly in the pot. The heavy ground coffee granules sink to the bottom of the cup, meaning the liquid can't be stirred after it is poured. Even in the throes of the canicule, coffees kept coming. A taste of home.

"It's so hot. Even late in the evening," they'd say. "Hotter than Syria."

The Five-Star Boarding School

The flashlight was getting closer. I crouched to avoid detection. My breathing was shallow. I knew the end was near. I tried to come up with a believable story I could use when I was caught. "I needed fresh air" just didn't sound like a reasonable explanation. It was 3:00 a.m. and I was drunk, though the run through the fields had sobered me up pretty quickly. The beam of light came closer. I froze. There was nowhere to go. Monsieur Mathe finally caught up with me. I knew he would. He shined the light on my face. "I'll give you a choice. You go back to your dorm now and we forget this ever happened. Or you're expelled." I got up and realized my friend Viviane, who had flattened herself behind me in the hopes of avoiding capture, hoisted herself up as well. She was struggling to keep her eyes open. The harsh beam of the flashlight was on my friend now. "There's two of you?" Monsieur Mathe asked. We promised to leave quietly and head back to our dormitory. Perhaps we'd gotten away with it.

The bonfire in the distance was what Monsieur Mathe was really there investigating. He had run into us by accident. Dozens of students had gathered in the rapeseed field on the last full day of school before the end of the academic year. It was my third year at the École des Roches boarding school in Normandy, where my mother and her second husband, Amr, had enrolled me while they lived part-time in Switzerland.

The students slept in grand nineteenth-century Norman-style manor houses set on fifty-five acres of land. They had access to tennis courts, a go-kart track, photography lessons, horseback riding, and, for an extra fee, flying lessons in a single-engine Cessna. The École des Roches, founded in 1899, had once been an elite boarding school modeled on English institutions, but its high tuition had since placed it out of reach of many middle-class French families. My mother and Amr were traveling too often for me to remain in school in Neuilly-sur-Seine, where they lived, and so I spent three years in a parallel universe of wealth and dysfunction with the children of financiers, aristocrats, celebrities, dictators, and swindlers.

Unlike in Britain and the United States, France's state schools have higher academic standards and better reputations than private institutions. I had spent two years at the publicly funded Lycée La Folie Saint-James in Neuilly-sur-Seine before being sent to the Norman countryside, and the abrupt change of scenery combined with my teenage malaise did me no favors. I turned into a lazy and underperforming student, took up smoking, and was generally uninterested in my studies. As usual, I felt like a visitor who'd landed in the wrong place. The fact that there were children from around the world didn't help me feel more acclimatized, in part because I knew it was a matter of time before I would have to leave again. Boarding was a temporary arrangement while my mother and stepfather split their time between Paris and Geneva, where they worked. A few years later, I was enrolled in a private high school in Paris that specialized in whipping poorly performing children into shape. A sort of rehab for wealthy underachievers. My grades very quickly shot up. I had two years of high school left, and I was eager to leave my teenage years behind. I wanted to make my own decisions about where I would live and when I would have to say my goodbyes.

The night we were caught running through the École des Roches fields, Viviane and I went back to our dorm room as instructed. From our bedroom window, we could see the cool kids' bonfire in the field, like the glow of a firefly's tail, enticing us to try to join them once again. We made our way out of the building the same way we had the first time, by tying sheets together and rappelling down the wall. We were caught before our feet hit the ground and expelled the next day.

The Train to Lille

"I'll give it to you one day," my mother said. I held the little ivory figurine in my hand, sliding my fingers down its smooth finish. She told me the story of the statuette: her parents, visiting the exhibits at the first Damascus International Fair in 1954, stopped at the Chinese stand when they saw a small sculpture of a girl playing the accordion. She wore pigtails and a school uniform almost identical to the one my mother wore to class at the École des Soeurs Franciscaines in Aleppo. They held it up, smiling. "It looks just like Nour," they said, and put it back on the table. A few days later, a package containing the little figurine arrived at their hotel in Damascus, with a note from the Chinese delegation. My grandfather Assad was justice minister at the time, and the Damascus fair was designed to showcase the best of Syria to the world. Limited-edition stamps were printed to mark the occasion, and more than a million visitors streamed through Umayyad Square during the monthlong event. It was the first forum of its kind in Syria, a celebration meant to mark the start of a prosperous and independent country.

Forty years later, the ivory statuette of the little Chinese girl had found its way to Neuilly-sur-Seine, where my mother and Amr still lived, in an apartment overlooking the large park of a nineteenth-century villa once belonging to the media baron Yves de Chaisemartin and later sold to one of the wives of a Saudi prince. Their building was a modern, postwar construction without the design features or quality of Haussmannian stone façades. Apartment blocks erected in Paris in the 1950s and '60s had clean, angular lines and used cheaper materials than the stone and brick of prewar residential homes. From my mother and Amr's apartment overlooking the mansion's park—and this was very unusual in Paris and its immediate suburbs—only trees were visible from every window. And so, with very little discussion, they made an offer on the property and moved in toward the end of 1987.

By the mid-'90s, I had already worked two years on and off as a freelance journalist. In 1992, I interned at the Agence France-Presse in Washington and in Paris. I was assigned to the French news agency's English-language desk, where I translated sometimes up to a dozen French wires every day. I was still only an intern, but my language skills made me a desirable free hand. It went both ways: in just a few months, I received an accelerated course on journalistic English writing and churning out news alerts and updates on tight deadlines. Once signed off by a senior editor, the translated wires would go out on the AFP's global subscriber network.

The following year, aged twenty-three, I freelanced for *La Voix du Nord*, a newspaper published in Lille, in the north of France, and one of the country's main regional dailies. Though television had been pushing newspaper sales down since the 1950s, *La Voix du Nord* was still a commanding presence in the city. Headquartered on the place Charles de Gaulle in a grand art deco building, the bronze statues of three graces on its Flemish gable rooftop overlooking the square, the paper was an institution. I was assigned to *La Voix du Nord*'s monthly business magazine and worked in a small office a few streets away from the paper's hub. For the first time, articles with my byline appeared in print. I cut out and kept each one, like precious jewels I was afraid of misplacing. Not every attempt was successful: "It's so strange," my editor, Maguelone Hedon, said to me after a few weeks on the job, "you either write really well or it's total shit. There's no in-between." It was valuable feedback. I was writing copy in French for the first time, and my work needed to improve. Maguelone, a sharp and attractive blond woman in her late twenties, gave me practical advice with good humor. Her barbs were never malicious, and her feedback was often valuable.

In more than one way, the north of France felt like a dark place. Disused factories and coal mines dotted the region after industrial work moved to Asia. In the 1970s, hundreds of thousands of coal mine, steel, and textile jobs were lost. The dank and chilly climate during the colder months made the region's economic despair appear gloomier. The thick cover of gray clouds on winter afternoons was so low that it seemed close enough to touch.

I lived for almost a year in a studio I'd sublet from a university student near the Lille train station in a run-down three-story building, which was also used as a base of operations by a prostitute who stood, most evenings, at the front door. We crossed paths often enough that I started nodding hello to her when I came home after work. She sometimes nodded back, at first wearily and, eventually, with an occasional smile. These unconventional living arrangements gave me an appreciation for a world I never had experienced in my privileged Parisian bubble. My nomadic upbringing had given me an ability to put temporary roots down anywhere, ready to pick up and leave after a short stay. I wanted to be as comfortable around the Lille hooker as I was around the Parisian prince. I wanted to navigate both worlds; to toggle from one to the other with ease.

I was lucky to have ended up in Lille because, as I came to realize later, some of the most intensely satisfying reporting happens at the local level. As a rookie, I was given freedom and responsibility I would not have had in a larger organization and at such a young age. I reported on everything from lace factory employees losing their jobs to a meeting of shipping bosses in Calais. I enjoyed the craft. I knew that whatever came next, journalism was my calling. The act of gathering information in its simplest form, pulling together the strands of a story and producing a finished product in a way that people could learn from was exhilarating. The journalistic process, before social media and multiple platforms splintered our attention and workflow, was almost meditative. It was also thrilling: seeing my initials at the bottom of a two-paragraph Agence France-Presse wire for the first time filled me with such joy that I ran halfway to my metro stop, transported by the elation of doing something that I truly loved. No one remembers the wire I wrote that day, a few paragraphs on a man charged with stalking East German ice skater Katarina Witt, but I will never forget it. I still have the yellowed paper it was printed on to this day.

After those first two experiences, I wanted more than ever to work as a journalist. I had a bachelor of science in economics from an American university, but I needed a French diploma if I wanted to pursue a career in France. I spent months studying for the top Parisian journalism school entrance exam but failed the admissions test. Instead, I got into the Institut d'Etudes Politiques de Paris—or Sciences Po as it's better known—and hoped that would be enough in the French system. It was an achievement: Sciences Po is an elite school that opens doors. It was founded in the 1870s and moved in 1882 to a Saint-Germain mansion bought with a million-franc donation by the Duchess of Galliera and has remained at the same location ever since. Almost every French president and prime minister in the last half century has attended Sciences Po, usually followed by the École Nationale d'Administration, a civil service school created by then president Charles de Gaulle after World War II. L'ENA was meant to democratize access to the top government posts but instead produced an elite class of career politicians and industry leaders cast in the same mold from one generation to the next. Graduates of those institutions, most often white men, would start their careers with an outsize advantage in business or politics. For the graduates who chose a civil service career, reaching the top jobs was not unusual. The more accomplished and ambitious became secretaries of state and ministers. The path to the very top positions in France was almost preordained: since 1969, six French presidents—Georges Pompidou, Valéry Giscard d'Estaing, François Mitterrand, Jacques Chirac, François Hollande, and Emmanuel Macron—have been Sciences Po / L'ENA graduates. A tiny members-only club with an established road map to the lavish gilded ministries fanned out across Paris, with the 365-room Élysée Palace, France's presidential residence, at the very top of the country's governmental power structure. The fact that I had gained access felt at once like I fully deserved a place in one of the world's top institutions and like I was a fraud. I applied as an American, my only nationality, and was admitted after a competitive entrance exam. Yet again, I was considered a foreigner in the only country I had ever truly called home. More than once, I was complimented, by professors and students alike, on how well I spoke my native tongue. I wanted to be part of the club, not treated as a guest enjoying a temporary residency. I would soon be on the move again.

Part 4

Cairo

The Revolution

People who don't work in journalism, specifically TV journalism, don't always understand a simple truth that those of us who've chosen this bizarre profession all tend to keep to ourselves: we love chaos. We don't love that people suffer, we aren't happy when there is misery around us, but what makes our job thrilling, what truly gets the blood pumping, is when stuff blows up.

Ideally, we don't die in the process. "You don't want to end up naked hanging upside down in a cellar," former CNN senior producer Robert Wiener once said. We avoid getting kidnapped or being forcefully escorted to the office of an overzealous intelligence officer who's honed sadistic interrogation practices over many years of working for one totalitarian regime or another. But when around us there is chaos—a war, a terrorist attack, an earthquake—and we are there, in person, smelling the sweat of the people whose lives have just been upended, really *there*, not on a balcony overlooking a skyline but on the ground, that is why many of us do this job.

Part of it is that we feel slightly more alive when we hear the bullets or feel the earth rumbling. And with each assignment, we test our limits. When the adrenaline rush wanes, we crave it like an addiction. Coming back home, doing ordinary things like going to the supermarket or doing laundry suddenly seems like time wasted, like being the only person who is truly living among the walking dead, because they can't understand—they will never understand—the intensity of emotions that we have just experienced. After an assignment, even speaking into a television camera in a TV studio in some ways feels like being a fraud. We aren't really reporters if we are just discussing something from behind a glass anchor desk; we are just relaying information others have gathered, possibly at some risk to themselves. Of course, not all journalism happens in the field. One can get to the truth through in-person interviews, by analyzing big events within the proper context, by programming the right types of stories in a newscast so that viewers feel enlightened and informed. But even though I've spent much more of my career in a studio, when I look back, nothing competes with the stories I covered in person, whether there was danger around me or not.

Sometimes, though, chaos is a violent lover. We run into a crowd, and the crowd closes in on us; it absorbs us and spits us back out because, as much as we think we can control events, we are powerless against the earth when it shakes or the mortars when they land, haphazardly, too close for comfort, or when a mob of angry men decides to tear the clothes off a female reporter and rape her in the middle of a revolution. The names of journalists who went into a conflict zone but didn't come out alive are well known in our industry. They serve as warnings to the rest of us.

On February 2, 2011, the day after I landed in Cairo to cover the Arab Spring uprising that had erupted across Egypt, I was filled with a kind of dizzying exhilaration. The protests that had started in December 2010 in Tunisia after a young fruit seller named Mohamed Bouazizi had set himself on fire to protest police harassment had spread to several countries in the Arab world. Eventually, demonstrations there led to the ouster of longtime dictator Zine al-Abidine Ben Ali on January 14 that year. In Egypt, the people were openly revolting against their abusers, as if they'd finally gathered the courage to punch a bully back. After decades of being muzzled, imprisoned, and exiled; after sham elections where the same autocrat wins with 99 percent of the vote; after years of corruption where resources and money were funneled to the offshore accounts of dictators: ordinary Arabs were publicly demanding freedom and accountability. Like a patient with a chronic illness suddenly bouncing out of bed screaming: I'm alive! It wasn't a fever dream. It felt like the impossible was happening.

CNN had rented a huge two-bedroom suite on one of the top floors of the Nile Hilton hotel, overlooking Tahrir Square, where thousands of anti-government protestors had gathered, demanding the resignation of then president Hosni Mubarak. *"Irhal,"* or "Get Out," was the leitmotif of the demonstrators. They chanted it. Spray-painted it on walls. They were fed up with decades of corruption, cronyism, and police violence. The CNN workspace was packed with reporters and anchors who'd flown in from New York, Washington, DC, London, Atlanta, Hong Kong, as well as with reporters based in the Arab world, who were experiencing the story both as journalists and as people whose personal lives and families were affected by the upheaval. There were also "fixers," local producers who speak the language and know the city and culture, there to assist correspondents on the ground. They act as translators and guides to journalists who are dropped into stories in countries they might know little about, and sometimes work at great risk to themselves. No international journalism of any value usually happens without them.

The day I arrived, I did not have a camera crew or a producer. There were so many CNN people covering the historic event that the network was dispatching staff as fast as it could, and I was told I would have to wait a day or two until I could be matched with a team. Had I been in almost any other city, I would have waited before venturing out into the crowd alone, but because I had traveled many times to Cairo before, I felt like I could safely navigate my way through the dense mass of protestors, filming my walk through Tahrir Square with a small handheld camera. I would have acted very differently covering a story in Caracas or Moscow or Nairobi; leaving the hotel on my own would not have been an option. Cairo, I thought, was a city I knew well, and, though I may not look like an Arab, I can easily and quickly identify myself as Syrian in Arabic, establishing a rapport with the people around me in a way someone who doesn't speak the language would have to rely on a translator to do. As someone whose origins were Middle Eastern, I was, in a sense, a member of the wider tribe of people whose historic moment this was. *I should be safe*, I thought.

It was a short walk from the Hilton to the outer edge of the square. On my way into the thick of the demonstration, walking into Tahrir, the crowd was still sparse. I was excited in the way a journalist witnessing history, to use a tired cliché, is excited. A young man with a bandaged hand and a black eye crossed my path. He smiled. I smiled back and immediately said a few words in Arabic, with a thick Syrian twang that he must have easily recognized. Though I'd never lived in Syria, I had learned conversational Arabic at home, where everyone spoke with an instantly identifiable Aleppine accent, which I picked up as well. "Hello, I want to see what's going on in the square," I said to the young man. A blond, blue-eyed woman venturing into the revolution's epicenter alone must have seemed exotic, perhaps even entertaining to him. Or, perhaps, he thought I was insane. I was wearing makeup in case I was asked to appear on air that evening. Fresh lipstick in a revolution. The absurdity of television reporting: reapply blusher before filming a piece to camera in a war zone. "I will escort you," he said, holding on to my right elbow. I wanted to shed him as quickly as I could without appearing rude. He felt my unease and let go of my elbow, but continued to follow me until I managed to lose him by melting into the crowd, a mass of people so tightly packed that they formed a single living organism. By then, I was about fifty yards from the central Tahrir roundabout, still on the side of the square where Mubarak supporters had gathered, sent by the regime to confront the protestors. There was tension, but not violence. I was making my way to the anti-regime side when a group of men riding camels and on horseback rammed their way into Tahrir, slicing the air with whips, galloping to the center of the square, knocking over anti-government demonstrators on their mad journey. I held up my camera phone and snapped a single photo: a man on camelback wearing jeans, a brown leather jacket, and a red checkered keffiyeh on his head, holding up a hand-written paper with one hand and his animal's reins in the other as he charged through the crowds.

I was *there*. The *there* that journalists dream of. The *there* that you talk about in hotel bars with other reporters, boozing and smoking, trading stories. Until I was in the wrong *there*. I was trapped. On one side, camels and horses trampling protestors, and on the other, angry pro-Mubarak supporters. I couldn't join the revolutionaries and couldn't retrace my steps back to the Hilton. I realized that by turning around and trying to escape, I had only drifted sideways against the iron fencing of the Egyptian Museum. I thought I needed to document the moment and started filming with my Flip Video camera, a sort of precursor to the modern-day cell phone cameras. Within a few seconds, men surrounded me, and I lowered the device. I don't quite remember what they said, but several men screamed at me and pinned me against the railing. I tried to speak to them in Arabic, but my voice was drowned out. The men came even closer. I could smell their breaths. Their faces so close to mine that spittle landed on my cheek. "She's with me," a voice behind me said. "She's with me," the voice grew louder. I turned around. It was the man with the bandaged hand and the black eye. He pulled me away and led me out of the chaos with his arms around my shoulders, almost marching me down the boulevard and below an underpass, letting go only when the mob was behind us. He said goodbye, left, and perhaps returned to the square. It's a man whose name I don't remember who probably saved me from being attacked or raped. It was only a few days later, when journalist Lara Logan was brutally sexually assaulted in Tahrir Square, that I realized how lucky I'd been.

The following day, pro-government thugs stormed the lobby of the Nile Hilton, searching for Westerners and journalists. The Mubarak regime was not going to go down without causing as much chaos as possible before it would be forced from power. CNN made the decision to evacuate part of its staff from the Hilton because it was a huge skyscraper only a few hundred yards from Tahrir Square that was too difficult to fully secure. We were told to head to the Marriott hotel, a smaller building on the other side of the Nile. Colleagues who stayed behind at the Hilton barricaded themselves in their rooms and hid under beds and in closets while several others prepared to evacuate to the Marriott. For no other reason than because we ended up in the same huddle looking for a ride, I shared a car with Joe Duran, a cameraman, and CNN anchor Anderson Cooper, who had also been attacked in the square the previous day.

On the section of the 6th October Bridge over the Nile, a mob forced our taxi to stop and encircled it. The men outside the car were angry. They waved sticks and shovels in the air. Their screams and insults blended into a single roar. I could see only parts of people from the back seat: a man's teeth as he opened his mouth to yell, another's mustache moist with spittle, another's hands and fingernails holding a weapon. Little snapshots of people flashing before me, like going through a roll of photographs on an old slide projector. They smashed the car windows, and glass shattered throughout the vehicle. Anderson, who was wearing a baseball cap, sank into the back seat next to me and tried to protect his head, arms, and hands as the crazed men threw rocks in through the car's broken windows. I used my carry-on suitcase to shield my face. Various projectiles bounced off the car, a few flew into the back seat. The driver, surrounded by the violent attackers, appeared to freeze.

In Arabic, I remember saying to him, "I will give you five hundred dollars for the windows if you keep going." I plucked that figure out of thin air. I still don't know why that number in particular came to my mind. I didn't care if he had to run someone over. I didn't want to be dragged out and assaulted. It was us or them. "Yallah, yallah, *go!*" I implored. The driver pressed down on the gas pedal, hesitantly at first, and then more forcefully. The crowd suddenly parted. We drove away as the men banged on the car's roof.

When we finally pulled into the entrance of the Marriott in our shattered taxi, dazed, we made our way into the hotel and registered at the front desk, without fully realizing how close we had come to disaster.

The *New York Times* columnist Nick Kristof, who had arrived at the Marriott without incident, told our group that some Western journalists were changing the names they checked in with so that any thugs coming into the hotel demanding guest lists wouldn't know which rooms the foreign press were in.

My name is Arabic, anyway, I thought, so I should be fine. "Does it say CNN anywhere on your form?" I remember Kristof asking me. I wasn't sure, but I decided to risk it. I was worried that lingering too long at the reception desk was more dangerous than asking the front desk to dig up my file.

We were told to stick together and not spread out immediately into individual hotel rooms. Anderson Cooper and I waited it out for a few hours, awkwardly sitting on a double bed, long periods of silence weighing on us like a cloud. I despise small talk and, it appeared, so did he, which suited me quite well that evening. I had no desire to engage in superficial niceties.

That night, we were joined by CNN's Ben Wedeman as we coanchored the network's special coverage from the floor of the hotel room, sitting on a lighting box with the curtains drawn behind us. I remember thinking it looked like a hostage video. I had been truly scared that day. At one point, I wondered if I would be physically hurt, but the elation of telling the story on the air with arguably CNN's biggest star anchor made it all worth it. I was forty years old, and I felt like every sacrifice I had made to get to that point in my career had been worth the struggle. I was *there*.

The Massacre

Waking up from a revolution feels a lot like waking up from an all-night party, where there is drunkenness and revelry and where promises of eternal friendship are made in the delirium of dance and music and exhaustion. The first rays of sunshine the following morning can reveal litter and broken glass, things that looked less problematic in the penumbra. The day after the night before, the hangover is etched on the faces of those who had let loose. Egypt, in one sense, had had a huge party in January and February 2011. It had been chaotic and violent at times, but it had ultimately been exhilarating for the revolutionaries who had achieved the near impossible: they had evicted a dictator. Rather, the will of the people was so strong that the military had not, for once, stood in their way. This didn't mean that the aftermath had been smooth: the problems the protestors had hoped would be resolved or disappear with the expulsion of President Hosni Mubarak and his cronies remained, stubbornly engrained. The corruption, the police brutality, the unemployment and poverty—eradicating those long-standing issues would take time and a more fundamental shift in governance and societal attitudes. What Egypt needed was more than the ouster of the man at the top. Egypt needed a revolution of its institutions, including a clear separation of power between the country's armed forces and its civilian leadership. This had not happened, and the country would soon pay a high price for it.

In May 2012, I traveled to Cairo to report on the country's first ever free presidential elections. I spoke to people who had been standing in line for hours to cast their ballots and dip their index fingers in purple ink to show that they had voted. But there was concern among some Egyptians that more than a year after the revolutionary uprising that led to the dictator's downfall, four of the five candidates running for president were either Islamists affiliated with the Muslim Brotherhood or had served as ministers in Mubarak's regime. Some among the more secular, urban revolutionaries who had participated in the movement from the beginning felt ostracized. Had they not fought for every Egyptian to be represented, including those who told me they wanted their country's politics to be unaffiliated with religious parties and free from the grips of the military? On the day of the vote, Wael Ghonim, a young Google executive whose Facebook page denouncing police brutality had become a virtual meeting place for regime opponents to organize, told me that he was "remembering those who died for us to live this moment." He had been held in secret detention for eleven days the previous year, and his emotional appearance on a talk show upon his release had made me cry. He had urged the revolutionaries to keep fighting for their rights. He was crying for his country, but all of us watching were also weeping for the entire Arab world. How had we all gotten to this point? I wondered. How did an entire region become hostage to authoritarianism? Ghonim's Facebook page was called "We Are All Khaled Said," named after a young man who was brutally beaten to death by police in Alexandria in 2010. Postmortem images of his bruised, broken face were posted on Ghonim's Facebook page and widely circulated, and it felt like the people of Egypt had decided, collectively, that they would not accept this type of humiliation anymore. *We are not animals, we are human beings,* they said.

The day of the first round of presidential elections in Cairo, I met with voters in a school on Mohamed Mahmoud Street near Tahrir Square. There had been violent clashes between protestors and security forces in that area the year before. Men waited in one line and women in another. This was a profoundly conservative part of Cairo where the Muslim Brotherhood had considerable support. At least two women told me they were casting ballots for the candidate their husbands had told them to vote for. This was not yet a mature democracy, but it was a democracy. Still, there was little doubt as to which candidates would get the most support there. Wael Ghonim and I talked live on CNN that evening about why this was a momentous event. He was publicly supporting an Islamist candidate, Abdel Moneim Aboul Fotouh, which I remember finding puzzling. "He is a moderate Muslim," he replied. I wondered if Ghonim had chosen to support the candidate most aligned with his views among an imperfect slate of contenders. "A crucial time for your country," I said, wrapping up the live interview. "And for the whole world, as well," he said, correcting me.

In the end, another Islamist candidate was elected. Mohamed Morsi became Egypt's fifth president. The era of Hosni Mubarak, a leader who, like a pharaoh, had once seemed imbued with the power to rule eternally, was forever in the past. He had just been sentenced to life imprisonment, and his two sons would also be put on trial and convicted. Morsi, an engineer who had earned a PhD at the University of Southern California, a devout man who'd been part of the Muslim Brotherhood and imprisoned under the Mubarak regime, was the choice of the people. Even the country's military leaders would have to accept the results of the democratic vote.

It didn't take long for that promise, too, to turn to rot. The corruption. The incompetence in providing essential services. The precipitous push to change the constitution. The persecution of independent journalists. The decrees granting Morsi unchecked powers. What was it, I wondered, that made so many leaders lose all sense of measure once they walked through the doors of a presidential palace? Morsi had lived in California and taught engineering at Cal State in Northridge for three years after his studies there. He had experienced a free society with a free press. Why then would he go back to his home country, run for the presidency, and almost immediately revert to Mubarak-era tactics? There were protests against the new president across the country. A few months into his term, his own defense minister, Abdel Fattah el-Sisi, ordered his arrest in July 2013.

The army was back in charge. It had stepped aside for less than three years, but had never really stepped down. When Mohamed Morsi supporters set up camp in two Cairo locations demanding their leader be reinstated as president, the military and police, under the orders of Sisi, tear-gassed and shot them when they refused to disperse. Nearly a thousand protestors were killed in what became known as the Rabaa massacre, named after one of the squares where protestors had gathered. Sisi had become the true successor to Hosni Mubarak.

Shortly after the camp was stormed, Muslim Brotherhood supporters were jailed en masse, some sentenced to death. Journalists and human rights activists who probed and openly criticized the Sisi government were persecuted and detained. Had this entire revolution been for nothing? we wondered in despair. In so many ways, the repression had become worse. When Mubarak was president, there had been a timid freeing of the press and a sense that mild criticism of the government, if not of the leader himself, was tolerated. During the Sisi era, even bloggers and social media activists have been jailed. "I wish none of this had ever happened," a Syrian friend told me. "I'm ashamed to say it, but I wish there had never been an Arab Spring at all."

One Night in Aswan

Egypt was empty of tourists. Ours was the only boat on the Nile as far as the eye could see. The United States–led coalition forces were about to launch a massive bombing campaign against Iraq for invading Kuwait the previous summer, and Western visitors, worried that violence would spill into other parts of the Arab world, were staying away from the Middle East altogether. At night, I looked outside my cabin porthole toward the banks of the river, with just the moonlight drawing the outline of palm trees and bouncing off the rooftops of the homes of the Nubian villages dotting the landscape. *The land of the pharaohs*, I thought dramatically. *I have it all to myself.* We had been told that there were fewer than a hundred tourists in the entire country.

My mother, Nour; my stepfather, Amr; my brother, Zaf; and a group of friends were spending a week cruising up the Nile on a small boat with only a couple of dozen cabins. In addition to our group, there was a wealthy American designer and his young boyfriend, a few Italian socialites, and an American diplomat posted to the region who referred to Egyptian locals as "these people," even though he knew there were both Syrians and Egyptians in our group. He had openly expressed a romantic interest in my mother, despite the fact that both her husband and his wife were passengers on the vessel.

I was twenty years old with long, blond hair and a fresh, youthful beauty that comes and goes so quickly in a woman's lifetime that it is a shame we don't know we had it until it's gone. There is a brief period in life when neither the complexes of childhood nor the pressures of adulthood matter, and I was experiencing that ease and self-confidence during that trip. The American diplomat had organized a camel ride during one of our stops close to Luxor. We rode to the top of a hill, reached some sort of ancient castle, turned around, and rode back to the boat. I had become best friends with the older American designer's boyfriend, who was closer in age to me than to his partner, and we laughed throughout the weeklong cruise, sitting next to each other at dinner like two naughty pupils in the back of a classroom. On New Year's Eve, we docked in Aswan in upper Egypt and, as if the mythical Egyptian gods had wanted our stop to be even more memorable, were showered with a winter storm so thunderous that the crew told us they hadn't seen anything like it in twenty years.

Even my brother, Zaf, who had sulked throughout the cruise because a girl he liked had ghosted him during the trip, was smiling widely as we ran through the muddy streets of Aswan, the dust turning into rivers of red-brown sludge with few drainage grates or underground sewers to absorb the rain as it fell in sheets. I had not changed out of my New Year's Eve outfit, and my wet hair stuck to my earrings and onto my sparkly top. My new friend took my hand as we skipped over puddles, and, for a moment, I wondered if he was really, irreversibly gay. I felt a surge of attraction for him; a beautiful man with a square jaw and the thick, slicked-back hair of a retro Hollywood star. Our group stopped at a coffee shop for shelter and, under a bright neon light, ordered a hot tea with sugar. The rain continued, the water pooling in the awning, sometimes rushing down in buckets when the tent above us couldn't contain it anymore. For the first time in my life,

I felt at home. Not because I was in Egypt, a country I barely knew, but because we were nearly all foreigners there, and the people on the trip with us knew the region well enough to not see me as some sort of curiosity.

The diplomat, some speculated, had been a spy before his posting. His perfect Arabic and knowledge of the Middle East certainly made him a good candidate. Looking out toward the riverbanks one day, he pointed at a group of men on camelback. "This is how they smuggle their drugs, you know," he told us. He seemed to be aware of even the most niche criminal practices in the Egyptian desert, as if he had developed an all-knowing expertise about every aspect of life in this part of Egypt. He sounded like a man who read secret briefings and would quickly be put through to important people in the US government on the phone.

I knew I wanted to come back. I wanted to understand this part of the world better. Did they really smuggle drugs on the backs of camels? We were on a small dinghy on the Nile sputtering our way back to the boat. I had started writing for my college newspaper in Virginia, and I felt excitement at the idea of writing stories about the Middle East one day. The world, after all, was clearly fascinated with a region featured on the front pages of newspapers almost daily. In January 1991, as we cruised down the Nile, we were all waiting for America and its allies to make good on their threat to force Iraq to pull back from Kuwait. The UN Security Council had given Saddam Hussein a deadline of January 15 to withdraw from Kuwait or face war. This "chronicle of a bombing foretold" filled us with nervous anticipation about a looming war just one country and the Red Sea away from our little luxury cruise boat. I didn't feel ill at ease, however, in the middle of a desert with spooks and designers as a thirty-nine-nation conflict was brewing in the region. I felt right at home.

"Making Us Look Bad"

As I look back on my years reporting in Egypt, I realize that almost every story I filed somehow foretold the 2011 revolution. The poverty, the overpopulation, the inequality. Even, sometimes, its beauty and its youth, its vibrancy and its exuberance.

When I met Hussein in a mobile health care unit in 2006, I immediately noticed his scarred hands. The skin, thick with an overlapping network of scar tissue, looked burned. "What happened to you?" I asked.

"A fire," he answered, laughing.

"Why is that funny?" I asked.

"Ha ha ha," said Hussein.

Hussein told me he was fourteen years old. Our first meeting took place in a converted bus where medical volunteers treated street children for wounds and skin conditions. Skin doesn't tolerate rough living very well. It toughens and putrefies and can develop rashes and infections. A charity named Hope Village Society ran two of these buses in Cairo, a city of fifteen million people.

I followed Hussein to a day shelter where kids like him were given food and a place to spend a few hours before heading back to the streets. He made faces at the camera, performing for us, sticking his chest out. He told me there was a fire in his home when he was seven years old, that the fire had killed his mother, and that his father was in prison, convicted of selling drugs. "They gave the dad ten years," the charity worker at the shelter said.

"Do you think about it often? The fire?" I asked Hussein again. He smiled. "It's better not to." I left it there. I didn't want to push it. I didn't want to make him cry. He forced himself to smile in the way people who hold back tears smile; it was more of a grimace. I know it took him exactly four seconds to compose himself, because I counted the time down on the interview tape twice.

That year, we were told up to a million children in Egypt were homeless or working on the streets to help provide for their families. Family breakup, overpopulation, poverty, and lack of shelters or government support were the main causes. I look at my notes from that shoot. "Great shot of dirty feet in plastic sandals," I had jotted down. It may sound heartless, but it's how TV news notes are taken. There is no time to word things diplomatically. At exactly 18:51:13 on the tape: "Fatma breaks down," I noted. "Daddy is on the street," I wrote on another page. "Most kids take drugs, sniff glue, sexually active..."

The seeds of the 2011 Egyptian revolution were planted over many years and in many different places around the country. The million children sleeping on the streets told the story of a country incapable, and perhaps unwilling, to give all of its citizens basic freedoms and opportunity. There can be an intolerance among officials in an authoritarian state to accept that there are problems that need urgent attention. Those who want to reveal or discuss or even resolve the problems are accused of wanting to make the country "look bad." Journalists, activists, humanitarians all risk being targeted by the government when exposing such abuses of power or even neglect.

A few months after my report on street children aired, the blogger Wael Abbas, who had been sharing videos of police torture online, uploaded a particularly disturbing one showing a minibus driver named Emad al-Kabir being sexually tortured by police officers. One of the officers had filmed it and shared the video with other minibus drivers. "They said they did it to break my spirit," al-Kabir said.

The Arab Winter

After every interview about Syria and every report on the war, I feel more removed from Aleppo. I realize that, as time passes, one can experience a loss of intimacy with places, as well as people. Perhaps that's not such a bad thing: Aleppo isn't the city it was before 2011, and seeing it broken and desolate would likely make me feel even sadder than if I just allow its memory to slowly fade. It's been so long. I haven't returned to Syria since 2011, the last time the government gave me a visa. I had spent two weeks in Damascus that summer, dodging secret police tails every time I left the Four Seasons hotel in the city's Shukri al-Quwatli District. *Mukhabarat* agents seemed to appear everywhere in the hotel, as well: there were men in suits in the lobby, in the room next to our workspace, in the restaurant area. They sat, they lingered, they suddenly appeared around a hallway corner. "Same guy with mustache in the lobby," I'd tell my colleagues, "holding up the same newspaper." "He should just cut holes in it," we joked. During that assignment, we were taken on an officially sanctioned tour of Douma, a Damascus suburb, where government minders showed us what they claimed was damage caused by rioters and looters. Their version of events was different from the reports we had heard days before that security forces had shot into a group of anti-regime protestors. On camera, none of the people we interviewed contradicted the official narrative. A large crowd of onlookers surrounded our crew. While our cameraman filmed street scenes, I stepped away. Just as I was ready to head back, I sensed a tickle on my palm, the feeling of something being slipped into my hand. I looked down: a tiny piece of folded paper. I turned around. A young man came closer. "They are lying to you," he said furtively, and disappeared into the busy street. I unfolded the paper. On it, an email address and a name: Zied. Later that evening, using VPN software to obscure our IP address, my producer and I contacted the young man via the Gmail account he had given me. I knew that his first name, "Zied," was likely a pseudonym, but I worried that our exchange could still be monitored. We agreed to meet at a shopping mall a few days later. Then CNN producer Jomana Karadsheh and I made sure we weren't being followed: we left the hotel early, stopped at tourist attractions, entered a museum through one door, and exited quickly through another. Every man in a suit behind us seemed suspect. Was he secret police?

Zied gave us a description of a T-shirt he would be wearing, so we would recognize him. In a café inside the mall, we sat together at a small table. After a few minutes of small talk, I started recording Zied's voice, making sure the camera did not reveal his face. He told us that some of the people who had demonstrated in Douma in the days before our visit there had been killed and injured by security forces and that the government version was a lie. We did not linger. After the interview, we spent time in the mall acting like unfazed shoppers. I bought a souvenir from a shop in the mall. The cell phone in my bag felt heavy with the weight of everything we had heard from Zied.

After that assignment, I was advised not to go back. My interviews with regime officials in the first years of the war were combative. During that time, I grilled ministers and Syrian government representatives like Bouthaina Shaaban or the deputy foreign minister, Faisal Mekdad, about the crackdown on peaceful protestors. In Washington, DC, my interview with Imad Moustapha, the Syrian ambassador to the United States, had been widely shared on social media in 2011. I was commended for pushing back against his claims that many of the Syrian demonstrators were Islamist terrorists serving foreign interests. Today, though I don't regret the questions, I sometimes wonder if my approach was the most effective one. Was I getting the most informative answers? Anchors are celebrated when they ask tough questions, interrupt when the interviewee stonewalls or gaslights, and challenge lies with facts and research. I still wonder how much more I could have gotten out of these Assad regime officials had I been a bit gentler, a bit more patient, allowing more time for pauses and silences. A big part of the challenge of being a woman in news is that we are often judged for not showing toughness. As a result, I wonder if I could have varied my approach with representatives of autocratic governments. Forceful objections when needed. Time for an answer to fully take shape, allowing the interviewee to lay out even the most ludicrous claim, giving it just enough oxygen to be slowly dismantled in a follow-up. As a relatively younger anchor, I wanted to prove to anyone who might doubt my capabilities that I was no softie.

This tough approach wasn't limited to my interviews with Syrian officials. One of my regular guests through the years was Mark Regev, spokesperson for the Israeli prime minister Benjamin Netanyahu. Interviews with him, especially when I asked questions about Israeli operations in the occupied territories, were as much about the back-and-forth between interviewer and guest as about the content of what was being said. Besides, what he came on air to say was always known in advance. Regev was a master spokesperson with unmatched longevity in his role in Israeli politics. He "did the rounds" on international news channels each time the Israeli government needed to get its message out. Those interviews, though among the most watched and shared on social media, were the least satisfying ones for me. Government spokespeople stick to talking points and expertly avoid offering new or useful information. I often came away from those made-for-TV clashes feeling like on-the-ground reporting was far more fulfilling than anchoring. In the end, I wondered, was I bringing anything more to the table than a television moment? Some reporters during the Donald Trump presidency, for instance, became superstars for using the same confrontational interview techniques with him and his supporters. There is a very fine line between journalism and spectacle. It is much more difficult than some would think to maintain the proper balance while live on air.

Today, there is no use regretting my on-air conversations with officials during the early days of the Arab Spring, perhaps because nothing I or my colleagues did to shed light on the story made any difference. I look back on that time with such sadness that it is sometimes unfathomable to me that a decade has passed since the people of Egypt, Libya, Syria, Yemen, Bahrain, Morocco, Algeria, and Tunisia rose up against their leaders. It is even more difficult to believe that variations of the same regimes are still in power today, most even more repressive than their predecessors.

Syria has been gutted, with more than half its population displaced or exiled, half a million killed, and tens of thousands disappeared. On the scale of a country the size of the United States, it would translate to over 150 million people fleeing. Since my last visit, Russia and Iran entered the war on the side of the regime, helping it destroy rebel-held territory in Aleppo and other large cities. Yemen has been in the grips of a vicious civil war, with Saudi Arabia and Iran both fighting each other using proxies in what was already the poorest country in the region. Egypt is back to its Mubarak ways, jailing and persecuting government critics. Even countries that didn't experience outright revolts or where demonstrations quickly petered out made sure the powerful wouldn't be held to account. The opposition movement, partially hijacked by Islamists in almost every country, gave some Westerners, Christians, and other minority groups reason to fear the rebellion and the possible consequences of these democratic upheavals. In many ways, I understand their fears, though I find it more difficult to understand how that justifies anyone's outright support for dictators who slaughter their own people with impunity.

The Arab Spring now feels like a trial run rather than a revolt. Perhaps future generations will pick up the fight, but, for now, the autocrats have won this round. Though the conditions that led to the uprisings across the Arab world were all largely the same in 2011—poverty, inequality, lack of freedom, corruption, repression—the outcome in every case was different, for reasons specific to each country. In Syria, the regime survived with outside military help against a splintered, increasingly extreme rebel force. The pro-democracy, secular, intellectual forces of the first few months of the revolution were killed, jailed, or exiled. The regime there never had any intention of sharing or ceding power, something made obvious when it cracked down on demonstrations with brute force from the beginning. How will the children of the generation that allowed this to happen to their homelands react when they read about this period in history books? Will they understand that for a brief, fleeting moment, we all felt free?

Nabil El-Araby, a soft-spoken man in his seventies who briefly served as the Egyptian foreign minister after Hosni Mubarak was deposed in 2011, smiled warmly as he greeted me in his office. It was a large room with the gilded décor of top ministries. On the wall above a large desk at one end of the room was the outline of a frame that had been taken down. "You haven't had time to print photos of the new president?" I joked. It was April 2011, only a few weeks after Hosni Mubarak had been deposed. I don't remember anything else El-Araby told me during our CNN interview except for a single exchange, which I wrote down in my notebook. "What is happening today is making my generation shameful," El-Araby, a former judge on the International Court of Justice, told me. "Shameful? What are you ashamed of?" I asked. "Because we didn't succeed in doing anything like this revolution. Our children and grandchildren succeeded in returning the spirit of a free country to Egypt." I remember this single sentence taking my breath away. I felt a lump in my throat. I looked down at my notes so that I could compose myself. This was an important moment, I thought. An admission that the men in power had, for decades, failed us. Surely, this meant they would not allow the tyrants to return. El-Araby soon resigned from his post and later became secretary-general of the Arab League, an organization that proved useless in stopping any of the calamities that plagued the region in the years after the 2011 revolts. Those in charge made sure that the spirit of freedom that had briefly returned to the region was extinguished. And indeed, perhaps they should all still be ashamed.

Part 5

Paris

Je Suis Charlie

Wednesday, January 7, 2015, was the day that two very different stories unfolded simultaneously: one of hope, and one of senseless murder.

In the first story, I am in a bridal shop in London, trying on a wedding dress, deciding that it is too virginal and princessy for a forty-five-year-old woman to get married in. In this story, I ask the shop assistant to shorten the lace sleeves and to take up the skirt, so that it is cut in a bias showing my legs at the front but keeping a longer train in the back. I also opt for a simple satin belt (which I remember thinking was wildly overpriced at around $500) and decide to forgo the tiara and veil. I was getting married relatively later in life and, I thought, dressing in a snow-white, virginal gown would look ridiculous. Still, I saw someone in the mirror that I thought was beautiful. I was in my midforties, and I was in love with just the right partner after many years of choosing exactly the wrong men. Like playing the same lottery numbers for decades, which unexpectedly come up, I'd felt like I'd won some sort of prize just as I had decided I would have to learn to love to live alone. In the first story, my mother is visiting from Paris to help me choose just the right dress. When we leave the bridal shop, having settled on a gown, my cell phone rings. It's CNN. Nothing good ever comes from work phone calls on a day off. It's usually a request to fill in for someone who's called in sick. "We have no one else. We literally will fall off air if you don't come in," is usually how those last-minute requests go. But in this first story, it's a call to tell me there's breaking news out of Paris. "Can you get on the Eurostar?" I am asked. "Do you know *Charlie*, I think it's *Heb...dow*? Have you heard of this place?" they ask me. "Yes, of course. It's a satirical paper. They're known for their cartoons. What happened?" I asked. "Someone shot the place up. We think maybe three dead."

The second story, which unfolds at the same exact time as the first, starts at around 11:20 a.m. local time when gunmen in a black Citroën C3 drive up to 6, rue Nicolas Appert in Paris looking for people to kill in the offices of the *Charlie Hebdo* weekly magazine. They had the wrong address. They realize their mistake and head to number 10, two doors down. They are masked and carrying Kalashnikov rifles. They are there to kill. The two men murder a maintenance worker in the lobby and force an employee who had just arrived to key in the entry code. They gain access to the *Hebdo* offices. In this second story, while I'm trying on tiaras for fun, brothers Cherif and Said Kouachi hunt down staff and cartoonists like prey. Survivors would later say they heard them shout, "Allahu akbar!" as they fired their weapons. They were there to avenge the Prophet Muhammad, which *Charlie Hebdo* had lampooned several times before. They burst into a conference room and killed eight people gathered there for an editorial meeting. In this second story, the shooting unfolds over five to six minutes, so we know that some of those who died witnessed the deaths of their colleagues and knew that their own time was up. By the end, eleven are dead, including the editor in chief, Stephane Charbonnier, and the famous cartoonists Cabu and Georges Wolinski. As the terrorists fled the scene, they encountered Ahmed Merabet, a police officer on patrol, and shot him in the head. This second story is the opposite of the first one. It is one of evil and hate. After getting the call from CNN, I run home to get my passport and take the first train out to Paris. I was there a few hours later.

The gunmen were on the loose for more than two days after the newsroom massacre at *Charlie Hebdo*. They hijacked a car, robbed a gas station, and were eventually surrounded by police as they holed up in a printing firm on an industrial estate twenty miles outside Paris. They were killed by police as they escaped, firing at officers. Almost every international media organization had deployed reporters to cover the aftermath of the murders at *Charlie Hebdo*. Just as we were covering the manhunt for the Kouachi brothers live on CNN, another terrorist, Amedy Coulibaly, took hostages and killed four at a kosher supermarket in Paris before being gunned down by police.

This was a time of extreme anxiety about terrorism in Europe in the name of radical Islam. The so-called Islamic State, better known by its acronym, ISIS, had conquered huge swaths of territory across Iraq and Syria over the previous two years. The terrorist army was originally founded in 1999 in Iraq and had morphed into an al-Qaeda-affiliated insurgent force against the US Army in Iraq in 2004. Three years after the Syrian uprising in 2011, it broke with al-Qaeda and proclaimed itself an Islamic caliphate from Mosul in Iraq to Raqqa in eastern Syria. The group made money by selling oil from Iraqi oil fields on the black market. Its fighting force was, at one stage, thirty thousand men strong. It imposed on the people it conquered an extreme, misguided, and brutal interpretation of Islamic law. Videos showing the beheadings of hostages in orange jumpsuits shocked the world. Western nationals from France, Belgium, and the UK, among other countries, had joined ISIS in Syria. Western countries were in a state of panic: If our own citizens will leave their country of birth to join the group that wants to annihilate us, then we are safe nowhere. We aren't even safe at home.

The worst was yet to come. Ten months after *Charlie Hebdo*, coordinated ISIS terrorist attacks across Paris targeted restaurant-goers, passersby, and, in the deadliest assault, a rock concert at the Bataclan, where ninety people were killed. The day after the massacre, I anchored live coverage of the attacks in front of the theater, where, unlike during the *Charlie Hebdo* coverage in January, when Parisians came out in defiance, holding "Je Suis Charlie" signs, an atmosphere thick with silent fear reigned. We spoke in hushed tones on camera. The dead of the Bataclan were still inside. On the night of Friday, November 13, 2015, gunmen had started shooting during the concert, and, for a while, the audience believed the shots were part of the show. When the American band the Eagles of Death Metal stopped playing, the shooters kept firing into the crowd. Survivors told me that the three attackers murdered people even as they tried to flee, that the dead fell atop the living, and that, during long stretches, there was silence when the assassins walked through the crowd, shooting one bullet at a time into their victims, with the calm determination of psychopaths. There is an audio recording of the attack. I have always refused to listen to it. Imagining it alone turns my stomach.

As I stood in front of the camera the day after the attack, telling viewers that behind me, in the Bataclan theater, were bodies still lying where they fell, I worried that other attackers, who might not have been caught yet, would come back to mow us all down. The thought of a secondary assault on journalists never left me.

What made this event feel different is that Paris is my city, and that in the confusing cocktail of ethnic and national identities that I carry within me, France is, almost by default, my country. Though I don't hold a French passport, Paris is the city I grew up in. Even when French people insist on calling me American, France is still the country where I feel most at home. Though some French people compliment my "perfect French" and say that they can barely detect an accent, which I don't think I have, France is still the country I love in the way one is attached to a first true love.

The day after the attacks, the world's media once again converged on Paris to cover the massacres. There had been three groups of men who carried out six separate and coordinated strikes. In addition to the devastating attack at the Bataclan concert hall, in another assault, three suicide bombers struck outside the Stade de France in the Paris suburb of Saint-Denis during a France-Germany soccer game that President François Hollande was attending, while another group of terrorists fired on crowded cafés and restaurants at various locations around the city. We anchored for a few days from locations close to where the terrorists had targeted. Eventually, CNN and dozens of other television crews set up positions at place de la Republique with tents and multiple cameras cabling semipermanent setups to satellite trucks parked nearby. Star anchors like Anderson Cooper and Chris Cuomo flew in from the US. It seemed as if the network had sent almost every reporter, producer, cameraman, and engineer it had to cover the attacks from Paris around the clock. I was on air twice a day, anchoring early mornings Paris time with the US-based anchor John Berman, covering the overnight domestic hours in America and, again, in the evening, hosting my own CNN International show. Paris felt suspended in time, still dazed from the death blows it had received, as if the entire city were holding its breath, afraid to exhale, so as not to provoke another attack. Parisians were urged to sit on café terraces, to demonstrate their defiance: "*Tous en terrasse!*" ("Everyone in outdoor cafés!") the slogan went. When what sounded like gunshots rang near the place de la Republique, though, hundreds of people ran, some falling down as they fled, in a panicked race away from what they feared was yet another attack. There were knocked-over bicycles and strollers, children's shoes scattered as their parents grabbed them in their arms to flee faster, café chairs and tables overturned as terrorized people ran, here and there, aimlessly, some hiding behind bus stops or under restaurant tables. Shortly afterward, when someone said they had heard an explosion near the Carillon, a café targeted by gunmen on November 13, a news report described people jumping into the cold waters of the Ourcq Canal a few hundred yards away.

"What's the difference between Islamist and Islamic?" then CNN anchor Chris Cuomo asked me during a commercial break, a few days after the initial attacks. For those of us who covered the region, the distinction between those two words was obvious, and I was reminded that we were responsible not just for reporting the facts but translating and contextualizing the terms and acts of terror of a group that called itself the "Islamic State." "Well, one—the Islamic State—is a political movement, and the other is the adjective that describes something that is Muslim," I remember replying. "So, what do you call a terrorist? An Islamist?" he asked. Cuomo was asking me to explain simple concepts and, though some CNN International anchors and correspondents were quick to dismiss him as naïve, I felt, on the contrary, that these questions were helpful. "Islamism is a political movement, so a terrorist can be an Islamist, but an Islamist is, in the vast majority of cases, not a terrorist." "Okay! Gotch-AHH," Cuomo replied. "It's great having you here to explain this stuff," he later told me off air. I was happy to do so, but I also felt pigeonholed as the "international" anchor, there to help explain complex foreign developments, but if a similar story happened in the US, then I was not seen as useful. It was frustrating. I wanted my network to see me as necessary on all stories, not just the ones that happened in certain parts of the world.

The November 13 terrorist attacks story developed over several weeks. Ultimately, many of the perpetrators were found to be Belgian and French citizens who'd traveled to Syria at a time the terrorist group ISIS controlled large parts of the country and had returned to their countries of birth to carry out the attacks against fellow citizens. The mastermind of the operation, a wanted man named Abdelhamid Abaaoud, was born to Moroccan parents in a suburb of Brussels in 1987 and killed in a police shoot-out outside Paris on November 18. Among the group of lunatics he had recruited to kill innocents in concert halls and outdoor cafés, there were petty criminals and ex-convicts who'd had run-ins with police before being recruited by extremists in neighborhood mosques. Others became enamored with ISIS online and had supported their cause virtually, on a computer screen, before traveling to Syria to join the group. They claimed to fight in the name of Islam; in fact, they were losers who did not speak Arabic and likely understood nothing of the cherry-picked scriptures their masters used to justify murdering civilians. "Allahu akbar," they proclaimed before pressing the trigger. "God is the greatest," they said before blowing themselves up. In an answer to the famous Proust questionnaire, two decades before November 13, 2015, the French Lebanese writer Amin Maalouf was asked what he hoped God, if he exists, would say to him when he reaches the gates of heaven. "I would like him to tell me: I am innocent of all the crimes ever committed in my name."

"Why Don't You Wear a Hijab?"

You could catch a glimpse of the Eiffel Tower from one of the corner windows of the apartment, located at the intersection of avenue Emile Pouvillon and avenue Elisée Reclus in Paris's seventh arrondissement. It was a short walk from the Champs de Mars, the vast stretch of green park space that extends from the tower to the École Militaire over the length of six city blocks.

The table was set for dinner. We were eight, perhaps ten. It was the type of grand Parisian apartment no one our age at the time—students and young professionals in our twenties—could afford. The parents of one of the young men were away that weekend, and he had invited friends over for a Saturday-night meal.

Some of the boys at the dinner party had inherited aristocratic titles from their fathers and so had officially been born counts or barons. The girls from the same milieu would likely marry into families of similar social standing. Pedigree was important to the point of making distinctions between Parisian and country nobility or aristocracy that predated Napoleon and the families who'd been given a title during the first Napoleonic empire. The former was seen as more upper crust and exclusive than the latter.

It was a world I had been introduced to through Antoine, an ex-boyfriend I met in 1991, brought together by Antoine's aunt and uncle, friends of my mother and stepfather. We separated amicably and stayed close for many years afterward. "Would you convert to Catholicism to marry me?" he once asked me. "I wouldn't convert to any religion," I replied. "Even my own."

Antoine was born a count, a title he had inherited from his father, and the family chateau a few hours' drive from Paris was grand enough to be open to the public. Proceeds from ticket sales went to the upkeep of a vast castle and sprawling gardens "*à la française*," which required a full-time gardening staff. Our lives and backgrounds were different, but we shared an irreverent sense of humor. "I don't believe in Frenchness; I believe in people of the same upper crust coming together," he had told me, to explain why his friends included Mexicans and Argentines. And me.

Meals at the chateau when Antoine invited friends to stay over for a weekend were served in a dining room with hand-painted ceiling frescos and crystal wall sconces. Antoine called the cook and women serving us at the table "house employees," signaling to me that he held domestic staff in high esteem. He wanted to establish that he was neither a snob nor a bully. Every aspect of life followed strict norms and rules, from the way to set a table to the way to greet a woman (lips should never actually touch the hand of a lady, one must bow and stop well above her outstretched arm). I learned through him that in France, a fork should always be placed facing down when setting the table, unlike in Britain, where it is placed prongs facing up, because French families would place their crest on the back of the handle. My great-grandmother Hikmat-Hanim would have no doubt approved of Antoine's attachment to etiquette. Perhaps she would have been intimidated by the grandeur of his family's castle, unsure what to wear, where to sit, how to serve herself when a maître d' bowed to lower a plate, the handles of the utensils facing toward her to allow for an easier grasp. From the Beit Kbeer to the Chateau Kbeer, there was a whole universe, separated by only two generations.

Antoine said he loved me, and I didn't quite understand why. I was brought up in relative privilege but not, strictly speaking, in his milieu. I was comfortable navigating the French aristocratic social scene, but, ultimately, I still felt like I didn't belong there. It was also a time when using certain derogatory terms to describe women or people of different religions or ethnicities was acceptable, and so questions about my ancestry hurt me. How Muslims married or how many times they prayed at Eid or Ramadan and many other subjects in between were topics I knew little about as an Arab born and raised in a secular family in the West. These questions and their subtext made me defensive and uncomfortable.

"Why don't you wear a hijab?" one of the young men at the dinner table asked me that night at avenue Emile Pouvillon.

"Why don't you wear a crucifix around your neck?" I asked.

"No, seriously, why?" the young man insisted.

I did not feel like the question was asked out of genuine curiosity. Rather, I believed, it was designed to single me out.

"Not everyone is religious, and even some practicing Muslims don't wear it." I felt heat rise up in my body. Every moment of that exchange made me want to scream. I kept smiling. I had no witty comeback at hand.

"Why are you getting upset?" he asked. The truth was that I wanted to be more like them and less like me. Their questions made me loathe my differences because I wanted my identity not to be a topic of discussion over dinner. That night, in the opulence of an apartment with a view of the Eiffel Tower, a slice of paradise for most people, I wanted to run away and never come back.

My relationship with Antoine did not last, but our friendship did. We were each other's first real romantic loves. We would always have a connection. Perhaps the French count with chateaux and titles and the American-Syrian-French-Muslim-whatever had a lot more in common than met the eye. Over the years, we stayed in touch. He and his wife came to my wedding. I look back at the avenue Emile Pouvillon dinner, though, with a measure of sadness. I allowed questions about my identity to hurt me; I did not tell Antoine, a generous and kind man, that they had made me uncomfortable. I'm certain no one but me remembers that evening almost thirty years ago.

My Brilliant Harasser

At the café at the corner of rue Saint-Guillaume, across from the main Sciences Po building, I ordered a coffee and waited for classes to restart after lunch. I was weary. I was in my last year of studies, sending off résumés to almost every newspaper, magazine, radio, and TV station in Paris. Earlier that day, I had spotted a classmate who had been pursuing me for months. He'd written a novel about a man named Nestor who spent a lifetime secretly following Helene, a woman he'd decided, at the age of twelve, would be the love of his life. Nestor does some crazy things, hoping to be noticed by the object of his love. In the novel, Nestor eventually only finds peace when Helene is dead and buried.

I would deliberately sit facing the window so I could see passersby. If I spotted him, as I had that day, I would slump into my chair and wait for him to disappear into the crowd. My former friend had started sending me handwritten letters after our brief friendship the prior year had turned into an obsessive, one-sided infatuation.

"I will dedicate the book to you when it comes out," Yann Moix had told me after I'd read the novel's manuscript, a few months before

I cut off contact with him. I had spent a weekend in the guest room of his family's home in Orléans, where I'd met his parents and brother, even though I knew his interest in me was romantic. I had found his promise of a dedication both flattering and terrifying. He wrote gorgeous, deep prose in a free-flowing narrative style that did not follow traditional storytelling structures. It wasn't so much that the plot was unconventional but that there was not much of a plot to speak of. The characters seemed to act out obsessive patterns, ruminating philosophical thoughts—over hundreds of pages—while doing little else. Though the novel's storyline lost me early on, his writing read like dense, buttery poetry. The lack of connective tissue in the book's narrative didn't seem to be an issue for his publisher, however. The novels carried by elite Parisian literary houses are sometimes exercises in philosophical wordplay rather than straightforward, linear tales. Yann Moix's style was all turn of phrase and panache, and when *Jubilations vers le ciel*, dedicated to "Hala Basha," was published in February 1996, it was celebrated with a top literary prize.

Moix's obsession with me coincided with a period of deep insecurity in my life about my future in journalism. Compared to my friends and Sciences Po classmates, I was getting very few responses to my résumés and even fewer interviews, even though I had done more freelance work than some of them. "You should put a picture on your CV and, if I'm being frank, remove the fact that you speak Arabic," one of my friends told me. I knew he was right. I had seen studies on how job applicants with Arab-sounding names were much less likely to be called in for interviews than those with typically French names. A full fifteen years after I graduated from Sciences Po, a study showed that when near identical résumés were sent to large French corporations, a made-up applicant of Senegalese Christian background named "Marie Diouf" received 21 percent positive responses from potential employers versus 8 percent for an equally fictitious Senegalese Muslim "Khadija Diouf." So, I "de-Khadija'ed" my résumé and removed what should have been seen as a desirable skill from my list of qualifications. I also added a photo, as I suspected that a blond, blue-eyed applicant would be less likely to suffer from the discrimination that more convention-ally Arab-looking job seekers from a North African background faced.

Today, I realize how abject this all was. At the time, I wanted to work in the journalism industry so badly that I was ready to whitewash my identity in ways I find heartbreaking today. Because it sounded generically European, I added my mother's last name to my father's and became Hala Basha-Gorani, which I then shortened to Hala Gorani. No one I asked in my circle of friends and acquaintances thought this was a bad idea. All agreed that Gorani sounded Italian or from a Balkan country and wouldn't be immediately associated with Arab ancestry.

On my résumé, I had become a blond-American-born-French-educated-fluent-in-French-and-English-ONLY Hala Gorani. Within a few weeks, I received roughly double the number of callbacks. It had worked. I was being given permission to fit in.

I was still living in my mother and Amr's Neuilly-sur-Seine apart-ment on the western edge of Paris when I started looking for work after graduating from Sciences Po. In between the sculptures my mother had created and the bohemian crystal vases she'd brought over from Syria, and surrounded by Persian rugs and the rich, colorful uphol-stery of her living room furniture, my mother had set Hikmat-Hanim's clock on one of the side tables, still stuck at 3:06 p.m. (or a.m., depend-ing on what time of day one believed Hikmat had passed). "I brought it back from Aleppo. Your nana Berine told me to give it to Zaf in Wash-ington," my mother had said, "because he likes watches."

Around that same time, Yann Moix sent flowers to Neuilly and once slid the card of a shoe store I had recommended to him under my car's windshield wipers just outside my parents' building. He also kept sending me letters to their apartment, dozens over the years, some of which I've kept. "I want to summit you with my fingers, from your clearing to your mane," he once wrote. My continued rejection ignited in him a sort of madness. There were weeks when Moix sent or dropped off several letters, left hour-long messages on my answering machine, and, in a particularly extreme fit of folly, traveled to Syria on a pilgrimage to visit the country of my ancestors. He landed at Aleppo International Airport and headed for the city center. He told me later that he asked a taxi driver to take him to the house of the "Ibrahim Bashas." After much confusion, he ended up at the wrong building, visited Aleppo for a few more days, sent me a postcard from the city's old post office, and flew back home to Paris.

"I am a monster, a loser, a jerk, self-obsessed, excessive and possessive, a harasser, a persecutor, whatever you want to call me, but I know that this monster will never abandon you," he wrote in one of his letters the following year.

As time went on, Yann Moix's fame grew as much as a result of his work as of the controversies ignited by his often gratuitous provocations. He wrote more novels, won literary awards, had a brief but very successful stint as a movie director, and became a bona fide celebrity. For a few years, he continued to send me early copies of his books, some with handwritten notes addressed to me, others to my mother, and invited me to the premiere of one of his films, which came out in 2004. By then, his obsession with me had long since fizzled, and I was curious to see what had become of him and interested in his ability to direct a film. We saw each other only once or twice after that and never spoke again.

From time to time, when I'd think back to this episode in my life, I'd sometimes google Moix's name to find him routinely mired in scandal and controversies. In 2019, a French magazine unearthed Holocaust-mocking anti-Semitic cartoons he had drawn and accompanying texts he had written as a twenty-year-old student ("These texts and drawings are anti-Semitic, but I am not an anti-Semite," he responded in 2019, apologizing for what he called a youthful mistake).

He became a late-night talk show pundit, often spouting divisive diatribes for effect. He wrote a book about physical and emotional abuse he claims he suffered as a child, something his family denied was true, which led to a defamation lawsuit and a cringe-making airing of dirty laundry in public. It all felt like a natural progression, in some ways, in the life of a man who had always wanted attention and fame above all else. In some ways, he had not changed much since our Sciences Po days. He had just been given a bigger platform.

Leaving It All Behind

The offices of France 3 Television on cours Albert 1er overlooking the river Seine were a short walk from the Champs-Élysées in the city's eighth arrondissement. I was an intern cataloging videotapes, before the digital age. Back then, an hour of programming weighed between half a pound and a pound and a half and required considerable physical storage space. I worked in a department that packaged and sold France 3 Television content abroad. The division's archives were kept in floor-to-ceiling rolling shelves, mounted on tracks. Every aspect of producing audiovisual content then was labor-intensive and required physical storage space. I would spend hours each day focused on repetitive and unchallenging tasks while looking for openings in the nearby newsroom. The real journalism happened a few doors away. I would cross paths with the reporters and producers but could never shadow them or observe them doing their work. I was twenty-five and had two degrees, including a bachelor of science in economics from the US in addition to my Sciences Po degree. I had also worked as a freelance journalist for over a year in Washington, DC, Lille, and Paris. Despite my experience and ambition, the office space I really wanted to work in remained, tantalizingly, only a few steps away. I was an intern in the wrong department. The door to what felt like a mysterious beehive where TV reporters spoke with urgency and walked with purpose between desks, holding tapes and pages of script, was sometimes ajar, and I would peek in, praying I would one day make it inside.

Despite my unfulfilled desires, I have fond memories of the time I interned at France 3 Television, either because I was twenty-five and everything is tolerable at that age because the bulk of one's life still lies ahead, or because a part of me found a meditative quality to the manual labor involved in my mindless work. I was lucky to be paired with Gaidz Minassian, a fellow intern whose impersonations of our boss made me laugh so much that I remember them to this day. After a few months, I was called into his office. "Would you like to work here?" he asked me. "Yes, I would love to. But I am interested in journalism, as you know." "Aha," he replied, "well, this is a good position. My assistant is leaving. Salary category C."

It felt like my entire being was suddenly emptied of its oxygen, like a balloon deflating, like the blood in my head suddenly dropped down to my lower extremities, preventing me from fully processing the information presented to me. I had spent six years studying economics, politics, journalism, and history; I had worked as a freelance journalist and an intern at Agence France-Presse, *La Voix du Nord*, and in various other places; I spoke three languages, and, after several months at France 3 Television, a middle-aged man was proposing that I become his secretary? Every ounce of goodwill I felt toward the internship that I thought would be a stepping stone job vanished. "I don't think you understand," I replied. "I want to be a journalist, not a personal assistant." "But you haven't been to journalism school. You will never become a journalist in France without a journalism school degree."

The established French track for journalists required a diploma from a school like the Centre de Formation des Journalistes (CFJ) or the École Superieure de Journalisme (ESJ). I'd taken the CFJ entrance exam during my time at Sciences Po and failed it. I had hoped—and even assumed—that I could overcome these perceived shortcomings with experience and the two university degrees that I already had. I realized that day that the system in France would not allow for any exceptions. I had the wrong diplomas, the wrong nationality, and the wrong pedigree. France didn't want me, and so I would have to not want France.

A few weeks after my decision to leave France 3 Television, one of my mother and Amr's friends slid an ad published in the *International Herald Tribune* under our front door in Neuilly-sur-Seine. It was for an anchor position at a new French-language TV network in London run by Bloomberg, a media group whose core business is selling data terminals to financial institutions. Bloomberg was expanding its television operations into international markets in local languages, including French, Italian, and Spanish. I applied for the position and sent a VHS tape of an on-camera report I begged a cameraman at a French cable news channel I'd interned at for a few months to shoot for me. I was sent a first-class ticket on a new high-speed train called the Eurostar for the interview in London. A few short weeks later, I was hired to anchor an early-morning stock market update segment. The French language channel launched July 1, 1996, with one manager and about a dozen twentysomething on-air presenters split between Paris and London. The London side would handle business news, and the Paris side, a collaboration with Agence France-Presse with French reporters who'd gone to journalism school there, would anchor general news.

A few weeks before launch, a journalist from the French weekly magazine *Paris Match* tracked me down in the Bloomberg newsroom, which was at the time in a high-end glass-and-chrome building in London's Finsbury Square, near the city's financial district. I can't remember if the reporter had called me on my cell phone or if they had asked to be put through on a landline. "Hala Basha?" the person asked. I had only recently become Hala Gorani, using my mother's last name for on-air work. I knew that anyone calling me Basha was someone who'd known me before my London move.

"I want to give you an opportunity to reply to Yann Moix," the voice said. In his book *Jubilations vers le ciel*, Moix was imploring me to return to him, the reporter added. I was told that the word *Reviens* ("Come back") was printed in large white letters on a red banner wrapped around the cover. He had dedicated the book to Hala Basha.

"We want to do a story about you," the voice continued. I refused. "But we would send a photographer, and we could take a picture of you under a tree in Hyde Park," the voice said. Nothing could have sounded less appealing to me at that stage. I refused again, saying no in the uncomfortable way women rebuff male advances gently, trying not to offend. "I want to be in your magazine for something I've done," I replied, "not to talk about a book I didn't write."

Moix had been promoting the book that had been published in February of that year on television and radio shows, describing me as an ex-lover, which was not true. In his version of events, I had left him because he had been too possessive and jealous, that he had somehow mistreated me, and that his passion for me was so overwhelming that he had to write a whole book to win me back. None of that was true, either. He'd himself told me that the book was largely written before we even met. We had never been romantic partners. The reality is that when I rejected his romantic overtures, Moix spent several years nurturing an obsession with me that I now realize was based more on his romantic, excessive notion of how a man whose love is rebuffed should act—a character in his own novel—rather than on any real affection he felt for me.

Over time, Moix became as known for his controversial statements, including the 2019 book accusing his parents of abuse, almost as much as he was fêted for his writing. He wrote provocative opinion pieces designed to illicit outrage. In interviews, he claimed and explained, in quite flowery terms, as was his habit, that he could not find a woman over the age of fifty sexually attractive. It made headlines around the world, and I imagine that rather than prompting him to think twice, he was amused, perhaps even flattered by the attention. When we first met at university, the young, twenty-five-year-old Moix told me that he was hungry for fame and recognition. "If we could, today, know that we would be avenged later in life, we would jump for joy," he wrote to me in one letter in 1996, "but when the longed-for love and revenge arrive, we are no longer there: we've already left. It's another person within us that will reap the rewards instead."

Allez Les Bleus

The flares and fireworks lit the night sky over the Champs-Élysées while below, thick smoke from the mobile merguez stands curled upward, hundreds of French flags floating in the wind above. Thousands of people had climbed on top of cars, drivers honking their horns in celebration, waving flags of their own. The flares shooting up in the air came back down in plumes of red mist, the silhouettes of fans jumping, dancing, and punching the air with their fists against the fires burning looked almost like the beginnings of another French revolution. There were no cell phone cameras, and there was no social media. There was no screen between us and the crowd's pure elation. France was celebrating as one. That night, it had beaten Brazil 3–0 at the Stade de France to win the soccer World Cup.

The night of France's victory, my mother, Nour, and I were watching the final alone in the Neuilly-sur-Seine apartment, and, after the final whistle blew, I had dragged her to the Champs-Élysées with me to celebrate *our* team's triumph. Growing up in France means that regardless of how little you care about professional sports, you know enough about the rules of soccer to follow a game and even appreciate some of its nuances. "Zidane glides on the pitch like a dancer," my mother said of one of France's star players. "He's an artist." I agreed, of course, and we both decided that he was particularly handsome. A Frenchman of Algerian Berber descent, Zinedine Zidane embodied what my mother and I considered to be perfection: the handsome, successful son of North African immigrants with the good looks and restrained behavior of a model citizen, whose mere existence sent the message that Arab Muslim immigrants can be what white French people want them to be. He never spoke about politics or religion, lived the life of a devoted family man, and had won France its first ever World Cup. His name had even been projected in laser lights on the Arc de Triomphe, the nineteenth-century monument France erected to celebrate its most decisive military victories.

The victorious 1998 French soccer team was being celebrated as the incarnation of French multicultural immigration. The team included Zidane, whose parents came from Algeria in North Africa, Lilian Thuram and Thierry Henry, who were of French West Indian descent, Patrick Vieira, who was born in Senegal, alongside white players like Laurent Blanc and team captain Didier Deschamps. For French people with immigrant backgrounds, the 1998 team became a way to tell France that they, too, could represent their country with honor and patriotism. Rather than doubt us, ghettoize us, they said, you must now recognize us as equal citizens.

For a few weeks, France seemed to have overcome generations of failed integration of its Black and brown minorities. Could a single tournament victory heal the wounds of decades of marginalization and exclusion? There were undeniable disparities in education and housing. Unemployment was still much higher among French people of Arab and African descent, crime rates where they lived were higher, their rates of being detained and other reports of police mistreatment higher than for white French citizens. For a brief moment, however, the dream of a unified country papered over these real and stubborn social and economic issues. Before France's win, Far Right politician Jean-Marie Le Pen had criticized the French team for having too many non-white players, several of whom, he said, did not seem to know the words of "La Marseillaise," the country's national anthem, which is sung before games. During the cup, a clip of an all-white French national team from 1984 surfaced, showing that they hadn't sung a word of it, either. Le Pen was widely rebuked for his words at the time, and with the historic 1998 win, the country appeared to be coming to terms with something important. Perhaps, some thought, it was not faith or politics that would represent the country's contemporary republican identity but eleven men in soccer jerseys. Perhaps football was the country's real religion.

Only a few weeks later, the divisions returned. "La Marseillaise" was even booed at a France-Algeria match, the first played in France since Algeria gained independence from France in 1962, at the same stadium where Les Bleus had raised the World Cup trophy three years earlier. It was clear that a sense of alienation was profound among some young French Arabs and Africans, and a sense of belonging to the country of their parents and grandparents was stronger than the confidence of being seen as a full citizen of France. A 2008 poll[1] of high school and university students from immigrant families found that almost half identified with their parents' culture of origin more than with their French identity. Previous generations, invited in from former French colonies after World War II to work in factories and fields, might have wanted and tried to blend into their new host nation, but some in the younger generation, despite being born and raised in France, rejected it as their primary country. A 2007 study[2] showed that unemployment among immigrants with African backgrounds was

1. Azzam Amin, Marjorie Poussin, Frédéric Martinez, "Le rôle du sentiment d'exclusion et des perceptions de la société dans le processus d'identification chez les jeunes français issus de l'immigration," *Les Cahiers Internationaux de Psychologie Sociale* 4, no. 80 (2008): 27–38, https://www.cairn.info/revue-les-cahiers-internationaux-de-psychologie-sociale-2008-4-page-27.htm.
2. "Part des personnes à la recherche d'un emploi en France de 2006 à 2021, selon le statut d'immigration," Statista, May 17, 2023, https://fr.statista.com/statistiques/505332/taux-chomage-selon-statut-immigration-france/.

twice as high as the national average. Those whose families came from more modest backgrounds were concentrated in suburban enclaves on the periphery of the higher-end urban centers. They felt ostracized, physically separated from the more affluent parts of the country, in charmless high-rises and concrete jungles. Their sense of identity, for many, could therefore never be proudly and exclusively French since they blamed France for treating them as second-class citizens by stigmatizing them and denying them equal opportunities.

For some immigrants of Muslim and African heritage, their rejection of a classic "French" identity had led to a romanticization of the culture of their ancestors. In recent years, I have started noticing some younger people of North African heritage increasingly peppering their speech with Arabic colloquialisms like "Wallahi" ("I swear to God") or "Inshallah" ("If God wills it"). This new slang, using words from a language they likely don't speak fluently, has become an almost separate sublanguage that I don't remember their parents' generation ever using. This strikes me as another blow to what French authorities call "integration," or the process by which immigrant culture should converge toward a French cultural "standard," but that some minorities see as imposing largely white and Christian norms on people of different faiths and practices. If France is about baguettes, the Eiffel Tower, camembert, and Sunday mass, why, one might ask, can't it also be about Eid and Ramadan? Integration, in the eyes of some children of immigrants, has really come to mean complete assimilation. Or else.

For decades, the notion of integration "à la française" and, by extension, what is expected of immigrants, has been exploited by the extreme Right and, increasingly, by more mainstream politicians. They have made immigration, often code for "North African Arabs" and Muslims, the central message that all other policies rest on. When I interviewed Marine Le Pen in 2015, who'd taken over from her father as the leader of the xenophobic and immigration-obsessed

National Front—later renamed the National Rally—she blamed glo-
balization and immigration for exacerbating almost all her country's ills. She also told me, "France is being attacked by radical Islam.
Clearly, French values are being attacked." Over the years, Le Pen has
given her father's party a makeover with new branding and sleeker
messaging, but the fundamental ideological pillars of the National
Front remain: immigration, diversity, and globalism, they say, are the
main causes of France's problems. When I started covering politics in
France in 2002, Le Pen's views were considered fringe. Over the last
few decades, however, anti-globalization populism has become part of
more conventional political messaging around the Western world. In
the United Kingdom, anti-globalization sentiment led to the country's
exit from the European Union following a 2016 referendum. Even populist politicians *within* the EU were exploiting these nativist impulses
for political gain. Hungarian prime minister Viktor Orbán often used
anti-Semitic and anti-immigrant rhetoric in his campaigns, blaming
outside forces for attacking his country's "Christian democracy." At its
core, Trumpist ideology in America is closer to Marine Le Pen's platform in France than that of the country's centrist president Emmanuel
Macron. Le Pen herself told me in 2016 that she and Donald Trump
were both anti-establishment candidates that "did not take money
from corporate sponsors" and that Hillary Clinton was synonymous
with "war" and "devastation." The populists of the world were uniting
using nationalism as their principal rallying call, blaming a globalist
system they had ironically often benefited from themselves. As Amin
Maalouf wrote in *In the Name of Identity*, nationalism's primary goal is
"to find for every problem a culprit rather than a solution," and their
message was a stark illustration of that idea. The Muslims, the immigrants, the Jews, the global elites and their institutions, they told their
supporters, have stolen your country and wrecked its values. Easy solutions to complex problems, brought to wide audiences on ideologically
aligned media networks and publications.

In France, the "integration" question has become so ferociously debated that both "sides," if we can describe the debate in that way, have hardened the attitudes of the other. For example, authorities in the country seem to have become fixated on regulating Muslim female dress. More than a decade after banning the headscarf in public schools in 2004, several cities in France banned the so-called burkini, a full-body swimsuit worn mainly by Muslim women who wish to preserve their modesty, in public pools and on beaches. The burkini ban was upheld in 2022 by France's top administrative court after an appeal by the city of Grenoble in a decision France's interior minister called "a victory for secularism." What some believe is a win for traditional French identity, though, others see as an attack on their own identity, which will surely motivate them to cling even harder to the very features of their culture they believe are under attack.

On these questions, I have been in a particularly interesting position. I could see how some of these bans, disguised as hygiene or secularism measures, were perceived as an assault on Muslims in particular. The spectacle in 2016 of women being fined for wearing full-body outfits on the beach in French resort cities like Cannes, for example, was grotesque. But as a secular Muslim who believes that a country should be largely united in terms of national identity, while allowing for cultural and religious differences, I could not understand how some young Muslims, born in France, with only a distant knowledge of their culture of origin, would want to embrace even more conservative dress and practices than their own parents. Muslim preachers in the outer suburbs have made huge headway in the last few decades, taking advantage of young Muslims' feelings of disenfranchisement to push extreme interpretations of Islam. What can start out as a desire to embrace North African identity has sometimes been exploited by these religious figures. In the most extreme cases, a small handful of young people have been brainwashed into acts of unspeakable horror in the name of God, believing they are avenging themselves—and therefore their identity—through terror.

❦

NOVEMBER 28, 2015
DRANCY, FRANCE

We squeeze into the small elevator of an apartment block in Drancy, a town in the Parisian suburb of Seine-Saint-Denis. We tell the van carrying the CNN crew and equipment to wait outside the nondescript building, part of a cluster of social housing mid-rises in this banlieue, best known for having housed a transit center during World War II through which seventy thousand mostly Jewish prisoners passed, destined for Auschwitz and other concentration camps. A memorial site with a museum stands in its place today, a reminder of the evils of the Nazi collaborators of the Vichy regime. I am feeling uncomfortable. I am about to interview the sister of Samy Amimour, one of the three men who took part in the execution of ninety people at the Bataclan concert hall fifteen days earlier. The front door of the apartment is open, its frame cracked and its lock pushed in with a thick gaffer tape holding the door handle up. Anna, who asks that her real name not be used, greets us. She looks distraught but eager to talk. "Do you want to see his bedroom?" she asks. I spot a framed picture of a cat on a shelf above a single bed, an Islamic calendar on the wall, and a Larousse French dictionary. "This is the way he left the room. We haven't touched it."

I want to believe that she was surprised to learn of her brother's involvement in the November Paris attacks, but part of me also wants to scream in her face: *How could you not know that about your own brother, who was already on a terrorist suspect list for trying to go to Yemen in 2012, who had left for Syria a few years later, whose own father unsuccessfully tried to extract him from ISIS the year before the Bataclan massacre, that this twenty-eight-year-old would commit the worst mass atrocity on French soil since the Second World War?*

We set up for the interview. Anna tells me her brother's radicalization began on the internet after which recruiters in the neighborhood took over. "They came to talk to him more and more and told him that he should attend the sermon at the mosque more regularly and that he should be more devoted to his practice of Islam. Then they led him toward mosques that were more radical," she tells me, crying. "He was a nice guy."

There are pictures of Amimour in frames in the small living room, a picture of a young boy playing chess, of a teen wearing a pirate's hat and mugging for the camera. I felt my chest tightening every time I looked at a photo of the boy that he was and pictured him as a twenty-eight-year-old adult, a psychopath, walking up to terrified concertgoers, taking aim, and executing them one after the other without mercy.

We left knowing we had a powerful interview; "great TV" as we call it in our business, a term that can describe everything from an explosive interview to footage of a live firefight erupting while a reporter is on air. "Great TV" is the industry term for sparks flying, theater, and drama. None of it is usually all that great for the people involved.

The Return

The problem with coming from nowhere and everywhere is that no matter how people describe you, even if they show tremendous goodwill and curiosity, you still feel mislabeled, misunderstood, sometimes even reduced. On the night of the first round of the French presidential elections in 2012, I was invited as a guest in France Television's gorgeous purpose-built studio, which featured a huge central desk, a three-dimensional Élysée Palace background, and multiple additional camera positions on two floors custom-made with transparent glass-like material. I was asked what Americans thought of François Hollande and Nicolas Sarkozy, the two front-runners in the election. Hollande, the Socialist Party candidate, had come out ahead of the incumbent, Sarkozy, in the first round of voting, and the French journalists in the studio wanted to know whether the United States government had any preference which candidate ultimately emerged victorious.

"La journaliste Americaine de CNN Hala Gorani (The American journalist from CNN Hala Gorani)" was usually how they worded their tosses to me. I was often complimented on how well I spoke French after my interviews regardless of how often I reminded them that

French was my native tongue. I was asked what people felt or said about France in the United States as if I had just flown in from New York when, in fact, I had made my way to the studio on the metro from my mother's apartment west of Paris. I was the American who spoke perfect French and so was the ideal interpreter of one world to the other. The fact that I had a top job at CNN, a network with tremendous brand recognition in France, gave me a journalism heavyweight aura that I didn't have in the US, not even within my own network. And so what I was unable to pursue in France after college, when I so desperately tried to work as a journalist but was told I did not have the right diplomas to do so, was suddenly available to me everywhere I went and in the most prestigious outlets. I was interviewed on top radio shows, made the cover of *TéléObs*, a high-circulation television magazine, was invited to talk shows on Canal+, and asked to pen columns in French newspapers. Because I worked for CNN as a prime-time news presenter, I was described as a "star anchor," a designation that both flattered me and made me uncomfortable. I was a "star" in France's eyes because I was a journalist working for one of the best-known news brands in the world. I could tell them what Americans, and even the world, thought of France in an authoritative and credible way.

On June 13, 2015, I was wearing the wedding dress I had first tried on in London the day of the *Charlie Hebdo* attacks, in Marrakech, Morocco, excited about walking down the aisle and into my husband's arms on our wedding day, when I saw a French number appear on my cell phone. It was a producer who'd seen me on one of France's top talk shows on Canal+. "I'll get to the point, we want to offer you the main presenter job on *Le Grand Journal*," he said. I'd heard that the network's ratings were tanking in part because of competition from streaming platforms like Netflix and Amazon Prime, and what was once a highly rated show was hemorrhaging viewers at a rapid pace. The billionaire industrialist Vincent Bolloré (sometimes described as the "Rupert Murdoch of France") had secured a controlling stake in the media conglomerate that owned Canal+, and its flagship show was rudderless and flailing. I knew even before hanging up that it would be suicidal to join a sinking ship just as I was launching my own prime-time show on CNN in London. A few weeks later, the producer who had called me was laid off, and a new team took over the program, appointing a new presenter who left after less than a year. The next host did not last much longer, and the show was canceled in March 2017. I wondered if the offer made to me was even discussed among top executives or if it was an idea that had come from a desperate brainstorming session to save the show. French anchors and on-air journalists don't use agents as they do in America, where even the most junior TV reporter either has or is trying to sign with some sort of representation, so I didn't think that the direct call was odd. I did, however, wonder how a job offer of that caliber could be funneled through a show producer on a cold call just months before a new team was put in place.

Many years later, I interviewed former French president Nicolas Sarkozy at an event in New York City. He is known to be a very close friend of Vincent Bolloré, whose decision to control Canal+ had caused so much turmoil in 2015. "I was a journalist in France before I joined CNN," I told him as we were mingling with guests before dinner and the sit-down interview that was to happen on a stage in front of a live audience. "You didn't miss anything, with the state of journalism in France," he said.

"I think France has some fantastic journalists, especially women," I added.

"Please," he said, "wearing a miniskirt on TV doesn't make them journalists."

There were at least two other people in our little huddle—one of whom was a serving ambassador—and I was surprised that Sarkozy felt comfortable saying something so insulting to female journalists in front of them, which is why I wrote his comment down later. In 2019, when this exchange took place, the #MeToo movement had swept through newsrooms across America and was starting to make headway in Europe. Men in positions of authority who had behaved inappropriately were reprimanded; some lost their jobs. In networks like Fox News, some of the most powerful male anchors and executives were forced to step down after allegations of harassment. There was a realization that women were still objectified and underrepresented in the executive ranks across the corporate world. In my industry, the notion that women should dress a certain way in order to be considered credible journalists, and that wearing short skirts stripped them of that credibility, was not a view that I expected to be aired in polite company, certainly not from a former head of state in such a public setting.

"I disagree," I said, trying to remain civil. I smiled.

"Oh yeah, who? Name one," I remember him saying.

I had to think quickly. I offered the first name that came to mind: "Ruth Elkrief of BFM TV." Ruth is a well-known, veteran political interviewer whose show I had been a guest on a few times and who I knew for sure did not wear miniskirts on air.

"Yes, Ruth is good, but who else?" he asked.

I didn't want to pursue that line of questioning, so I changed the subject. What should have been idle banter before a chat onstage had turned into something rather uncomfortable. We moved on to other topics.

He looked me up and down. "Very elegant tonight, by the way."

Part 6

London

A Fresh Start

The interiors of the Bloomberg London office on Finsbury Square were all chrome and glass, shiny and new, the architectural equivalent of a fancy space station. When I walked into the grand 1930s-era building for my screen test in the spring of 1996, wearing a powder-blue suit I had borrowed from my cousin Samar in Paris, I had never seen a more glamorous newsroom. Coming from France, it felt like I had gone from old-world aristocracy to the glitz of the one percent. If Ferrari had tried its hand at designing office space, it would have looked like Bloomberg London in the 1990s. "Money is no object," the man in charge of TV operations told us during an introductory lunch before the network's official launch in Europe. We were bemused rookie TV anchors and didn't quite understand what "no object" meant in the real world, but the message was that our new employers were flush with cash and were ready, if necessary, to weaponize it. Bloomberg's London office design and high-end finishes were about communicating wealth and status. The lobby offered a wide selection of fresh fruit, snacks, and drinks on display. There were also giant stainless-steel refrigerators and microwaves and, dotted throughout the building,

149

giant aquariums with tropical fish calmly drawing circles in the water, little islands of serenity and self-reflection in sharp contrast to the frenetic buzz of the 24-7 Bloomberg newsroom. Years before Google and other tech companies created self-sufficient campuses, employees at Bloomberg never had to exit the ecosystem during their shift: everything they could possibly need was at their fingertips.

The company founder and owner, Michael Bloomberg, had made billions selling real-time data and analysis terminals to banks and financial institutions. Shortly after leaving Salomon Brothers in the early 1980s, Bloomberg had launched his own firm, and the quality of the product he developed quickly made the terminal an essential tool for anyone working in the financial industry. Though Bloomberg LP is still privately held, it's estimated that renting out terminals for $25,000 a year to hundreds of thousands of subscribers has helped push Michael Bloomberg's current net worth to around $95 billion. To this day, the terminal is a must-have in the banking business, and the media company's reporters—often highly specialized beat journalists—are some of the most respected in their field.

In 1996, though, Michael Bloomberg wanted his name to expand beyond terminals, his business newswire service, and his company's English-language television network. His plan was to launch Bloomberg TV channels in several international languages, including French, Italian, German, and Spanish. The recruitment process was dizzyingly quick. The launch of Bloomberg France was set for September 1, with the trial run starting on July 1. Rehearsals had only started in May. We were so young that most of us had no real idea what we were doing. The average age of Bloomberg France's team of young on-air journalists could not have been higher than twenty-eight. We were all in our twenties, and the oldest among us, the team leader, was somewhere in his midthirties.

We had all signed contracts for salaries well above what a starter job would normally pay in 1996. I was earning enough to rent a one-bedroom apartment in London's ultra-high-end Chelsea neighborhood while preparing for the launch of a network nobody had heard of in France but that had the backing of a huge American multimedia powerhouse. I went from being an intern in the obscure *vidéothèque* of a French network to becoming a full-time television anchor. Bloomberg France would initially broadcast only in the morning hours, which meant working a full overnight shift and anchoring from 5:00 a.m. to 7:00 a.m., a brutal schedule, especially for people who couldn't catch up on sleep on weekends or had trouble napping during the daytime hours.

Before the first show had even aired, we had heard tales of the intense work culture at Bloomberg's American offices. We were made to sign a promise that we were nonsmokers, which, for a group of young French journalists at the time, was almost comical. We were warned that if we chose to leave the job, we would never be allowed back. Bloomberg, it was implied, did not like deserters. We were also told that the big boss detested offices and closed doors, and that everyone, including senior managers, was expected to sit in an open-plan office space. Anyone who attempted to seal off a corner behind a divider or a bookcase was promptly made to dismantle the structure and return to the open-plan fold. There were rumors of employees who had not been able to withstand the grueling hours. Tales of nervous breakdowns and, in one instance, an oft-repeated story involving a junior employee who had handcuffed himself to a radiator at the New York office in a public display of mental collapse. The anecdotes were shared and repeated so many times that it was impossible to know which were true and which were fabricated, urban tales designed to make light of an office culture that demanded uncompromising loyalty and dedication from its staff.

Bloomberg's television operation was entirely computerized, which was unusual at the time. There were no control room directors or camera operators. We cut our own video and wrote our own scripts. The screen was divided into several boxes of data and text that updated in real time with only about a third of the space left for actual television programming. Foreign exchange and stock price quotes flashed and updated in one section, the weather forecast in another, and, every once in a while, star sign predictions for the day would appear in a box while news and business news updates aired in the upper-left portion of the screen. Some of the data on the screen needed to be inputted manually. Typos and mistakes from tired overnight data typists were common. I once wrote my own horoscope and watched it go out live on air a few minutes later, alongside the weather forecast for Shanghai, the FTSE stock index, the dollar-to-yuan currency exchange rate, a prerecorded sports segment, and whatever else happened to be flashing on the screen during the few seconds that it appeared on-screen.

We were like university students working an overnight shift with the energy of beginners and the impulsivity of youth. A random assortment of staff—Rym Brahimi, who became a Jordanian princess, and Letizia Ortiz, the queen of Spain, were both employed as Bloomberg anchors during that time—infused the newsroom with a party atmosphere. Pranks were common, including trying to destabilize each other on air by crawling under anchor desks and slowly removing a presenter's shoes while they read the prompter, or ordering cabs for *Mr. J. Christ* just to hear the receptionist announce over the Bloomberg loudspeakers that a taxi for Jesus was waiting outside for pickup.

I knew my time there would be brief. The French-language network was a start-up that had very limited distribution. It had such low viewership numbers that when I once missed my live slot and the computerized camera switched itself on automatically, broadcasting only an empty chair, no one watching television at 6:37 a.m. central European time appeared to have noticed. Its format was lampooned as a visual mess in 1996 by *Charlie Hebdo*, the same satirical magazine that was attacked by terrorists in 2015, with a caricature of me rattling off stock indices surrounded by a confusing constellation of flashing numbers, symbols, and weather forecasts. Moreover, I did not want to specialize in business news. My ambition to work in the field had only grown in the two years I spent at Bloomberg. Despite all my frustrations, my experience there gave me the kind of anchor training no journalism school could have provided. I ad-libbed on live television for several hours every day, five days a week, without a prompter for more than two years. It was repetitive and uninspiring, but the best real-world practice I could have hoped for at that stage in my career.

When it was time to look for the next opportunity, I again worried that my assorted patchwork of identities would make me undesirable no matter where I applied. As far as I could tell, the BBC did not hire anchors with American accents. I had given up on France entirely. Even after my Bloomberg stint, my qualifications did not include a degree from the journalism school my bosses in Paris had told me was essential to joining a French channel. In the US, my country of birth, I was often treated as a foreigner with an exotic name people struggled to pronounce correctly. In the '90s, women with international backgrounds who had achieved mainstream success in America were so rare that, to this day, I can't think of anyone other than Christiane Amanpour, whose reporting from Bosnia during the war in the former Yugoslavia had made her a household name. Years later, after meeting her at CNN and observing her at work, I realized that what helped her succeed was a combination of talent, raw drive, and not taking *no* for an answer. Amanpour picks up the phone and calls bosses. She doesn't ask, she announces. As a result, no one really messes with Christiane. Her qualities are usually those lauded in men but scorned in women. Her approach is one I wish I had embraced more, though I know that not all women are rewarded for similar behavior: we are told to be more aggressive, only to be punished when we are. We are told to say no, only to be described as uncooperative when we do. I know this because it has happened to me in every company I've worked in and no matter how senior I became. The thrill of being one's own defender is seldom followed by professional rewards. It is an act of love toward one's self with the knowledge that there may be a price to pay for speaking up.

When a Bloomberg colleague told me in 1998 that CNN International was looking for a financial news correspondent, I updated my show reel—a tape featuring work I thought illustrated my range and on-air abilities—and sent it to CNN's offices in London. After Bloomberg, I desperately wanted to leave financial news, but working for CNN, which I saw as the highest level of achievement for anyone wishing to be a television news journalist, was worth making the sacrifice for. I'd have to work my way out of that division, even if it meant filing market updates for a few years.

"Lou Dobbs said to hire you," the man in charge of the CNN Business News unit told me when I was called back in a month after taking a writing test. "He watched a minute of your tape and said to hire you. He didn't want to see your résumé." Dobbs, the head of CNNfn, CNN's now defunct financial news network, was described by some of his staff as a tyrant in New York, where he anchored the prime-time business show *Lou Dobbs Tonight.* Producers and correspondents who had worked with him told me that he would sometimes stop them in the hallway and quiz them on the news of the day, berating them if they didn't know the answer. "What's the fed overnight lending rate?" a colleague was once asked. She remembered freezing like a possum, cornered, unable to recall her own name. When she couldn't produce the correct answer, he scolded her: "He basically said I was an idiot and walked away." I imagined that man looking at my tape and, like a Roman emperor, turning his thumb up toward the ceiling, barely raising his head from his computer, smoking at his desk years after it was banned indoors in New York, refusing to quit because *screw everyone, Lou does what he wants.* I wondered how luck lies at the intersection of so many different paths, those in your favor and those working against you. The bully who torments can ruin the day of one and then make the life of another. There is so much randomness in how one moment leads to the next, our destinies disconnected from anything we do or say, out of our control. How often have we been overlooked or dismissed because the person behind the desk in charge of making decisions that affect us was having a bad day?

The CNN London bureau in the late '90s, housed in a small art deco building on a narrow street in the city's Soho district, was unremarkable, especially compared to the Bloomberg offices. A small lobby, dated décor, an anchor desk with, in the background, a colorless newsroom. Still, I couldn't believe my good fortune. The network I had watched daily since I was old enough to realize that I wanted to be a journalist, the home of rolling breaking news, the brand so recognizable that anywhere in the world announcing that CNN was on a story opened doors. CNN was still the only real dominant cable news channel at a time when Fox News had only been broadcasting for a couple of years. The big names of cable TV news like Bernard Shaw, Christiane Amanpour, Peter Arnett, Walt Rodgers, and Richard Blystone had all become colleagues. I felt as if I had achieved something beyond even my most ambitious dreams. I was hired to file business news reports, but I had resolved to do everything in my power to transition to general news. For two years, I reported on banking mergers and the bond market, cut off entirely from the news division, frustrated that I was pigeonholed in the financial news beat. I wanted to travel to the Middle East, to report on US politics, to interview world leaders. I was too nervous to approach the news assignment desk and pitch myself for nonfinancial stories. I would occasionally anchor business shows but never general news. I was almost thirty and felt for the first time in my career that I needed to speed things up. I saw the big names I wanted to call colleagues so infrequently that we could have been working for different networks entirely. But on September 11, 2001, everything changed. On that day, everyone at CNN became a news anchor and reporter. The terrorist attacks on the United States, one of the biggest stories in history, meant that networks needed journalists from every department to cover the attacks and their aftermath. I was in London that day and was sent to Paris to cover any 9/11 reaction there. It was a sidebar to the central event, but I felt like I was doing the job I had always dreamed of. I visited Paris's Grand Mosque and interviewed worshippers there after Friday prayers. Our car was surrounded, and men spit at us, calling us Islamophobes for asking them for a reaction to al-Qaeda's attacks. I was not in New York, but I felt like the work I was doing there was important. No one was asking me to interview financial analysts on that day's stock market activity. Those days were behind me.

Live from the Studio

I felt sick to my stomach. The alarm clock had gone off at 2:30 a.m. and, as was often the case, it was the taxi driver's call that had woken me up. I was on my second year of overnight shifts, copresenting a CNN morning show with business news anchor Richard Quest. The program was called *BizNews* and was meant to be a mix of both business and news, but ended up being a straightforward breakfast show, with almost no financial news content. We had been told that sponsors were more likely to advertise with programs that included the word *business* in the title, rather than risking brand association with a death-and-destruction broadcast. "Today's civil war, brought to you by Lastminute.com!" would not have been an ideal way to promote a business. For the network's sales division, what went into the show, in the end, seemed to be less important than how it billed itself through its name. Quest, a financial news correspondent, was a showman with the on-air persona of an eccentric Brit. I was eight years younger and his counterweight at the anchor desk; the more restrained, serious news presenter. I handled the interviews about the Iraq War. He grilled CEOs with amusing turns of phrase, rolling his *R*s for effect, occasionally using props to

157

inject extra visual appeal into his segments. We weren't friends off air. I can't think of a single time Richard Quest and I went out for lunch, but on live television, we were ideal partners. Our interests never overlapped. Our styles were different but compatible, and there was never competition for the same guests or stories. Quest was a generous coanchor, despite his seniority, and always graciously offered to divvy up anchor scripts and live reporter segments. We were like a vaudeville act in which one comedian slips on a banana peel and the other nods at the hollering crowd with a knowing smirk. Morning shows are about news, but they are also about entertainment and chemistry and, in that regard, *BizNews*, despite its unappealing and perplexing name, was a successful product.

I couldn't tolerate the hours. My body rejected the middle-of-the-night wakeup call with every ounce of energy it could muster. I did not have the strength to socialize outside of working hours. I could never enjoy after-work get-togethers or dinners. Weekends were for catching up on sleep rather than spending free time seeing friends or going to the movies. Fridays, after my shift ended at 8:00 a.m., were entirely dedicated to sleeping on and off until the next morning, only to jet-lag my body all over again on Sunday nights. I would often cry in bed when the time came to go to work. I wanted to be a journalist, but I didn't want to do it at the expense of my physical and mental health. I was so sleep-deprived that I wasn't able to enjoy the fact that I was a CNN anchor in a desirable time slot. I also felt like I had not spent enough time in the field. In my early thirties, I was once again feeling like time was slipping away.

During that time, I was also hosting another CNN show that aired on weekends. In 2002, when the network found a sponsor for a monthly show called *Design 360*, one of the CNN International bosses in London called me into a meeting to tell me I was chosen to front it. By then, we had left our offices on Rathbone Place and moved into a more modern building close to Oxford Street, one of the city's busiest shopping districts.

It was prime real estate in the heart of Soho with state-of-the-art studio space, a huge upgrade from our previous location. Sitting across from a desk, face-to-face with men who controlled my destiny (they have been men most of my career) was always intimidating. I objected meekly. I did not want to host a fashion and architecture show. I wanted to go to the Middle East and report on the lead-up to the expected Iraq invasion. "I'm not asking you, I'm telling you," was the answer. The voice pronouncing the edict was flat and the directive clear. The conversation ended soon after, though it could hardly have been described as a conversation at all.

It occurred to me then that there was no use protesting anyway. Whatever skill I needed to argue a convincing point in my favor seemed to be a talent that I lacked. How had other women before me been able to say, "No, I won't do this," and managed not to be punished or ostracized for it? During that period, I started developing low-grade self-loathing that plunged me into a sort of depression. I was working shifts that were ruining my health, and I would soon have to host a monthly show I had no interest in working on. I could grill a head of state on live television but was scared to advocate for myself with an executive whose power was only great when measured by its impact on me.

By summer 2003, the United States' invasion of Iraq had already descended into chaos. The Middle East and its crises were at the center of every editorial network meeting. The vast majority of international news coverage in the decade following 9/11 came from the Middle East, a part of the world with a smaller population than the United States and fewer Muslims than in Asia. Since the Lebanese civil war in the 1970s and '80s, the Middle East conflicts had attracted Western journalists, many of whom settled in Beirut or Baghdad after the invasion. Finally, I felt, my fluency in conversational Arabic and my knowledge of the culture would be useful to my network bosses. I was willing to go to war zones and ready to sacrifice my private life for the job. I may not have had the skill for office politics that seemed to be essential for advancing in the industry, but I had talents that made me valuable in the field. I would soon be sent out into the wider Arab world. After years of working the wrong shifts and hosting studio-based shows, I felt like I was finally on the cusp of fundamental change.

On the Road

The Four Seasons Amman reception desk staff knew us well. My producer, Schams Elwazer, and I traveled regularly to Jordan to film episodes of *Inside the Middle East*, a monthly feature show on Arab and North African affairs. After I spent a year reluctantly hosting a design program, the network needed a presenter for *IME*, as we called it, and asked me to front it. I went from feeling like my career was stalling to living the most rewarding years of my professional life from one day to the next. I had moved to CNN headquarters in Atlanta in 2004, mainly to escape the exhausting London overnight shift that came with anchoring the morning show with Richard Quest. I was first a floating anchor but was quickly assigned to anchor *Your World Today* and, later, *International Desk*, two shows that aired in prime time in the Europe / Middle East and Africa regions on CNN International. My CNN job during that time involved an ideal combination of in-studio work and fieldwork in the Middle East: between studio-anchoring stints, I was given the freedom to spend weeks at a time in the region, anchoring *Inside the Middle East* from a different country in the Arab world every month. When there was breaking news that interested

Western audiences, and there was a lot of it in that part of the world at the time, I would be diverted to day-of reporting.

"It is probably a gas explosion," the assignment editor in Atlanta told me over the phone. It was around 9:00 p.m., and Schams and I were sitting in the Four Seasons hotel lobby. I had had a drink and felt sleepy and groggy after a long flight to Jordan from Atlanta. "It's never a gas explosion," I remember saying. We called our camerawoman, Margaret Moth, a veteran war photographer who'd been badly injured in Sarajevo during the war when a sniper bullet shattered her jaw. "Get the gear. There are reports of a gas explosion at the Radisson." We took a small yellow taxicab from the hotel. A police checkpoint at the top of the road leading to the Radisson stopped us from driving farther. There was an unusual silence in the air. No sound of traffic; the wails of multiple ambulance sirens overlapping, some closer, some more distant, echoed through the nighttime chill. *This isn't a gas explosion.* We took the camera equipment out of the taxicab trunk and continued on foot, walking at first but soon running the half mile that separated the checkpoint from the Radisson with dozens of pounds of equipment, the tripod I was carrying digging into my right shoulder. We arrived at the hotel, panting, but were stopped at the outer perimeter gates. Though we couldn't confirm it yet, we knew this was an attack. My old Nokia phone rang. "Can you go live?" I was patched through to the control room in Atlanta. I started reporting from outside the hotel with a description of the scene and the possibility that there had been an explosion at the Radisson. I was in one of those rare states where the body is fueled by a mix of adrenaline and stress. Heart pumping, breath quickening. I started noticing that though some ambulances turned into the Radisson driveway, many others were driving past our position, down the street, toward another part of the city. I hung up with Atlanta. "They're saying another hotel was hit," Schams said. "Which one is down there? What's the building?" I asked her, pointing to a tower in the distance. "It's the Hyatt. That's the Grand Hyatt."

At dawn, it became clear that the bombing at the Radisson was one of three coordinated attacks on hotels across Amman. We had been sitting in one lobby when three others were blown up by terrorists. The next day, we were given a tour of the Philadelphia Ballroom at the Radisson, where an Iraqi suicide bomber detonated explosives strapped to his body, killing twenty-seven people at the wedding party of Ashraf al-Akhras and Nadia al-Alami. (The couple survived, but the bride's parents and Akhras's father died.) There was a haunting stillness in the gutted and blackened room where, hours before, there had been revelry. There were pieces of skin still hanging from the walls. Blood spatter in all sizes and patterns formed constellations on the ceiling above. This is what a terrorist does, I thought. And all for what? It had been four years since 9/11, when al-Qaeda terrorists had crashed passenger planes into the Twin Towers in New York, into the Pentagon in Washington, DC, and in a field in Pennsylvania, and Osama bin Laden was still attacking innocent civilians around the world. This was the work of the foot soldiers of the mastermind hiding in a cave. The followers of the deluded commanders of a bogus army of God, promising eternal salvation in heaven. The men and women who buy it all. If it wasn't for the brutality of their acts, you would almost laugh at their gullibility. But instead of sharing lunatic conspiracy theories in closed circles, they chose to explode their own bodies and kill innocents around the world. As reporters, understanding the terrorist path from fundamentalism to terrorism means being able to understand how militant groups brainwash recruits and send them to kill in the name of God and tribe, even if it comes across as an apologia, an exercise sometimes mistaken for excusing, even justifying the acts of the attackers.

In the United States, when a white, Christian man shoots up a supermarket or a primary school, the coverage often tends to unpack the perpetrator's upbringing and family life, trying to comprehend how a person who, from the outside, looks nothing like the devil, could stand over a trembling stranger and pull the trigger, killing them on the spot. When Muslims are radicalized and commit atrocities, there has been less of an effort to understand individual motives. The tendency has been to point the finger of blame at Islam as a whole, asking questions about why and how this one particular religion is used to justify barbarism, in some cases even implying that it promotes violence in its scriptures while others embrace tolerance and peace. Attempts to individualize a terrorist attack as an act of singular radicalization are sometimes seen as excusing violence, perhaps even condoning it. There are often fundamental differences in how two perpetrators of the same type of crime are described in media coverage and treated by law enforcement. The identity of a suspect can therefore be as significant as the identity of the journalist covering the story. If we see in the physical features of the attacker a potential neighbor or family member, we are more inclined to try to understand the root cause of the violence. When attackers look like foreigners and their religion and ethnicity are to us exotic and unfamiliar, are we not more likely to see their acts as representative of a whole group?

The Amman attacks story was one of many I covered in the field during those years. In the Middle East, I reported the effects of America's invasion of Iraq but also, thanks to *Inside the Middle East*, I spent time filming non–news of the day stories: profiling a priest in Gaza, a cancer treatment center in Jordan, the film director Nadine Labaki in Lebanon. In Europe, I covered elections, demonstrations, and the occasional human interest story. Slowly, though I was professionally more fulfilled than ever, I started yearning for a bigger platform and a higher-profile position. I felt like CNN Domestic was still reluctant to air international content produced by its overseas presenters and that those in charge of the network's American feed viewed CNN International anchors as less glamorous, less worthy of airtime in the prime television markets. Once again, I wondered if my identity was a hindrance. More than once, I had to correct domestic producers when they asked me to analyze a story in the Middle East "because you are of Syrian origin." Why did that matter? "I'm a journalist with work experience in the region, that's why you should ask me," I would reply. Besides, I was American, just like they were. Would I ask a US journalist with German roots to explain the functioning of the Bundestag because their father was from Cologne?

Bad Decisions

I gathered Francesco's leather satchel, trousers, and socks and threw them down the spiral staircase. The satchel tumbled down, bumping once or twice on the banister on its way, before crashing on the ground floor below. The clothing seemed to float, taking its time, as if the pants had been waiting for a chance to escape and wanted to take full advantage of the opportunity. Francesco, in his boxer shorts and shirt, was in a state of paralyzed shock. I was throwing him out of my apartment on New Year's Day, ordering him out, in fact, after he had told me, for the second time in as many months, that we were not a couple and that what we had was a nice but casual relationship. A few weeks before, after ordering me never to salt the pasta water while it was boiling, he had said something similar about what I meant to him, and so I had told him that it was over.

Francesco, a tall and fair northern Italian lawyer, was one of the prettiest men I had ever seen. I had met him at one of the many parties the twentysomething European expats threw in '90s London. There was an internet boom, Tony Blair was the newly elected prime minister, and the city felt like it was powered by a sort of collective energy that crossed social and economic barriers. All young professionals newly employed in law, banking, tech, and media, we had the energy and optimism of the newly emancipated. And it felt like we had it all: good looks, youth, and enough disposable income to party with panache.

A few months after our first separation—though I suspected Francesco would not have called it that; it implied a real romantic commitment that he had not made—I had seen him at a New Year's Eve party in an apartment not far from where I lived in the Earl's Court neighborhood of London. We had spoken briefly and then ended up on a pile of coats in the guest room, kissing, his eyes on mine. I had felt the connection of true love. A man surely doesn't look into eyes like that if there is no emotional draw. His long fingers on my cheeks. His angular face, the profile of a marble statue, the thick hair he would wipe away from his face, the teeth, clean and white. He kissed me, and I let out a giggle. I hated sounding like the chuckling damsel, but it was a role I took on when I wanted with all my being to please and seduce. Isn't that what men want? I didn't know. I was just hoping he had realized that his life without me was poorer and that seeing me across a room of New Year's Eve revelers by chance had reminded him of what he was missing. We walked back to my apartment from the party, arms locked, through the fine misty night air, hopping over puddles, slightly wasted from too much bubbly, then the key in the door, the clothes on the floor, and the night spent finally in the embrace of a man who had come back to me after the near tragedy of ending things too soon. "I don't want you to think something," he said the next day at dawn. I was thinking of coffee and pastries. "Think what?" I replied. It was the first day of the year. It would become one of the best days of the year, I thought. "That this is a relationship," he replied. "That this is serious." The charm of his Italian accent suddenly dissolved. The way he pronounced it "see-rioos" made me angry. It felt like a stab in the abdomen, like I would double over in pain if I allowed him to see me suffer.

Francesco wasn't really at fault. I realize this now. It wasn't just Francesco with whom romance had fizzled after sometimes barely having started at all. There was the French banker, the British television producer, the American real estate executive, the star reporter on French television who absentmindedly called me Patrick one day and didn't call me again after that. The younger American CNN producer and I lived together for a while until I found a Prada thong in my dirty clothes hamper, which would have been fine if I had actually owned a Prada thong.

I chose the wrong men, or allowed them to choose me, and tacked onto them fantasies of romantic love. Who they were seemed to be almost irrelevant. I grew attached too quickly. They pulled away. The breakups would inevitably bring up feelings of rejection from early childhood, when my parents' divorce forced regular relocations, ripping me from schools and friends. I feel today great sadness at the years spent yearning for the attention of men who either weren't available or too preoccupied with themselves to be genuinely loving partners. I realize, too, that I wanted to be desired and loved so badly that I allowed myself to get lost in the fictionalized version of a man I knew little about. The separation wounded so much because I was giving up on the idea of a relationship I had constructed in my mind rather than losing the person I was involved with. None of the men I was involved with during those lonely years were particularly kind or cruel, intelligent or slow, loving or heartless. They were a canvas I painted my own feelings of inadequacy on. They were mirrors in which I saw my own pain reflected.

There were men who loved me, some had even fallen in love with me, but those I rarely wanted in return. I was once invited to Venice by a man I was trying to find attractive but, in the end, had to accept would remain only a missed connection. We shared a hotel room "as friends," as the dreaded saying goes. He had booked a gondola ride through the city's canals, hoping, I'm sure, that we could share a first kiss in the most romantic of locations. That trip must have been such a bitter disappointment to him. He didn't let it show, though, and I realize today what an act of kindness that was on his part.

It was as if the lives of most of the women in my group of friends during that time mirrored London's frenetic pace. We had the freedom to do what we wanted and go where we pleased. But what initially felt like a privilege started to feel like being unmoored. Slowing down and finding a place to call home seemed ever-more difficult to grasp as I continued to run from one night shift to another and from one social gathering to the next, living far from family, unable to form attachments in my adopted city. "What's wrong?" my mother asked when I called her one day crying from my one-bedroom apartment in Chelsea. "I'm just depressed," I replied, crying. There was silence. "Why?" She sounded a bit fed up. I had been calling often with similar complaints. I thought about how to word my answer but couldn't find the right turn of phrase. "No reason. I'm just tired."

Full Circle

Anchoring is a rather lonely business. There are meetings before a show with a producer or two, a few conversations with colleagues in the newsroom, but when all the editorial and technical steps are completed, the day ends with a single presenter in a studio facing a camera, usually robotically operated by someone in a control room in another part of the building or, on occasion, in another country altogether. Guests are seldom in the studio with us. With today's videoconferencing technology and home studios, they are most often somewhere else, in another time zone, dressed for work on the top and whatever makes sense to them on the bottom. Anchors speak into a camera, read news updates, and toss to prerecorded segments. During remote interviews, we ask questions and nod, but we are not looking directly into our guests' faces. What goes out on air, what we call the *return*, is on a screen under the camera lens, so it is only perceptible in our peripheral vision. Viewers see two people chatting to each other in a split screen when they are, in fact, staring into the void. It takes some time to become accustomed to conversing in this way and enjoying the interview rather than focusing on its technicalities. Interrupting someone who speaks for too long presents some specific challenges during remote exchanges. There are no physical, in-person cues that allow us to cleanly jump into a discussion. There are no body language indicators to signal that we are about to interject. I imagine this is how a dog measures time, not by looking at a clock but by sensing that a certain amount of time has passed. With enough experience, the number of seconds and minutes that elapse register in some sort of internal body clock, at which point we try to find a natural place to come back into the conversation so that the exchange is informative and fast-paced. There is a limit to how long most people can focus on a monologue. TV news isn't Shakespeare or Edmond Rostand. Over the years, I have calculated that, in most cases, a break of some sort must occur after about two minutes. It doesn't matter if that interruption comes in the form of a question from me or a sound bite that the guest can react to, but, like in sheet music, the rhythmic pattern of the conversation needs to change. There are exceptions, of course, in the case of highly charged dramatic moments or breaking news, but for routine on-air interviews and correspondent live reports, talking too long is as useful as saying nothing at all.

The solitude of the studio anchor is made more peculiar by the fact that he or she is alone while also talking to thousands of people who are, to them, faceless and nameless. Being on one's own in a room while being watched is a singularly odd phenomenon. The challenge is therefore to be friendly with viewers we can't see, to make eye contact with an invisible person, to manifest an interlocutor, like a child speaking to an imaginary friend.

On the first Monday of November 2017, I had reached a pinnacle in the career of any news anchor. CNN International management had agreed to change my show name from *The World Right Now with Hala Gorani* to *Hala Gorani Tonight*. Anchoring an eponymous program on a mainstream network is an achievement by any measure. It wasn't the domestic network, where programming and talent, as presenters are called in the United States, have much bigger budgets, but it was something I could be proud of. I had become, and this was crucial, an Arab American with her own show on CNN. No one had done that before I had. For someone like me, who is atrociously lacking in the skill of office politics, to have progressed that far seemed to me even more reason to celebrate. I have always felt awkward at office gatherings with network presidents and their entourage. I have watched with great envy some of my colleagues engage in perfectly timed small talk, approaching the executives at the right time and retreating when their time was up. After an Emmy Awards event in New York in 2018, I tried and failed to engage with CNN Worldwide president Jeff Zucker twice, each time beaten to him by someone else, forced to retreat to try again, like a general calling his troops back mid-operation. We eventually did exchange a few words, but I was unable to plead my case with him to cover the upcoming midterm elections in the US for CNN International. I was not shy, nor was I particularly low on self-confidence, but I often lacked the timing and skill of small talk, and I found myself that evening without a natural conversational pause during which I could ask for what amounted to a relatively expensive assignment. Before his tenure, I reported on American politics on my show often, but Zucker had all but stripped CNN International anchors of such assignments, favoring domestic reporters and presenters in Washington and simulcasting their programming on the international network. Many of us felt like international programming was being sidelined in a Trump-centric world when we were told to sit out exciting stories while our colleagues in America handled big news.

The launch of my new show coincided with a long period of diminished on-air responsibility for CNN International as domestic programming originating in New York and Washington was increasing on the worldwide feed. Ironic, I remember thinking, that the most journalistically thrilling moments of my career happened when I didn't have a prime-time show at all but anchored dayside or floated around on the schedule filling in for others. The Iraq War, the Israel-Hezbollah

War, the Arab Spring, US and French elections, the Haiti earthquake, crisscrossing the Middle East for a decade. There was no *Hala Gorani Tonight* then, yet those were some of my most rewarding professional years.

I blamed the lack of travel and the ennui of studio anchoring for some of my unhappiness during those years in London because personally, I was more fulfilled than I had ever been. I had married Christian Streib, a CNN photojournalist I'd known for years and with whom I'd reconnected when we both found ourselves single at a wedding in Lebanon. It had happened relatively late in life, this perfect love, but it had happened, and that was all that mattered to me. But I was holding a secret, keeping something from even my closest friends and family: that despite having the high-profile job, a loving marriage, a beautiful home, and a cute dog, I had started experiencing panic attacks that would come in waves, washing over my entire body and head, overwhelming me with a sense that I was having an out-of-body experience. Convinced I was dying, I made my husband drive me to the emergency room every few months, including on a Saturday night where he waited with me for seven hours until a doctor could see me. I underwent a few superficial tests and was released without diagnosis or further treatment. Surely, I was having a heart attack or a stroke, I thought. They must have missed something. For several years, I visited cardiologists, neurologists, endocrinologists, pulmonologists, and gynecologists. I didn't know what was happening to my body and, perhaps even more mysteriously, why my mind seemed to have developed a mind of its own, as if it controlled me rather than the other way around. I felt like I was losing my sanity. Before going on air, I would take deep breaths, terrified that one of the attacks would happen on live television. I was not sharing any of this with my colleagues: professional women who show weakness, even now, can be seen as liabilities. Women who cry are "emotional," while men who cry are commended for being "in touch with their feelings." Women who, like me, were experiencing anxiety were often seen as unable to handle the stresses of a demanding job. A female colleague who had returned from Gaza with obvious stress in 2005 was not sent back into the field for years after she had felt ready to return. I worried that admitting any of what was happening to me would give my employer even more reason to keep me in the studio rather than send me on assignment. Men who admitted to mental health struggles, meantime, were often praised for their bravery, and I have noticed throughout my career that they are more likely to be sent back to war zones after taking time off to recover from post-traumatic stress. Social media, mental health–awareness campaigns, even corporate human resources emails were all encouraging people to speak up about anxiety and depression. The messaging was everywhere. We were meant to be entering a new era of tolerance—understanding, even—about what was once a taboo subject. Despite reassurances that women would not be judged for coming forward, I still believed that speaking frankly about this at work would have ultimately harmed me. What I needed was a leave of absence to deal with my issues. Instead, I made a point of working even harder. I accepted extra shifts. I pitched more projects and ideas. It was like walking on a broken leg, every day, making the injury worse, until the fracture was at risk of not properly healing.

Solutions to the most overwhelming problems are sometimes so simple that we are almost angry when they finally materialize, like searching frantically for a pair of glasses that was on our heads the entire time. A gynecologist who patiently listened to me explain my symptoms as I cried uncontrollably, one of the last doctors I saw, told me that she would order a blood test to make sure but that she already knew what the issue was. I was suffering from the hormonal swings that accompany perimenopause, that hellish period that precedes menopause, when a woman reaches her post-reproductive years. "You still have your period, you are still ovulating," she told me, "but your body's hormones are on a roller coaster. Blood tests are pointless anyway. In these cases and at your age, we must treat the symptoms first." She reassured me that HRT (hormone replacement therapy) was not as dangerous as a study conducted a few decades ago had made it out to be, especially on women who are young and healthy. At that point, I was in such a state of distress that I would have swallowed ten horse pills to feel better. After a few months, my panic attacks stopped, and a few months after that, my anxiety became completely manageable. I realized that the hormonal constellation inside a woman's body is like a sort of precise microscopic miracle that does not tolerate imbalance for long. A dip in one place causes chaos across the spectrum. So many have suffered needlessly in the past, and I feel fortunate to be alive at a time when there are treatments available to help women navigate what can be a difficult transition in their lives. I have wondered since if many of the women that history recorded as having gone insane in the past, who ended up in nineteenth-century Victorian-era sanatoriums, simply hadn't just needed a proper course of HRT.

CNN LONDON, APRIL 28, 2022

I had already moved the few possessions I kept in my office space out. I had donated some of my anchor outfits, old dresses and blazers that had become too small when I couldn't shift the weight I had gained during the COVID lockdowns, and thrown away most everything else. I do not get attached to things, except for letters and photos. I have a very difficult time throwing away old photos, even when they're out of focus and I can't quite remember the names of everyone in them. But a pair of diamond earrings? I will sell them or give them to a loved one without a second thought. Books, clothing, even homes, I shed and I move on. I kept a single red CNN mug, branded *The World Right*

Now with Hala Gorani, the title of the show I anchored from 2014 to 2017 before I was promoted to *Hala Gorani Tonight*. I had never truly embraced that show title, but it represented an important period in my life, and I wanted a keepsake to remember it by. I threw away all my business cards, as well. Whatever television job I would get after this one would require new cards anyway.

I had prepared a little monologue I was going to read at the end of the show. It was only forty-five seconds long. I told viewers on my last show that if I had been told as a young woman that a Syrian American woman who didn't feel like she truly fit in anywhere would one day anchor her own prime-time show on CNN, I would have not believed it. I added that I was also immensely grateful for the opportunity. I meant every word. But there came a time when reading the news in the studio was making me feel like I was missing out. There were muscles I wasn't flexing. There were stories I wasn't telling. International news channels were cutting back on travel budgets for anchors, and CNN's US network was facing unprecedented ratings challenges. By leaving, I wasn't giving up on journalism. I was giving myself another chance to feel passionate about telling stories again. I thought of the day I wrote my first wire for the Agence France-Presse in Washington, DC. That day, June 2, 1992, seeing my initials, *HB* for *Hala Basha*, at the bottom of a tiny dispatch, had filled me with such joy that I had run several Washington, DC, blocks, holding a copy of my piece in my hand, fueled by sheer elation.

I wanted to feel that way again.

Part 7

Istanbul

Love on the Bosphorus

He was not as physically imposing as I'd imagined. I had seen him on television reporting from various Middle Eastern countries and had pictured a bigger man. Television often magnifies people. I have often been told that I am more "petite" than I appear on air. Simon had the square jaw and thick hair of a European television network correspondent and the swagger of someone who's not short on self-confidence. I noticed him as soon as he walked onto the apartment terrace overlooking the Bosphorus in Istanbul, where a group of reporters had gathered for an evening drink. I remember later hoping that this would become the story of how I had met my husband, perhaps even one we would both share. "I was on a balcony at a *New York Times* party, and he walked in," I would say. "I recognized her from CNN and made a beeline for her," he would add. The fact that it was a moonlit night, that we were in Turkey, looking out onto the Asian side of Istanbul from across the Bosphorus Strait, that the story sounded almost like it came right out of a romance novel, added to the fairy-tale aspect of it all. I had spent years going from one romantic disappointment to the next for no other reason than because I projected onto each man I met the idea of a perfect partner, with little regard for who they actually were. During those years, I was what might unkindly be called desperate for genuine affection. People yearning for a romance tend to aim low. They rarely attract caring partners. From the outside, however, I doubt that anyone could tell: I projected strength and individuality. I was quite pretty and active. I was a television journalist who traveled the globe. Inside, however, I craved love and attention in a way that made me vulnerable to the types of men who make the first move, men who enjoy seducing and are adept at making women feel noticed and desired.

That night, Simon and I drank tepid white wine out of plastic cups and chatted about war reporting. Istanbul, like Beirut, was a common base for foreign correspondents covering the Iraq conflict and other hot zones in the Middle East. For Western journalists off the clock, hardship postings in the region often came with comfortable living conditions. The American dollar goes a long way in some parts of the world. It was also a time when Iraq was a huge story in the United States because of America's enormous military involvement in the country. Networks sent their top reporters to Baghdad and kept permanent bases in the city. This came at considerable cost and risk both for the news channels and the journalists on the ground. The Iraq War turned young, intrepid correspondents into television stars. They went from relative obscurity to being featured in *Vanity Fair* magazine. Simon was one of them.

A woman who has remained single into her thirties can be a particularly vulnerable creature. I was thirty-five years old when I met Simon, and I felt time ticking by so quickly that I worried that if I didn't soon couple up, I would never find a suitable life partner. At that time, though I wasn't opposed to the idea of having children, becoming a mother wasn't my primary goal. It wasn't a burning desire for me in the way it sometimes is for other people. I deeply longed for a life partner, however. I wanted to create a home with someone. I yearned for the intimacy and companionship that only a spouse can provide.

My cell phone rang. "It's the CNN International desk," someone on the other end of the line said. "Tristan is trying to reach you, but he can't dial an international number from his US phone." Tristan. A CNN colleague I had dated intermittently for a few years, whose attachment to me seemed to vanish when he romanced other women but suddenly grew when I started pulling away. Could he sense I had met someone new from three continents away? "Tell him I'm busy," I said and hung up. Simon looked at me. "Work?" he asked. "Sort of," I joked, with only myself.

We spoke of the Middle East, of Iraq, of the beauty of Istanbul. I was mesmerized. A Western man who spoke fluent Arabic and who understood the region deeply. We exchanged numbers. I was surprised when he texted me the very next day. He wasn't playing it cool, I thought. What was the point of delaying things? Perhaps we both knew the attraction was undeniable. I was flying back to Atlanta, where I lived at the time, and he was traveling back to Iraq, where he was based on an almost full-time basis. Simon was displaying a level of commitment to the story that not all journalists who covered the region did during the height of the conflict. A permanent base in Baghdad was as dedicated as a reporter could get.

We met again in Morocco, in New York, in Paris, and in Jordan, where he had followed me on one of my assignments. He read poetry on top of a hill in the ancient city of Petra while I filmed a piece to camera below. The Nabataeans had used Petra as a major hub for the incense trade in the second century BC, and here we were, I thought, in the rose-hued valley of one of humanity's most prosperous nomad tribes, thousands of years later, allowing love to flourish within its carved sandstone cliffs. My Arab colleagues on that trip nicknamed Simon "Lawrence of Arabia." My producer, Schams Elwazer, rolled her eyes whenever I mentioned his name—"Something about him," she'd say in a wince. Schams seldom embraced strangers, and wariness could be her default setting, so I ignored her qualms about Simon.

I had never been comfortable with public displays of affection, but I behaved differently with him. I finally felt like I had met the right partner. He was from Europe but had lived years in the Middle East. He spoke and read Arabic and therefore, I believed, could appreciate and understand someone with my complex set of overlapping identities without prejudice. I had never been romantically involved with someone who had been to all the places that made me who I am: Syria, the US, France, and Britain. Simon understood the difference between being Muslim and being an Islamist, a distinction that should be basic but that many don't make in the West. He knew that being Syrian or Iraqi could also mean being worldly and cultured and didn't reduce non-Westerners to one-dimensional stereotypes. We were both in our midthirties and at an age when two people who find themselves in love might want to plan a future together.

Sometimes, the most mundane incidents alert us to the most serious impending catastrophes. The first crack before a building collapses, the first drop of rain before a typhoon. When, after several months, I sent Simon a care package to Baghdad, I started realizing that I was more invested in the relationship than he was. A FedEx parcel sent to a war zone sounds like an absurdity, but in many ways, life always seems to go on even in the worst of conflicts: delivery drivers make their rounds doing their best to avoid bombings and flying bullets. I had carefully chosen some DVDs, a few high-priced delicacies that I can't quite remember now. He had asked for some multivitamins, which I also included in the big box. One of the movies was *Spanglish* starring Adam Sandler. The vitamins came in individually wrapped baggies with the exact number of pills that needed to be taken daily. "My pee was bright yellow from those vitamins," he told me on the phone. "That movie was cheesy," he said when I asked him about the DVDs. I was realizing, slowly, that a man in love would find every reason to hide his disappointment at a gift sent halfway across the world to a country in the midst of sectarian warfare. In a matter

of a few weeks, Simon's behavior changed. "In general I do worry...
however...that you deserve and want more than I can offer...which is
terrible," he emailed me toward the end of our relationship. I held on
in my mind. I hoped there had been some sort of misunderstanding. I
blamed myself. Had I been too pushy? I reread our email exchanges,
went over telephone conversations in my mind. What about the weekend in Marrakech, where we played roulette at the Mamounia Casino,
or the whirlwind trip to New York, or the plans we made to go back
to Turkey together but, this time, as a couple? Those trips and those
plans, which had meant so much to me, did not hold for Simon the
same meaning. "miss u" was the subject line of the email he sent after
I told him I could no longer continue. "am a big hala fan," he wrote in
another. Sometimes, after a few months, I would receive another note:
"love that turtleneck on you, looking hot on air." I would answer, leaving the door open for more. Even then, I wondered if perhaps there
was still interest on his part and if I had acted too precipitously. Had I
ended the relationship too abruptly? Was I, ultimately, responsible for
my own heartache?

BRUSSELS, MARCH 24, 2016

I had seen him on other stories in the field before, but this time, we
were in the same small room, waiting for the Brussels mayor to sit
down for an interview in his city hall office. The mayor was speaking
on camera to a small group of foreign news networks about the
terrorist bombings at the Brussels airport and in the city's metro a
few days before. By then, I had covered so many of these attacks that
I felt almost numb to them. There was a routine to them and to our
coverage. How many attackers? How many killed? Wounded? Claim of

responsibility? ISIS? How were they radicalized? Ten years had passed since I had cried over the end of our affair. I had married Christian the year before. Simon had also gotten married and had started a family that year. He showed me holiday snaps on his phone. Our exchange lasted only a few minutes. In the years after our relationship had ended, I had learned of his liaisons with other women while I hoped that he still nurtured an exclusive interest in me. Over time, I had learned to laugh about it. Later, I found the extent to which I had been mistaken about Simon to be genuinely bewildering. "The day you called him after your breakup, he was in the Caribbean with another reporter," one of our common acquaintances told me several years later. "How do you know?" I remember asking, suddenly experiencing a tinge of heartache again. "She posted a picture of the two of them on Facebook," he replied. Simon and I had talked about going to the Caribbean together that winter. After our separation, he had evidently invited someone else to take my place. "If I was a dog breed, I'd be a Labrador," he had told me during one of our vacations in Morocco. "They love everyone!"

I wondered when I saw him in the Brussels mayor's office that day in 2016 how someone who holds vital importance to us one day becomes, on another day, just another social relation, whose physical features suddenly appear foreign to us, on whom we notice imperfections we missed in the initial throes of romantic love. Feeling nothing at all for a man I once traveled the world to spend three days with really makes no sense at all, I thought. That first conversation on a terrace with a view of the Bosphorus Strait, the exchange I hoped would lead to true love, was, in the end, just another conversation. We said our goodbyes and then each took our turn interviewing the mayor. We did not speak again after that.

The Little Boy on the Beach

There was something grotesque about the photo of the little boy lying face down in the sand, dead, in the tiny clothing of a toddler—a red T-shirt and a pair of blue shorts—still wearing the little Velcro-strap sneakers his mommy had slipped on his feet just a few hours earlier. His body had washed up on a beach close to several vacation resorts. You could buy a ferry ticket from Bodrum, where Alan Kurdi's body was found, to the Greek town of Kos, where the refugees were headed, for $20.

Alan Kurdi was two years and two months old when he drowned in the Mediterranean Sea. His parents had paid smugglers around $4,000 to transport them and their two sons from Turkey to Greece during the massive refugee wave in 2015 in which nearly half a million Syrians fleeing the war tried to make their way to Europe.

The father, Abdullah, was the only survivor in his family after the dinghy they were in capsized. "He told me the boat hit the first wave and the Turkish captain jumped in the water and ran away," Tima Kurdi, Abdullah's sister, told me in an interview about ten days after the picture of the little boy caused consternation around the world.

187

She felt overwhelming guilt, she told me in a flood of tears, because she had sent her brother the cash for the trip. Maybe, just maybe, they wouldn't have attempted to cross had she not given them the money.

Even those who cared little about refugees couldn't ignore this image. Alan Kurdi's bottom was slightly raised and his arms outstretched by his side, his palms facing up, in the way very small children sometimes sleep in their cribs. I remember thinking that if European countries could tolerate the death of a two-year-old, then there was no hope for the people fleeing persecution and war in the home country.

The initial wave of sympathy for the refugees who had arrived by boat in Greece, many of whom had walked thousands of kilometers to seek asylum as far as Germany and Sweden, soon fizzled. Some countries, like Hungary, refused entry to the exhausted migrants. The government of Viktor Orbán rejected every single asylum request made at its border with Serbia. It deployed the military to block refugees, lobbing tear gas at them, arresting anyone who attempted to cross. A razor-wire fence was erected. Some migrants trying to get through shredded their skin on its sharp edges. We aired the images on CNN with reporters following the migrants on foot through several countries. On the way, Hungarians opposed to the Orbán anti-immigration policy handed refugees water, baby strollers, clean socks. Some were crying as they did so. How could one stand by the side of the road, watching this stream of human misery, and say, "Go back to where you came from?" I wondered as I anchored hours of coverage. We at CNN, like all the other news outlets covering the story, called it a refugee "crisis." Half a million people in a continent of 300 million seemed to me like less of a crisis than the 1.5 million migrants in Lebanon, a country of 4.5 million. At what point does something go from being a tragedy to being a crisis? Seven years later, many more Ukrainians fled to Europe after the Russian invasion of their country and were absorbed with enthusiasm as neighbors. Why did razor wires go up for one group of refugees but not the other?

The year 2015 was particularly brutal for Syrian civilians. Russia had entered the war on the side of the regime, and civilian areas were being increasingly targeted with aerial bombings and indiscriminate weapons like barrel bombs and artillery shells. ISIS and other extremist groups were also targeting civilians, kidnapping them and committing other atrocities. By 2016, four hundred thousand Syrians had been killed. Millions more had felt like they had no choice but to flee. Despite ample evidence that civilians were being targeted, I had started noticing online that any mention I made of the conditions the refugees were fleeing from in Syria, particularly those in areas still controlled by the rebels, brought out a subgroup of self-proclaimed journalists, analysts, and internet attack dogs accusing me of siding with terrorists. Other reporters covering the conflict faced similar insults, and many of them were women. My CNN colleagues Clarissa Ward and Arwa Damon, who had both spent time in rebel-held parts of Syria where Islamist fighters were largely in charge, could hardly mention the suffering of ordinary civilians without being charged with being terrorist sympathizers. This bizarre army of trolls cast themselves as anti-imperialist truth tellers. Their hatred for Western interventionism turned them into apologists for the worst of humanity, so that they were either justifying attacks against civilians or claiming that they were outright fabrications. A year or so ago, I stumbled on an unhinged online discussion between two Syria YouTube "analysts" who denied that the 2018 chemical attack in Douma had ever taken place, that whatever transpired there was actually a false flag attack by Islamist rebels, and that Arwa and I should be ashamed, as women with Syrian roots, of perpetuating falsehoods about the war.

"CNN's Hala Gorani is just another Jihadi Fake News Media Whore," tweeted one account. "I'd rather have a colonoscopy than watch your pro-ISIS propaganda," offered another. The accusations of "fake news" were lifted straight from the Donald Trump lexicon and used to discredit fact-based journalism if it went against the trolls' worldview. There were Syrians who sided with the Bashar al-Assad regime who took part but also, increasingly, Western academics and journalists who could no longer draw the line between legitimate critique of Western foreign policies and support for dictators.

A truly strange shift took place within this class of former commentators and intellectuals. One well-known journalist, whose father had once been an American presidential adviser, claimed that the Assad government was being blamed for the chemical attacks because the US's goal was regime change in Syria. He also baselessly claimed that the first responders and medical staff who rescued civilians in rebel-held areas in Syria were all jihadists. When Barack Obama failed to enforce his own red line on chemical attacks in 2013 after Assad forces dropped sarin gas on civilians in the Damascus suburb of Ghouta, most Syrians I knew were disappointed. When another attack took place in the Damascus suburb of Douma, the former *Rolling Stone* reporter Matt Taibbi linked to an article by the veteran journalist Robert Fisk doubting that a chemical attack even took place, implying that anyone who believes the Assad regime could target its own people is a naïve Western stooge. Later, several reporters, including the *Times of London*'s Richard Spencer and Catherine Philp, confirmed that the journalists traveled to Douma on a government-organized trip and that the doctor interviewed by Fisk in his story admitted to not having been to the hospital where the chemical attack victims had been treated. In fact, other journalists on the same trip that Fisk based his reporting on found survivors who said they had inhaled toxic gases. Was it a case of confirmation bias, when a reporter is so intent on proving their theory that they willfully ignore evidence that contradicts their preconceived conclusion?

The fascinating thing about this phenomenon is that soon a bizarre overlap between Left-leaning anti-imperialists and Trump Republicans started to emerge. After a while, both groups were basically echoing each other and arguing the same points. Some journalists like

Glenn Greenwald, who had gained worldwide praise for his reporting on the NSA whistleblower Edward Snowden, the contractor who'd leaked documents exposing the US government's surveillance machine, also began opining that the US had no moral standing to say or do anything about the atrocities committed by the Assad regime. His work exposing Western hypocrisy had, for a time, earned him a reputation as a champion of the anti-establishment left, but he was becoming increasingly abrasive and insulting to his critics. It seemed his mistrust of Western mainstream media and government institutions was overriding all his investigative journalist faculties on Syria.

What happened to Greenwald and other journalists like him around the time Donald Trump was elected was even more perplexing. Their foreign policy reporting went from holding Western leaders accountable for their interventionism and double standards to casting all intervention to save civilians in Syria as imperialism. Some of them cited or "liked" articles and tweets about whether Syria's White Helmets rescuers were, in fact, jihadists funded by the CIA and the British foreign service. Greenwald started appearing regularly on *Tucker Carlson Tonight*, then Fox News's highest rated prime-time show, where the two men's views on Russia, Syria, and the Democratic establishment appeared to be in perfect synchronicity. The Far Left and the Far Right had come together in agreement on a wide range of foreign policy issues. In their view, anyone supporting intervention in Syria was a supporter of a corrupt establishment, guilty of parroting "deep state" narratives. I don't personally know of a single Syrian who was not critical of Barack Obama for failing to enforce his own red line after the 2013 chemical attack on Ghouta with a no-fly zone. It would have been an act of war, but one that had been leveled at Iraq for a lot less for over a decade. The argument, used by some a posteriori, that this was a direct confrontation with Moscow was nonsense, because Russia had not directly entered the conflict yet. There is little doubt that it would have saved lives and prevented the deaths of hundreds of thousands of people in aerial bombings of densely populated urban areas under rebel control.

I had to create another Twitter account to find Greenwald's tweets on Syria because he had long ago blocked me on the social media platform. Notoriously thin-skinned, he has viciously attacked fellow journalists for their views, their abilities, their choice of subject matter, and their analysis, only to block them from access to his account after even the most benign pushback.

The British-Syrian writer Leila Al-Shami calls this phenomenon "the anti-imperialism of idiots" led by a Left that "seems blind to any form of imperialism that is non-western in origin. It combines identity politics with egoism. Everything that happens is viewed through the prism of what it means for westerners—only white men have the power to make history."

For Syrians, these debates are about more than politics; they are about identity and not allowing the truth about who is really responsible for the misery of millions to be buried. No one who is seriously following the developments in Syria denies that the rebel forces soon became dominated by Islamist fighters, but they also know that the vast majority of the misery inflicted on Syrian civilians was perpetrated by the regime and its allies in Russia and Iran. The civilian, pro-democratic opposition to Bashar al-Assad was basically decimated or sent into exile in the early months of the uprising. Thousands were disappeared, and the gruesome images taken by Caesar, a military photographer known only by his code name, provide evidence of how many were tortured and killed in prison. Millions have been internally displaced or forced into exile. The people who fought for their freedom, who were jailed for their struggle, rarely made it into the point-scoring tweets of the anti-imperialist Left.

Former Syrian political prisoner Yassin al-Haj Saleh described the views on Syria of another intellectual and anti-imperialist, the renowned academic Noam Chomsky, in broadly similar terms, writing that his "Americentric perspective tends systematically to minimize the crimes of states that are opposed to the U.S."

For the victims of the war, ultimately, none of these debates matter. They are the background chatter of the privileged Twitterati, the discussions of people who rarely mention the names of the victims in their analysis. The self-proclaimed anti-imperialists primarily view Syria through the prism of political argumentation. For them, supporting any kind of Western intervention means being an establishment shill. Period. There is no nuance, no gradation to their analysis. I have found this approach infuriating because it is intellectually myopic and far too often drifts into apologism of dictatorships.

The children gassed to death, whose limp bodies were displayed in a row in a hospital basement after the Ghouta attack in 2013, their eyes closed and their mouths agape, would not have cared either way. Sarin will kill you, but it won't leave a wound. There is no blood splatter, no dismembered bodies, no bones and guts scattered on the ground: the murderers come and go in silence, go back home to their own children, tuck them in bed, and deny to the world that they were ever there.

Part 8

Baghdad

The Green Zone

I had been warned that the landing would be brutal. I looked out of the plane window: Baghdad. It was my first time flying into Iraq since the 2003 American invasion. Pilots landing at Baghdad Airport, formerly Saddam International Airport, used something called *the corkscrew approach*. At around eighteen thousand feet, flaps positioned and landing gear out, they would execute the exact opposite of a slow drift onto the runway. Instead, the aircraft hovered above the airport for a moment before spiraling downward in an almost vertical descent. The American military had used the corkscrew technique in Vietnam. It was designed to shorten the amount of time a plane was within range of a surface-to-air missile. Early in the war, a DHL Airbus had been hit by a shoulder-fired missile soon after takeoff. The occupation forces had blamed insurgent groups loyal to the deposed president for the attack. After that incident, in which, miraculously, no one was killed, most pilots flying in and out of Baghdad did not take any more chances.

Royal Jordanian Airlines was one of the only operators flying civilian aircraft into the country at the height of the war. Most often, South African crews manned these civilian flights. Pilots who performed this type of landing usually had some sort of military training. The flights from neighboring Amman, Jordan, to Baghdad carried almost no regular passengers. They were filled with reporters, diplomatic staff, aid workers, and the security personnel needed to protect all those people from attacks, IEDs, random shootings, kidnappings, and whatever other gruesome fate awaits those who run out of luck in a war zone.

"Welcome to Iraq!" said Mohammed Tawfeeq, an Iraqi producer who worked at the CNN Baghdad bureau as I exited the baggage claim. His wide smile, high energy, and chattiness put me at ease but also came as a surprise. I had pictured a pickup crew with sullen faces and no time for jokes. We were about to embark on a stretch of highway that had been nicknamed "the most dangerous road in the world," the seven miles that connected the airport to the Green Zone, where coalition forces had carved out a walled security area in central Baghdad.

In the airport parking garage, they opened the trunk. "We were told you weren't bringing your own body armor, so here, you can wear this one," they said, handing me a flak jacket. In addition to Mohammed, there were two security guards, each carrying a concealed handgun, escorting us back to the CNN Baghdad bureau. In the car, there was also an MP5 submachine gun resting between the driver's seat and the passenger seat for easy access in case of an attack on the vehicle. CNN had purchased fully armored cars to transport its personnel into and around Baghdad after attacks on so-called soft cars became common a few months after the war began. In January 2004, an assault on CNN correspondent Michael Holmes and his convoy had ended in the deaths of two team members: translator Duraid Mohammad and driver Yasser Khatib. The armored vehicles used after that were converted old-model Mercedes sedans with heavy, reinforced doors and bulletproof windows. Avoiding detection was the primary goal, so media and humanitarian workers learned quickly to stop using the more conspicuous black SUVs associated with the occupation forces. "You can always tell an armored car by how low it is to the ground. All the extra weight," the bureau chief there later told me. I learned to look out for them in traffic in Baghdad when we were out on assignment. If the body of the car almost touched the ground, I tried to figure out if it was because the car was armored or if it was just because it was an old jalopy.

There were dangerous assignments, and then there was Iraq in 2007. The sectarian war that broke out after the United States entered the country had exploded into a conflict so brutal that almost every part of the nation was in flames. The American idea, in President George W. Bush's words, of "spreading liberty and democracy" was coming up against the reality of a catastrophic, badly planned invasion based on the lie that Saddam Hussein's regime was developing weapons of mass destruction or that it was somehow linked to the 9/11 attacks. When Americans spoke of "democracy," Arabs heard "invasion." When they spoke of "liberty," Arabs heard "hypocrisy."

No one I talked to in Iraq over the years believed that America's war was about finding and destroying weapons of mass destruction. Those who knew the region had warned that the ripple effects of a poorly executed invasion would lead to chaos. But even the most seasoned observers couldn't have predicted that within the first few months of the invasion, Paul Bremer, George Bush's envoy and the inept head of the Coalition Provisional Authority, would dissolve the Iraqi military and other security forces, in effect firing the entire police force, the army, and the presidential guard. Many of the dismissed Sunni officers went on to join the nascent anti-Western insurgency, al-Qaeda-affiliated groups that later morphed into ISIS. Bremer's decision helped create a ready-made insurgent army that would fight with deadly force for many years after the invasion and destabilize the region for decades. We are still suffering from the effects of those decisions today.

After the end of the Saddam Hussein dictatorship, which had favored members of his Sunni sect, an informal power-sharing arrangement was initiated along ethno-sectarian lines: the prime minister—the head of the Iraqi government—would be a Shiite, the parliament speaker a Sunni, and the president, now a nominal post, a Kurd. But the Sunni insurgents who had backed Saddam Hussein felt ostracized after decades of total control under Saddam. Sunni militants increased attacks against the majority Shiite population: truck bombs exploding in a packed crowd of Shiite pilgrims one day, a suicide bomber targeting a market in a Shiite district another. Shi-ites were retaliating, in some cases killing dozens of Sunnis. In March 2007, after a truck bomb explosion in a Shiite neighborhood of Tal Afar killed more than 150 people, Shiite attackers gunned down 70 people in a Sunni neighborhood the very next day. Tal Afar, inciden-tally, was the city George W. Bush had, the year before, hailed as an example of counterinsurgency success. "The people of Tal Afar have shown why spreading liberty and democracy is at the heart of our strategy to defeat the terrorists," Bush told an audience in Cleveland in 2006. Condoleezza Rice, his secretary of state, had claimed that Tal Afar was an example of America's "Clear, Hold, and Build" counterin-surgency strategy working. But it was already too late. A few months later, Sunni insurgents, Shiite fighters, American soldiers, the civilian population, and everyone in between were once again caught deep in a sectarian bloodbath that would tear the country apart and destabilize the entire region.

As we left the airport, I looked out of the window. So this was the deadliest stretch of road in the world? The Americans had nicknamed it "IED Alley" for the improvised explosive devices—bombs and sui-cide bombers—that went off on an alarmingly regular basis on the seven-mile stretch to and from the airport. Others called it "Death Street." Insurgents would drive cars with darkened windows and fire into moving traffic, aiming for vehicles that appeared linked to the US military, its diplomats, or anyone connected to Western interests. They would bury bombs under roadways and trigger them with cell phones just as their targets drove past. Marla Ruzicka, a twenty-eight-year-old aid worker from California, whose car was stopped behind an American Humvee convoy, was killed in April 2005 when a suicide bomber drove his explosive-packed car into traffic. Three others died in the attack. Every car was a potential threat. Every overpass. Every embankment. While I eyed cars and military vehicles nervously, Mohammed, his eyes sparkling with excitement, ran through the stories we could film together. He was from Baghdad, knew the city intimately, and had been working for CNN since the beginning of the war. Over the years, he had become one of the best field producers in the country, full of energy and the kind of resilience only the strongest among us show when reporting on the destruction of their own homeland. It would take years for me to understand what it takes to not break down when watching your own home destroyed, your own country in flames, your own family torn apart.

Baghdad then was a city no one visited unless they had to. The humanitarians, journalists, and diplomats who flew in and held their breaths on the airport road were there because they had jobs to do. Most would count the days until they could leave again. What Baghdad really was, what it had meant to the world, was lost on many of us during that time. We were in the city to report on a war and its effects, not to write history tomes. Baghdad, where science, learning, and poetry flourished for centuries, a city of light and riches, where the Abbasids, the Mamluks, the Mongols, the Safavids, and the Ottomans had all jostled for power, had given to humanity some of its most foundational riches. Did people who dropped in on reporting assignments know that a library in Baghdad once had the largest collection of books in the world in the ninth century? Or that, in the city, the method for writing numbers that we all use today, using positional notation, with single digits in columns, was perfected there, forever revolutionizing mathematics?

At the height of the civil conflict in Iraq, we talked about, wrote about, and heard about death and destruction all day, so, when Mohammed made jokes—and he made them often—they were always welcome.

"HELLO, TODAY IS WEDNESDAY," he once printed out on an A4 paper he pinned to my desk in the CNN Baghdad bureau when I got the day wrong during a live report earlier in the morning. I looked up and saw him smiling at me from across the newsroom. His mere presence lightened the mood.

There were no incidents on our way into the bureau from the airport on that first day, and we eventually drove off the highway, into side streets, finally reaching the compound CNN shared with other media organizations. It was located behind blast walls and barbed wire, with a security crew manning the front gate. The car stopped; a man checked the chassis for explosives with a mirrored device and waved the car in. What was once an enclave of private villas had become a walled-off enclosure of TV networks, newspapers, and press agencies all clustered together for maximum security. It was like a medieval village sealed off by ramparts; Western journalists based in and around the CNN bureau lived together in a sort of cooperative with joint safety measures and intelligence sharing. If there was a threat against one, it was treated as a threat against everyone in the compound.

This makeshift Baghdad newsroom occupied about half the ground floor of the villa CNN used as its base in Iraq—a few desks pushed together at one end of what had once likely been one of the house's living rooms and, on the other, a bank of television screens linked to our satellite returns. It was difficult to tell what the original floor plan looked like before the property was turned into a wartime news-gathering facility, because there were sandbags stacked in and around the external doorways, and many of the windows had been boarded up. On the other side of a massive marble staircase, there was a large kitchen, where local staff prepared three meals a day. There were also Iraqi cleaners, drivers, and local security personnel. Many would return home after their shifts. Others would stay overnight in the villa, including the security staff, who completed rotations of four, six, or eight weeks. I was shown my room: a large space with Formica closets pushed up against the windows to protect from glass shards and shrapnel in case of an explosion outside.

So here I am, I thought. Strictly speaking, this wasn't my world. I hadn't spent any time in Iraq since 2003. I put down my things and looked around. I was excited to start working. Eager to tell stories of Iraqi civilians and to spend time with US troops on the battlefield. In the most unlikely of places, I felt like I was exactly where I belonged.

Baghdad Beautiful

As I waited to go live on CNN one evening, I watched American choppers in the air above the compound firing off colorful flares to protect against surface-to-air missiles, flying against the pastel-tinted Baghdad sky, and thought they were beautiful in a way, these helicopters, creating red, green, and blue circular patterns before heading out to other parts of the capital. They were also equipped with high-caliber automatic machine guns, a thought that made them seem suddenly less poetically alluring. Aboard the Black Hawks the US military used in Iraq, I would often watch the young gunners, one eye pressed against the rim of a visor, scanning the landscape below; only they stood between us and whoever was trying to shoot us down. Whatever your opinion about a war, you quickly become a fan of soldiers with good aim when people are trying to kill you.

In the bureau, though, the atmosphere was rarely one of existential contemplation. When one US network bureau chief pursued me openly, visiting the CNN bureau almost daily and asking for me often, one of the female correspondents told me he was the kind of guy who "cheats on his mistress." Being on assignment in Baghdad was like being posted to another planet, where the rules of polite society did not apply. There were all-night compound parties, booze, and late-night poker games. There were hookups and pranks and dancing on tables. Grown men with wives and families back home sometimes behaved like they were letting loose at a frat party. Women, because they were in a distinct minority, became objects of fascination and desire. "If you can't get laid in Baghdad, you can't get laid anywhere," one of the male producers joked, though I wondered if it was meant to be some sort of challenge. "Doesn't matter what you look like on the outside; if you're a woman here, you're 'Baghdad beautiful.'"

Working in a war zone meant that for many on assignment there, there was no need to show decorum, and standards for what was considered socially acceptable behavior slipped considerably. We were in a place where we were in danger at all times, and so the act of living itself was a provocation that needed to be executed with maximum intensity and at maximum speed. Working in a war zone was also a way to leave the tedium of real life behind. The school runs, the commutes, the routine: all of it dissolved during a Baghdad rotation. Though a large part of wanting to cover a story like the Iraq War was about the journalism, for many of us, it was also about confronting the fear that we were not living intensely enough at home. It was about the romance of reporting on the worst of humanity in a faraway, exotic land, Ernest Hemingway–like, sending dispatches back to base while all around us burned.

Covering a war comes with some perks. There is the admiration of colleagues and friends back home, the congratulatory emails from network bosses, and, perhaps, a year-end bonus or two. Every year, industry award nominations come out. It's hard to imagine anyone reading faster than we did when scanning the names of people included on the short list for an Emmy or a Peabody. As international reporters, we could come and go as we pleased. Dodging bullets one day, and the next, flying to New York to mingle with colleagues. The option to leave was always there, a luxury local staff workers rarely had.

※

Michael Ware was sitting on one of the chairs on the landing outside his bedroom and mine. "Want some wine?" he asked.

"No, thanks. I hate red wine."

There were hours during which nothing happened in the communal house. Ware, an Australian journalist, had been *Time* magazine's Baghdad bureau chief for three years before joining CNN in July 2006. We were villa neighbors, our bedrooms side by side, and had become close. "She came the other day," he told me about a journalist based in Iraq he was locked into a volatile relationship with. "She keeps telling me she loves me but can't commit."

I nodded. "Well, she doesn't love you enough, then, does she?" In some ways, I was envious of his lover, though I did not share this with him. She had managed to marry femininity and the no-nonsense toughness of reporting from an active war zone. She wore skirts, the type of clothing it would not occur to me to bring to a hardship posting. She carried herself with the confidence of a woman whose entire being is a gift to the human race. I felt a bit dowdy in comparison. I didn't dive headfirst into a dangerous story. I took my time. I assessed the risks. I wore sensible shoes. I stood back and made sure I wasn't going to die for a story, because no story was ever worth dying for. The object of Ware's affections was criticized by some of the people she worked with for taking unnecessary risks and being journalistically shallow. I had also noticed, when she visited the CNN house from her own villa near the compound earlier that summer, that she was wearing strappy summer sandals and that she had a fresh pedicure. This required a kind of mindset I didn't have, I thought: the choice to wear delicate, even frilly clothing and paint my toenails pink in a place where there is misery all around me. At the time, I thought it was admirable. I realize now it was likely a sign of detachment from reality, a lack of empathy.

Among the wider group of journalists who covered Iraq was a unique coterie of veteran war reporters, whose entire professional lives had been spent in the worst conflict zones, bouncing from Bosnia to Chechnya to Afghanistan to Lebanon to Iraq and to various other places people were being bombed and tortured. Often, they were photojournalists, who always need to be close to the action. They cannot take pictures otherwise. Print and television reporters can choose to stay behind, dip their toe into battle, and retreat to a more secure base, like a hotel or a safe house, to file their stories. Ware, with the broken nose and rough face of a prizefighter, was one of the journalists who got close. In 2004, he was dragged out of a car in central Baghdad and nearly executed by fighters loyal to the terrorist leader Abu Musab al-Zarqawi. In the spring of 2007, he filmed the shooting of an Iraqi fighter who died slowly, on camera, for twenty minutes in Diyala Province while American soldiers hurled abuse at him, translated into Arabic by their interpreter. "You're going to die," they said in English. "You're going to die," the translator repeated to the mortally wounded fighter in Arabic. The target was legitimate, Ware later said, but the inhumanity of the soldiers' behavior was difficult to watch. The translator, too, appeared to be tormenting the dying man gleefully. Ware's producer showed me the video. It was sickening. CNN had refused to air it.

Ware and I continued to correspond over email, sporadically, for many years after first crossing paths in Iraq. We spent time together on a few other stories in Lebanon and Paris. A decade after our first meeting in Baghdad, he sent me an email: "I still love you, by the way." I didn't understand what he meant, and I didn't reply. Perhaps what he still loved was that time, the one he associated me with, the few months we spent together in the CNN Baghdad villa or the summer before in Lebanon where we both covered the Israel-Hezbollah War. There was a freedom to being there, far from the tedium of office life and management overreach. The danger all around imbued us with a sense that we were deserving of special treatment by our peers. We were doing important work, and so we had a sense of purpose. And we were young, still many years away from midlife, either without strong ties to the outside world or willing to ignore them. It created an intensity, an intimacy in our relationships with colleagues. Perhaps when he said he still loved me, he meant he still loved *it*, that life that was now behind us for good.

I did not answer Ware's message, for no other reason than because I didn't know what to say, but, thinking back, I should have replied that I still loved *it* too. That time. It was a sort of tribe that we belonged to, a kind of dysfunctional family; a traveling circus. It gave many of us a sense of belonging. The Iraq and Lebanon wars and the Middle East revolutions of that era tended to be covered by the same group of English-language traveling reporters, and so, a big story meant that many of us were reunited, often sharing the same hotels, bumping into each other in airport lounges. On the American side, there was CNN, NBC, CBS, ABC, Fox, NPR, and a few others. We would also often cross paths with correspondents who worked for Al Jazeera English, the new English-language network launched in 2006 by Qatar's Al Jazeera media network. Later, newcomers like Vice and video units from legacy newspapers like the *New York Times* would add themselves to the TV and radio journalists on the ground. Their reporters tended to be even younger and nimbler. They produced visually appealing pieces with smaller budgets, often as one-person operations. Television networks, with their expensive satellite trucks and three-, sometimes four-person crews were initially slow to react, dismissing some of their competitors as upstarts producing second-rate journalism. But in 2007, we were not quite there yet. American cable news networks had spent millions of dollars covering the US-led war in Iraq because their audiences were watching and ad money was coming in. Those of us working in the field during those years knew we were at the center of the biggest story of our generation.

For some—perhaps even for most—covering human misery for too long comes at a price. Only psychopaths can cover death and devastation without being affected, and our profession has them too. But people with standard emotional responses to trauma will only keep going until they can't. Some of the most hardened among us, those who seemed unmovable, reached a point beyond which exposure to the worst in humanity had become unbearable. Michael Ware was one of them. He quit CNN in 2010 and in 2015 released *Only the Dead*, a powerful documentary using footage from his years in Iraq. Though he still works as a journalist, he is no longer on the front lines. Even prizefighters, after years of taking punches, have to retire one day.

The Surge

I climbed up the concrete steps of an isolated house comman-
deered by a small US Army unit near Yusufiyah, a predominantly
Sunni town outside Baghdad, right behind Lieutenant General Rick
Lynch, commander of the Third Infantry Division. We had flown to
this remote position from Baghdad on a chopper, landed in a dusty
field, and made our way on foot to a mini-base where a couple dozen
American soldiers, exposed and overwhelmed, were trying to hold
it together in the middle of nowhere, Iraq. I was working with Cal
Perry, one of the CNN producers who was based full-time in Baghdad, and we were on what was called an "embed," short for *embedded*.
This meant we were attached and given access to the military units we
were covering, provided we didn't divulge their combat positions or
any other sensitive information. This was a loose agreement, but one
that, by and large, reporters abided by. The few who broke the rules,
most often by revealing their location before they were allowed to do
so, were asked to leave.

Embeds were sometimes criticized for being dependent on creating too cozy a relationship between journalists and the troops they

are supposed to be covering. Reporters could, if they chose, travel autonomously, but the embed strategy provided a minimum level of security at a time unilateral coverage in Iraq's Sunni heartland would have been a good idea only for those with a very strong death wish. In Baghdad, there was no such relationship between reporters and the US military. We reported completely independently, outside of the US military bubble. For safety, we usually limited our outings to two hours in the city. Leaving the armored car was always a risk. "You've got twenty minutes," Mohammed Tawfeeq would tell me. I would remove my body armor to film a piece to camera and hop back into the vehicle. I played a game with Mohammed: "If I walked in Sadr City alone, dressed in jeans and a T-shirt, how long would I last?"

"In a T-shirt? Thirty seconds. They would kidnap you."

Sadr City, a poor, sprawling Shiite neighborhood in eastern Baghdad that had seen nearly daily clashes between US troops and the Mahdi Army of the Shiite cleric Muqtada al-Sadr since the spring of 2004, was considered a no-go zone for Western journalists.

"How long would I last if I were dressed in full hijab?"

"Probably twenty minutes."

At the small army outpost in Yusufiyah, in a part of Iraq dramatically nicknamed "the Triangle of Death," Lieutenant General Rick Lynch told me that the base we visited that day was part of America's new surge strategy: put more boots on the ground, spread them out, and link up with Iraqi army units to patrol the heartland. "But there is a problem," I told him. "There is no Iraqi security presence here." He agreed: "That is indeed the problem, but to take this land and this area away from the enemy, you need to have a persistent presence, and that persistent presence can't be coalition forces; it has to be Iraqi security forces." Later, I wondered how a man in charge of a strategy he could not implement thought of his role in a country like Iraq. Did he realize, then, that America's long-term goal of nation-building was unattainable? Arabs viewed the US invasion as folly at best and a criminal act at worst. Four years after the start of the war, it sometimes didn't seem like coalition forces were closer to understanding that a nation is not built from afar and a political system is never successfully imposed overnight by an occupier. The notion that the West, that very diffuse term, can school Arabs on democracy, that with money and benevolence, they can turn decades-old dictatorships into functioning democracies was one so deeply engrained in American political culture that it took almost a decade for it to fizzle out, to be replaced with the polar opposite idea among many ordinary Americans that *all* intervention is necessarily bad.

On the rooftop of the house turned army base in Yusufiyah, a twenty-one-year-old American specialist named Gerald Leeks scanned the horizon. It was his turn to warn others in case of an attack. A few weeks earlier, insurgents attacked their position, killing one man in his unit. "You wanna kill every motherfucker you see out here, excuse my language, but that's the truth of it. You just hate seeing these people every day after one of your buddies dies." The fact that he said this on camera, with his superiors within earshot, was revealing. Would he go back home and continue to believe in the mission his country had told him was his reason for being there? To, as former US president George W. Bush told them, "liberate an oppressed people"? Would he one day think that the hundreds of thousands of dead Iraqis were killed in vain, or would his hatred for *these people* remain, expand, and take on new forms?

"I can't believe he said that on camera," Perry said after we finished our interview with the young specialist.

"I wonder how much they still believe in this mission," I replied.

"Hala, why do you hate freedom so much?" he asked jokingly.

A few days later, driving through the streets of Baghdad, we passed a giant billboard in front of the Iraqi Ministry of Youth that read, in Arabic, "Forgive and be merciful for a unified Iraq."

The streets were busy with pedestrians and shoppers. We drove down Saadoon Street, a wide central artery with twenty-foot blast walls cutting off one side of the street from another. Painted over the concrete, there were images of pink flowers, flying doves, river and mountain scenes.

On Saadoon Street and everywhere else in Baghdad, most cars had bullet holes. I counted more than twenty on one vehicle as we stopped in heavy traffic.

Inside the car, looking out, I occasionally remembered the threat of car bombs. It was a lottery. Was that man a suicide bomber, alone in his car? Would those four young men in another car kidnap me if they had a chance? In the distance, I thought I heard a thud. Was it an explosion? Whatever it was, it didn't happen on Saadoon Street that day. I also tried to picture my great-great-grandfather Husni Bey Gorani, who was sent to Baghdad as inspector of the Ottoman courts in the vilayets of Baghdad, Mosul, and Basra in the late nineteenth century. He would have traveled down the same streets our armored car navigated that summer. During Husni Bey's time in Iraq, the empire was attempting to modernize its judicial system, which had until then been a confusing mixture of religious and secular laws with different sets of rules and standards for Muslims, Christians, and Jews. The new Ottoman judicial system—known as the Nizamiye courts—was part of an empire-wide project of judicial and administrative reform, which was inspired in large parts by the French model.

I was in the same place over a century later, watching war zone life somehow roll on. While Westerners traveled in armored vehicles, Iraqis had no choice but to keep going, in the open air, with no flak jackets or bulletproof cars. We passed a market with stalls selling fruits and vegetables. I couldn't help but imagine the scene if a car bomb exploded in the middle of the hubbub.

How many would die if it went off here?

Or here?

I noticed a shop called Beirut Shoes and, one after the other, three stores that sold only wheelchairs and crutches. The Ministry of Health at the time had told me that the number of stores selling medical equipment had more than doubled in the previous four years in Baghdad alone. When bombs went off, people died, of course, but many more were injured. I decided then that I wanted to cover the wounded and maimed in my next story. They are more than the second, afterthought number listed following the death counts when casualties were tallied. They had lost legs and arms. They became the wheelchair merchants' most loyal customers.

We continued our drive down Saadoon Street toward the Palestine Hotel. The building once favored by foreign journalists and security contractors had been almost completely abandoned a couple of years before. In October 2005, a coordinated attack involving a truck packed with explosives caused such devastation that it drove the remaining Western reporters and other organizations out for the duration of the war.

As we reached the Palestine, I noticed that it was completely locked in by blast walls and that the street in front of the hotel entrance was almost entirely deserted. "Can I get out here and do a stand-up here?" I asked our security escort as we approached Firdos Square. "You can do whatever you want," he replied. "My job is only to advise you." I rolled my eyes. "Fine. *Advise* me." He and Mohammed laughed. "Sure, but just a couple of takes." Mohammed took a photo of me in the car before I stepped out. "Hala is a one-take wonder!" he said enthusiastically.

I stood close to the spot where the Saddam Hussein statue was torn down a few weeks after the invasion. I remembered the jubilant scenes more than four years before when even those who opposed the war had no other possible reaction than glee at the sight of a tyrant coming down, pulled off its pedestal by ropes, the forty-foot statue resisting at first until it finally gave way, its arm still outstretched to the sky. A few years later, Saadoon Street and Firdos Square looked nothing like the Baghdad that fell to the Americans in 2003. Saadoon Street, with its gouged-out sidewalks, its razor wire, its concrete blast walls, thinly disguised by colorful, amateurish murals; Firdos, the once glorious square, abandoned and degrading in the sun.

Today, Firdos Square, Saadoon Street, and the surrounding areas have returned to a kind of normality. Where I could step out of a bulletproof sedan for only three minutes, now, an American female journalist friend told me she can take walks alone and shop for groceries on Saadoon. The threat of suicide bombers and truck bombs no longer constantly weighs on the minds of people there. The wounds of the war, however, have not healed. The successive governments that have ruled the country since the invasion have been ineffective, corrupt, and sectarian. The dream of a stable and democratic country is still, for many Iraqis, out of reach.

The Pullout

"I'm Don Lemon at the CNN world headquarters in Atlanta with special coverage on the end of the US war in Iraq. Joining me now for the entire broadcast, CNN International anchor Hala Gorani."

I was sitting alone in a studio in Washington, DC, coanchoring CNN's coverage of the US troop pullout from Iraq with CNN anchor Don Lemon, who was, that evening, hosting from Atlanta. I readied myself to speak, as we were on air together, but before I could, Don tossed live to then CNN correspondent Arwa Damon, who was in Baghdad reporting on the American withdrawal. Instead of introducing myself, I ended up smirking awkwardly in the split screen, while Lemon launched into a live Q&A with Damon without giving me an opportunity to speak.

It was a Saturday evening, a cold and lonely place to be in a newsroom when there isn't significant breaking news. The event, the bookend to the "shock and awe" of the Bush administration's invasion in March 2003, was covered by CNN with a short, unremarkable special a few minutes before midnight eastern time the week before Christmas 2011.

Michael Holmes, who was live at the Iraq-Kuwait border, announced the departure of the "last of the fighting presence in Iraq," once the US military had lifted a reporting embargo on images of the convoy of military vehicles driving down Iraqi highways in the dead of night, crossing in the early-morning hours into Kuwait through a heavy metal gate and driving onward into the dusty desert to anywhere but the Iraqi battlefield. Damon, with palm trees and Baghdad rooftops behind her, reporting live from the CNN bureau in Iraq, talked of the people left behind, reminded viewers that "many Iraqis wanted to see Saddam Hussein gone but say they were the ones who had to pay the price for America's mistakes." Martin Savidge, another CNN reporter, had traveled nine and a half hours with one of the last American convoys, reporting via cell phone from inside a cramped MRAP vehicle. "Now they are out, they are safe, and they know that soon, they will be on their way home and they have witnessed history," he told us of the last remaining US troops departing the country. I remember thinking that night that the same story, the same pullout, even the thud of the metal gates closing behind the last American MRAP, the oorahs of the marines at the crossing, the photographers and journalists gathered to witness it all, seen as a moment of relief and celebration for the departing occupiers, was a much more complex story of trepidation and uncertainty for the occupied. Iraqis would be left to pick up the pieces.

America vacated military bases that would soon become ghost towns in the desert. During the occupation, sleeping quarters for hundreds of thousands of troops, heavy machinery, mess halls with Burger Kings and Taco Bells, and fully equipped gyms had been flown over to Iraq. In Camp Cooke, twenty miles north of Baghdad, decommissioned tanks, too costly to fly home, were abandoned. The Iraqis were supposed to take care of all that was left behind, the new custodians of the US military's misadventure in their country. "All that American money, all that American sacrifice, all that American idealism—trashed, dumped in the ancient, unchanging, Mesopotamian dirt. We were so naïve," the ABC News correspondent Terry Moran said in 2014 of the Kirkuk air base, a camp the Americans had turned over to the Iraqi army in 2011. Moran told viewers that the Iraqi soldiers had fled, leaving their uniforms behind, fearing the advancing ISIS fighters that had taken over Mosul a hundred miles to the north a few days before. The air base had been looted and vandalized by the time Moran arrived. The Iraqi soldiers tasked with manning it had already melted back into the general population, and the Kurdish Peshmerga had taken over. "In a way, this is your tax dollars at work," Moran told his American viewers, pointing to a room with upturned furniture.

I could understand his obvious revulsion at the sight of what had cost billions of American dollars, years of investment in troops, technology, and lives seemingly so disrespected by Iraqi soldiers. I wondered, though, whether Arabs watching the destruction of the base would have felt similarly appalled. Were Iraqis meant to feel grateful that the US had transferred ownership of its military infrastructure to them? This was never their camp. It was never their war. The Iraqi army posted at the air base had folded and fled the moment the smallest amount of pressure was applied. They hadn't asked for this base, and when it was time to defend it, they bolted and didn't look back. Later that year, Kurdish Peshmerga fighters took possession of the site before Iraqi forces regained control of it in 2017.

The soldiers who had abandoned the camp in Kirkuk in June 2014 were fleeing from a terrorist group that would never have existed had the coalition invasion not occurred. In July of that year, the world was faced with the unimaginable spectacle of the terrorist leader Abu Bakr al-Baghdadi giving a sermon in one of the world's oldest and most revered Islamic holy sites, the twelfth-century Grand Mosque of Mosul. I remember feeling a sense of intense dejection because this disaster had been entirely avoidable. After all, Baghdadi, who had been held by the Americans in Camp Bucca in 2004, had only joined al-Qaeda in Iraq, which later morphed into ISIS, after being detained with other like-minded insurgents there.

In the end, the war was not just a disaster for America, the United Kingdom, and its allies but for the entire world order. The invading countries had disregarded "the principles of the UN Charter in 2003" and had therefore "ceded their moral authority to promote the rule of law," former British diplomat Peter Ricketts, who served on Prime Minister Tony Blair's intelligence committee, wrote on the twentieth anniversary of the conflict. The fact that many years later, Iraqi troops, who were expected to continue the fight in an impoverished, sectarian, and divided country, found themselves unmotivated should have surprised no one.

What is America's legacy in Iraq now? It's certainly not the country they thought they would create when the US and its coalition partners went in, all tanks blazing. One of the US's mortal enemies, Muqtada al-Sadr, the man accused of forming death squads to hunt down and kill Sunnis during the country's civil war and who waged an armed insurgency against coalition troops, has become a kingmaker in Iraqi politics. Other Shiites, like Nouri al-Maliki, who is aligned with Iran, have led the country almost continuously since the US withdrawal. America's war, which cost more than $2 trillion, some 4,400 American soldiers' lives, and almost half a million Iraqi deaths, ended up bringing to power leaders allied with one of its biggest adversaries in the region. The incompetence of it alone is breathtaking. The cost in human lives still, all these years later, overwhelming.

After the war's declared end by the United States, many of the political, military, and intelligence officials who had supported the invasion have remained in prominent positions. Former army men, like Mark Kimmitt, who served as the chief military spokesman in Iraq during the first year of the war, are routinely asked for their opinions on other wars, including on CNN. "What we would tell the children of Iraq is that the noise they hear is the sound of freedom," Kimmitt once told an Iraqi journalist who'd asked him about Iraqi kids frightened by the sound of low-flying helicopters. John Bolton, former president George W. Bush's irascible ambassador to the United Nations, said in 2007 that the only mistake the United States made was to not leave earlier after the overthrow of Saddam Hussein and tell the Iraqis, "You're on your own. Here's a copy of *The Federalist Papers.* Good luck." That kind of arrogance and flippancy makes a mockery of the lives lost and enrages critics of US foreign policy. Bolton, who later served as Donald Trump's national security adviser, is still asked to appear on cable news channels to provide analysis on other conflicts.

David Frum, a George W. Bush speechwriter who supported the invasion and said he believed intelligence that Saddam Hussein was developing weapons of mass destruction, has opined that the alternative to the invasion and the devastation it caused was a Syria-like scenario had the Iraqi dictator remained in power. Without US intervention, "we can only guess how the Saddam Hussein story would have ended. But what happened next door in Syria is a clue," he wrote in March 2023. The analysis of former neoconservatives like Frum acknowledges that regime change in Iraq was an abject failure and that the invasion was ill planned. They even claim to regret the hundreds of thousands of Iraqi deaths. What they almost never do is question the mindset that led to the invasion in the first place. Iraq was not a limited humanitarian intervention, in the way establishing a no-fly zone over Syria after Bashar al-Assad used chemical weapons against his own people would have been. Iraq was a war of choice, a postcolonial invasion whose architects felt they had a right to launch, despite the fact that there was fervent opposition to it among Western democracies like France and Germany. Critics of Frum and other former Iraq invasion supporters like journalist Max Boot, former secretary of state Condoleezza Rice, or former British prime minister Tony Blair say the media's choice to still air their views is ignoring the misery the invasion unleashed on millions, whitewashing the war, speaking of it in terms of how it was a strategic disaster for the West and almost never about how it destroyed millions of lives and continues to destabilize the region to this day.

Would Iraqis have brought down Saddam Hussein on their own in 2011 when other Arab Spring countries toppled their leaders? I asked Mowaffak al-Rubaie, Iraq's former national security adviser, if he believed the dictator would have been removed by his own people. "It doesn't matter. Only what comes next matters," he said.

"And that concludes our special coverage," Lemon and I both announced, after an hour of live reports and interviews that night. America was officially out. Iraq, broken and divided, was on its own.

Part 9

Washington, DC

The White House Press Corps

I placed my bag on the x-ray machine belt and showed my ID to the security guard at the gate. It was my first time on White House grounds, where then president Barack Obama was hosting Middle East heads of state, and it felt like a momentous event. The United States is the most powerful country in the world and its president the most powerful political leader. I was only a few feet from the center of all of that global influence and decision-making. The White House Rose Garden, the Oval Office, the First Family residence. In some ways, the White House itself looks like a sort of movie set façade. Its pristine white rendered walls and columns are so perfectly maintained that it is as if, behind it, there are actors, extras, and soundstages. Unlike other centers of administrative authority, the White House has been featured in so many films and television series that most of the world has some sense of what it looks like. Seeing it in real life is like meeting a celebrity for the first time. I was starstruck.

The James S. Brady Press Briefing Room in the West Wing of the White House is so much smaller than it appears on television that, for a moment, I wondered if there was another press conference area and this one was some sort of backup to a larger venue somewhere else. There were only about half a dozen rows of fold-down seats, not enough on big news days for all the accredited reporters to sit down, with the first few rows assigned to mainstream outlets like NBC, CNN, Fox, the *Washington Post*, and NPR. Reporters are seated close to each other and only a few feet from a stage with a small lectern, recognizable around the world, adorned with the US presidential seal on the occasion of addresses by the American leader. There are television and agency cameras in the very back of the space as well as allotted positions for still photographers.

It is a long and narrow room built in 1970 on top of a swimming pool that Franklin D. Roosevelt once used as part of his physical therapy to manage the paralyzing effects of polio. There are still remnants of the pool in the basement under the briefing room. A staircase behind the stage leads to what used to be the deep end of the pool, now crammed with transmission equipment and miles of cables supporting the television and radio operations on the floor above. The tiles that once lined the basin are now covered with the signatures of journalists, celebrities, and White House staff.

The White House press corps is a uniquely American institution, and it is, relatively speaking, a rather recent creation. The *petite histoire* is that US president Theodore Roosevelt one day spotted reporters gathered outside the White House gates on a rainy day, trying to gather information by flagging people exiting the compound, and, taking pity on them, told his secretary that a room should be set aside in the building exclusively for the press. Journalists had been reporting from a corridor inside the White House for several years already, but now they'd have a designated office. More reporters joined the beat and, a decade or so later, the White House Correspondents' Association was founded in 1914 to represent them on access and other issues affecting their coverage of the presidency.

Before my first visit to the White House, I had spent about ten days with part of the press corps on a trip George W. Bush had made to the Middle East in 2008. Journalists who cover the president work in a sort of bubble on these assignments. It was a cooler-than-normal January in the region as we country-hopped from Kuwait to Riyadh to Jerusalem. On the ground, we all shared buses from the plane to our hotels after traveling together in the back of Air Force One with the president and his entourage at the front of the plane; we even filed our stories from the same workplaces, set up in advance, in various hotel ballrooms across the region. I was very much an outsider in this environment. I had been sent by CNN International to cover the trip because George W. Bush, who had ordered the invasion of Iraq in 2003, was profoundly disliked in the region, and the network wanted a reporter who had covered the effects of US foreign policy in the Arab world to tag along. His tour was unprecedented in scope, covering about a country every day or two. It was like being on a London hop-on/hop-off double-decker for tourists, except that each stop was an Arab capital with its own issues and demands of the Bush administration.

In Abu Dhabi, as the press corps gathered to film the American president seated at a table with his local hosts, Bush's eyes scanned the journalists in attendance and landed on me. He looked quizzical, clearly unused to seeing reporters not usually assigned to the White House beat. I looked behind me, wondering if there was something else catching his attention, but there was not. I did not know what facial expression I should adopt when locking eyes with the "leader of the free world," so, after a shared glance lasting a few seconds, I looked back down at my notepad.

As a news anchor, I have met and interviewed presidents and prime ministers and men and women who've launched wars and others who've signed peace agreements. I've always felt embedded deep within me a sense of solemness when in the presence of someone whose orders can either destroy or, alternatively, build up the lives of millions of people. When I sat down with Turkish president Recep Tayyip Erdoğan in Ankara in 2015, I remember thinking that, with his permission that year, Syrian refugees, millions of whom were being hosted by Turkey, were allowed to leave and flood the shores of Europe, causing a sort of generalized hysteria across the continent. In 2016, after European nations promised aid money and the possibility of visa-free travel for Turkish citizens, he turned off the taps again, reducing the refugee flow from his country to a trickle. Erdoğan's power play, which involved using human beings as pawns, was clever. Syrians, once victimized by weapons, were now being weaponized themselves.

My job as a journalist took me from presidential palaces to the smallest of makeshift shacks in a war zone or in a refugee center. I could follow a policy from the moment it was announced in a gilded serail to when its effects were felt in a flimsy refugee tent on the island of Lesbos in Greece. Nowhere are the decisions made more consequential than in Washington, DC, where journalists gather in that tiny press briefing room seconds away from the Oval Office, and nowhere does the physical space between the political leaders and the reporters who cover them feel so small.

During my first White House visit and on assignments covering the same presidential trips abroad as Washington press corps journalists, I felt like an exchange student on someone else's school trip. My visits to the CNN Washington bureau were similarly awkward; I was not part of that milieu. I had cordial relations with the bureau staff in DC and even made good friends there, but I did not take part in the same rituals as the city's political reporting elite, the most prestigious of which is the White House Correspondents' Association annual dinner. It is held every spring at the Washington Hilton and is usually emceed by a celebrity comedian like Trevor Noah or Stephen Colbert. Journalists who attend the dinner have nicknamed it the "nerd prom," reinforcing the notion that the people who cover the American president are, in some ways, a clique whose members belong to a single organization. The self-deprecating "nerd" appellation is added in jest, as a way to poke fun at themselves and send the message that the people who report on the president do not take themselves too seriously. The annual dinner, traditionally attended by the president, has become the highlight of Washington's social calendar and has outgrown its original purpose. Over the years, television networks, radios, newspapers, and their star reporters have gotten into the habit of inviting celebrities to their tables. There is now a red carpet with TV cameras providing live coverage of the event, and some White House journalists have become household names, almost on par with the actors and singers invited to the dinner. In 2022, the reality show star Kim Kardashian and her then boyfriend Pete Davidson were guests of Disney and the television network ABC. That evening, Drew Barrymore, Miranda Kerr, and Brooke Shields also attended the event. The *Daily Mail* and other papers published photos of the guests along with information on the designer gowns they were wearing.

This increasing blurring of lines between politics, journalism, and celebrity is not celebrated by everyone. The *New York Times*, for example, forbids its employees from attending the event. "It sends the wrong signal to our readers and viewers, like we are all in it together and it is all a game. It feels uncomfortable," the paper's former executive editor Dean Baquet said in 2011. The British newspaper the *Guardian* published an opinion piece around the same time that may explain, at least in part, why the distrust of mainstream media in Western countries has exploded, allowing populist leaders to cast journalists as purveyors of fake news: "To send the message via C-span that the Capitol, the Fourth Estate and Hollywood are all in it together, if only for one night, hardly helps accusations of elitism."

Then, the tsunami that was the Donald Trump presidency crashed into Washington, DC, upending decades of established Washington standard operating procedure. The White House Correspondents' dinner, the elite cocktails at the homes of newspaper editors in Georgetown where one would routinely bump into Alan Greenspan, Wolf Blitzer, and Sally Quinn, the friendly relationship between White House staff and journalists, lobbyists, diplomats, and think tank analysts: all disrupted. There was a wild, new, untested crowd of vandals in town, intent on burning the establishment to the ground. Even those among them who had spent decades dodging taxes and living billionaire lifestyles were joining them, led by the self-proclaimed billionaire in chief, Donald Trump. They claimed to represent the "other America," where the perceived injustices against ordinary citizens were being righted. These Americans, a vast majority of them white, believed what they were fed: you are being taken advantage of; America is being stolen from you by the Blacks, the browns, the Jews, the gays, and the Muslims; your country is getting kicked around on the world stage. We will bring all that is lost back: we will make America great again.

What this meant, this promised return to a simpler, wholesome Americana, was really just a return to the supremacy of the groups that had run the country for centuries. Much has been written about how the changing demographics in America has led to white anxiety and to the popularity of a brash and vulgar man who promised to give white Americans back some of the control they felt they had lost. As I watched US politics from abroad, I saw another major factor behind the unease that Trump was tapping into: the system itself. The lobbyists' money, the corporate influence on politicians of both parties, the tax code favoring capital gains rather than salaried employees, the widening gap between the superrich and everyone else. To many Trump voters, the system felt rigged. That the man at the top was blaming all the wrong people hardly seems to have registered with his supporters.

There was another phenomenon that I found both fascinating and on some levels more difficult to comprehend just before and during his presidency. In each of the groups Trump disparaged, he had supporters. Among Muslims, according to one exit poll, 35 percent had voted for him in 2016.[1] White women of every socioeconomic class had, in their majority, supported him, despite his on-the-record misogynistic remarks. A sizable proportion of Hispanics voted for him, as well. They were willing to overlook his prejudice toward them because they saw in the brash reality television host some sort of no-nonsense businessman who would control government spending and dial back the interventionist policies of previous presidencies.

When Donald Trump first announced his candidacy, he had an open mic with news networks. His rallies were carried live, including on CNN, and journalists covered him with the kind of enthusiasm Formula One commentators cover a high-speed race with. The day he suggested banning all Muslims from entering America, I felt a personal revulsion that I hoped my fellow journalists would share. I imagined Trump proposing to ban all Jews or all Black people and the kind of reaction that proposal would get. Instead, I saw cable news shows airing the views of paid contributors defending this racist and blatantly illegal policy proposal. Why was this question being treated as if there are two sides to the issue? And why was the idea that Muslims coming from abroad were a potential national security threat so often the premise of the question journalists asked? None of this was remotely true, yet the word *Muslim* itself came to mean something dangerous, even in mainstream discourse on supposedly Left-leaning networks in America. But the notion that Islam equals danger or depravity long outdates Trump's original 2015 call to ban all Muslims from entering the United States. During a town hall in 2008, Republican presidential candidate John McCain was lauded for his response to a woman who claimed that his opponent, Barack Obama, was an Arab. *Arab* and *Muslim* have become frequently interchangeable words, even though

---

1. "AP VoteCast: Trump Wins White Evangelicals, Catholics Split," Associated Press, November 6, 2020, https://apnews.com/article/votecast-trump-wins-white-evangelicals-d0cb249ea7eae29187a21a702dc84706.

many Arabs are not Muslim and most Muslims are not Arab. I found McCain's answer, seen in the post-Trump era as decent and fair play, personally insulting. "No, ma'am," McCain said, "he's a decent family man and citizen that I just happen to have disagreements with on fundamental issues, and that's what the campaign's all about. He's not."

Obama is decent. Obama is not an Arab.

When Trump unexpectedly won the presidency in 2016, the press corps from liberal-leaning mainstream networks and platforms went from giving him seemingly unlimited coverage to assuming the role of the ethical and moral counterweight to his agenda, openly arguing with him in news conferences and airing long monologues discrediting his numerous lies on cable television. Many of the journalists he had disparaged and insulted had stopped straightforwardly reporting on him and had started sparring with him. Trump's supporters lapped this up. They had another bête noire they could blame for all their woes and perceived injustices. Journalists were seen as "enemies of the state," as Donald Trump had so often labeled us.

Over the years and with hindsight, I've wondered what the best way to cover Trump would have been. I had covered dictators, and I had covered presidents in democracies before, but never a man with autocratic tendencies *in* a democracy. This odd overlap of the two was new to me and to everyone else. Should we be butting heads with the president in news conferences or, through questions and reporting, highlighting his misogyny, his disrespect for science, his Islamophobia, his flirtations with and endorsement of the Far Right without positioning ourselves as his direct antagonist? When, in May 2023, CNN held a live Trump "presidential town hall," giving the then Republican front-runner a prime-time platform and filling a college auditorium in New Hampshire with his supporters, there was widespread dismay. Had news networks not gained any insights from 2016, when Trump rallies were carried wall-to-wall live with little pushback or context? This was 2023, an insurrection and several legal cases against the former president later, and many critics said media organizations should have learned some important lessons about how to cover the former president. Then CNN chairman and CEO Chris Licht, who'd replaced Jeff Zucker in the role after Warner Bros. Discovery's takeover of the network, was widely panned for giving Trump what amounted to a free, de facto live campaign rally. Several of my former CNN colleagues privately told me they were upset that their new boss had given Trump a megaphone with which to spew lies and misinformation. Discovery brass initially defended Licht, but the criticism grew louder by the day. A lengthy Licht profile in the *Atlantic* magazine, in which he was described as having willfully stacked the audience with "extra Trumpy" spectators, proved to be the coup de grâce. He was out after only a year in the top job. In one important way, at least, 2023 would not become a repeat of 2016.

"You're Banned"

Corey Lewandowski's jaw appeared to clench more tightly with every question I asked. His face hardened, his brow furrowed, and I could sense anger rising up through his body as the veins in his neck swelled. "Donald Trump fired you," I started by asking him on camera. "Why do you still support his candidacy for the presidency?" I had run into Trump's former campaign manager at the Republican National Convention in Cleveland, Ohio, in 2016, outside one of CNN's make-shift studios at the Quicken Loans Arena. Donald Trump, the bombastic, populist, Islamophobic, anti-immigrant reality television star most everyone had dismissed when he had announced his presidential run, was about to become the Republican party's official nominee. Lewandowski, who'd worked on congressional campaigns, as a lobbyist on Capitol Hill, as the head of the New England Seafood Producers Association, with Americans for Prosperity, a Koch brothers–backed advocacy group, before joining Trump's presidential campaign, had just come off the air. CNN had recently hired Lewandowski as a contributor, reportedly paying him hundreds of thousands of dollars a year to argue the Trump position on the network. It was soon revealed that he was still collecting severance payments from the Trump campaign during the same period.

I knew of his reputation as a hothead. In March 2016, he had grabbed a female reporter by the arm at a campaign event and was later charged with simple battery by the Jupiter, Florida, police department. He wasn't ultimately prosecuted, but the incident had made headlines for days. A few days later in Arizona, video appeared to show Lewandowski grabbing a protestor's shirt collar at a Trump rally.

I kicked off my chat with Lewandowski that day the way I would with any interviewee. I have had unsavory people on my show throughout my career, and I was not intimidated. My approach to television interviews is to never waver and to never tell myself that the person in front of me is cleverer than I am, even if they are more knowledgeable. In my mind, I am never in a position of inferiority. The questions must be clear and help viewers understand a story better. I listen carefully to the answers and establish eye contact in order to ask the most journalistically useful follow-ups. Sometimes they are very basic questions. Early in my career, I tried to showcase my own knowledge rather than elicit the most illuminating answers. I wanted to prove that I was well prepared. Later, and this took many years, I started asking simpler questions and follow-ups that were as straightforward as "I don't understand what you mean. Can you elaborate?" It takes more confidence to ask questions that may sound elementary rather than fact-laden, complex ones. It's an approach that I have found often yields more newsworthy exchanges.

Lewandowski and I were standing at one of the entry points of the main floor–level seating area inside the arena. One of the CNN guest bookers had introduced me to him as someone who could be trusted to do a fair interview. Perhaps he expected softball questions. Perhaps he believed that I would treat him as some sort of independent analyst or use him for sound bites on the appeal of Donald Trump. The fact that I mentioned his dismissal from the campaign, a verifiable fact, seemed to elicit in him a kind of rage. After the camera stopped rolling, I thanked him for his time. We were left standing face-to-face, with no one recording the conversation.

"What the FUCK was that?" he screamed at me. "What do you mean?" I asked. "Fired? FIRED? I wasn't fired. What the FUCK were those questions about?" he said. He pointed a finger of me, close to my face, and almost spat the words out: "You're banned, you hear me? BANNED." He walked away, about to go into the seating area of the arena, but turned around and came back to me. He looked at me with so much anger in his eyes that, for a brief moment, I became concerned that something physical was about to happen. A shove? A slap? "I'm not kidding. You're fucking BANNED," he repeated. He walked away, still mumbling profanities, and rejoined the rest of the Trump supporters, Republican delegates, and journalists gathered inside the arena, on the verge of witnessing an event virtually no one had predicted: Donald Trump was about to become the Grand Old Party's nominee. The man who had called Mexican immigrants rapists, who wanted to ban Muslims from America, whose campaign was run by men later convicted of obstructing justice and of being in contempt of Congress, was about to be crowned the modern-day leader of the conservative movement in America. The party of Abraham Lincoln and Dwight Eisenhower had morphed into a sort of anti-globalist populist movement, skeptical of anything associated with the "establishment," that catchall word that applies to everything from journalism, to sciences, to academia, to celebrities. Supporters of the new candidate followed him from rally to rally as if he were a messiah, lapping up rants that were a laundry list of unfounded accusations, including the notion that the Democratic Party was an extension of the media: "Hillary Clinton is also given approval and veto power over quotes about her in the *New York Times*," he told a rally in West Palm Beach during the 2016 campaign.

Political conventions in America are rowdy and colorful affairs. They are usually held in huge arenas that can accommodate tens of thousands of people. Each state sends party delegates to the convention to vote and confirm the nomination of the candidate who has already emerged victorious from a series of contests called *primaries*. The number of delegates each state sends depends in part on its population, though the math differs depending on the party. There are huge signs, foam hats, banners, and pins. There are singers and celebrities invited to show support for the candidate. Outside the arena, there are pop-up memorabilia stands selling stickers, T-shirts, and baseball caps. Supporters who don't have access to the convention itself gather around the venue as well. In Cleveland that summer, some held up signs, others formed huddles of like-minded Trump fans. The outlines of the unexpected Trump presidency were starting to emerge more clearly: the convention had also attracted the conspiracy theorists, the attention seekers, and the odd, lower-grade celebrity who hadn't received an invitation to the main event. It felt more like a traveling circus than a political rally. A lot like the Trump presidency would be.

I have always loved covering political conventions. CNN, as a huge name in political news coverage, had some of the most elaborate and expensive setups. The network built several studios with massive glass desks designed to accommodate, in some cases, a dozen guests and contributors. CNN International, as the sister network with the much smaller budget, typically occupied positions in one of the boxes above the stage, with a bird's-eye view of the convention floor below. The Democratic Party booked top performers to celebrate the official nomination of their candidate. In July 2016, we ran down to the floor when Paul Simon rehearsed "Bridge over Troubled Water" at the Wells Fargo Center in Philadelphia. We listened, only a handful of us in a virtually empty stadium, as he conducted a sound check. The atmosphere in Philadelphia that year was one of elation, so sure the Democrats were of victory. Women, in particular, imagined a world where three Western democracies would be led by female heads of state or government: Hillary Clinton in the US, Angela Merkel in Germany, and Theresa May in Britain. No one I knew expected Donald Trump to become the forty-fifth president of the United States.

Laurel Hill Road

The drive to the house felt long from the interstate road, deep into the Washington, DC, suburb of Vienna in Virginia, the manicured lawns, one after the other, past the tennis courts, each house with its own mailbox, the smell of cut grass and barbecues. I was nine years old and had been plucked from Neuilly-sur-Seine and sent to live with my father and brother, Zaf, and in the throes of an adolescent desire for independence that would leave me feeling isolated in a home far from everything I knew.

"You said you wanted to go live with your father, and I didn't want you to blame me later for holding you back," my mother said when I asked her why we were sent to live outside of DC after three years in France. The culture shock was so intense that it was dizzying, especially at an age where both my environment and body were changing at the same time and with the same intensity. Girls around that age can feel a loss of control that can cause overwhelming anxiety. Their body, morphing into something foreign and controlled by forces beyond their own under-standing of the world, imposes its own will on them. Watching myself in the mirror of our downstairs half bath in our suburban new build, I saw another face struggling to emerge from behind my childhood features. My nose widened, my jaw strengthened, my neck thickened. It felt like another being had found its way inside my body and was slowly expanding, changing the outline of my silhouette, taking over.

The two years I spent in Vienna before returning home to my mother and stepfather in Neuilly-sur-Seine felt like a prolonged whiplash, one that neither of my parents had willingly imposed on me. Their childhoods had been stable and consistent in Aleppo, with the close village-like family and social ties. They felt that children were adaptable, and perhaps some of them are, and that another move would mean little to me in the long arc that is a lifetime.

Today, as I look back at the brutality of the change I endured at such a young age, I can only wonder how differently I might have navigated my teenage years had I stayed put in France. For those two years, I attended a French language school in Bethesda, Maryland, where teachers accredited by the French ministry of education followed a curriculum identical to the one taught in France. My classmates included children of diplomats and francophone journalists posted to the US capital. I made a few friends that I barely remember today, so brief was my time at the Lycée Rochambeau.

On March 30, 1981, twenty-nine days after my eleventh birthday, John Hinckley Jr. shot and wounded then president Ronald Reagan outside the Washington Hilton hotel. One of the bullets Hinckley fired bounced off the presidential limousine and entered Reagan's body under his left arm, puncturing a lung and causing life-threatening internal bleeding. "What the hell's that?" Reagan asked when he heard the *pop pop pop*s of Hinckley's firearm. Struggling to breathe and coughing up "red, frothy blood," the president was driven to George Washington University Hospital and wheeled straight into the emergency room.

Television networks in the US interrupted regular programming to broadcast news of the shooting. "The president was not hit," reported the ABC News anchor Frank Reynolds. ABC had interrupted the soap opera *One Life to Live* with the breaking news about fifteen minutes after the shooting. CNN, then a fledgling twenty-four-hour news network, also went live with Bernard Shaw at the anchor desk. "We cannot say it too many times, the president of the United States is okay," Shaw said. Producers were sliding papers onto his desk as he struggled to piece the story together live as the news was coming in.

I must have been watching daytime television when the news broke because that afternoon when he came home, in the pre-internet era, my father had not heard of the president's shooting. "Yeah, sure," he said, standing at the kitchen island, in disbelief. I remember a spark in his eyes when he realized I was serious and that something exceptionally significant had occurred; something historic. I felt a rush of excitement: I had broken important news. It was my first time experiencing the thrill of it. I had spent all afternoon listening to news updates on the major networks. We didn't have access to cable at the time. Very few people did in 1981, and CNN was a startup most people dismissed as the wacky vanity project of a Southern billionaire.

I remember March 30, 1981, not as the day president Ronald Reagan was shot but the day, with hindsight, that I realized something important about myself. I wanted to tell people what was happening in the world. I wanted to be among the first to do so.

My two years in Virginia with my father and brother were almost up. I would go back to Neuilly-sur-Seine to start school there a few months later. On summer visits to Vienna over the years after my return to France, I felt like I was shape-shifting from one world with its codes and rituals to another. From the bourgeoisie of Neuilly to the cutoffs and outdoor lifestyle of '80s kids in an American middle-class suburban subdivision. We rode bikes and skateboards, drank Tab, styled our hair with curling irons. Returning to Neuilly, everything about how I lived snapped back, like letting go of an elastic extended out to its maximum length. The language, the way I was expected to dress, my home with my mother and stepfather's paintings and art and their circle of friends. Every few months, I was physically and emotionally jet-lagged, not just because I traveled through time zones but because I traveled across worlds.

The Big Leagues

W e sat down for dinner at a seafood restaurant in Georgetown. He had emailed me a few weeks before informing me he would be in Washington and asking if I was available to meet with him. I had just returned from another trip to Egypt after my first assignment that year covering the revolution. I was eager to connect with a high-level television executive. I could leverage any offer from a network when renegotiating my contract with CNN.

After more than fifteen years in journalism, I was finally appearing regularly on CNN's domestic network after anchoring, for a few years in Atlanta, my own program alongside industry veterans like Jim Clancy and Michael Holmes. I was anchoring prime-time shows on CNN International, had received nominations for and won major industry awards, including an Emmy for coverage of the Egyptian uprising. I felt like all the work I had done and all the sacrifices I had made had been worth it. I assumed he had seen my work on air and wanted to discuss a possible job offer.

The conversation flowed naturally. He had traveled to many of the places I had reported from. He spoke several languages. Around midway through the meal, I was surprised that the talk hadn't turned to work yet. Perhaps, I thought, he was playing it cool. It was possible, I also hoped, that this was just an introductory face-to-face and that the more formal professional approach would come later.

I didn't have the typical profile of a network news correspondent, but I felt that the work I had done in Egypt and Syria that year had helped me break through into the American mainstream. A few years before, in 2004, when my agent pitched me to ABC News, I was given a writing test and was interviewed by about a dozen people before I was sent into star anchor Peter Jennings's office in Manhattan. I was told this was usually just a last sign-off before an offer was made. I sat on an office chair opposite his desk. He invited me to move to the sofa in another part of the room and inserted my VHS show reel into the tape player. "Do you know how many women cable news anchors have sat in this very spot saying they want to be correspondents?" he asked me. I smiled, more of a wince, trying to hide my annoyance at not knowing how to reply to a question that I felt couldn't apply to me, considering I was already a correspondent and had worked as an on-air journalist on CNN International for several years already. I tried to make my case. "I was just in Iraq," I offered. He appeared unmoved. "I speak Arabic?" I said in a way that sounded involuntarily like a question. I was sitting across from a man I idolized. He embodied everything about journalism that I hoped to achieve one day: an anchor with field experience and gravitas, a living legend with the handsome good looks of a movie star. I was a woman from a different part of the world than most of the correspondents on air in the US but, I thought, I could be one of the first. Why not? What was standing in my way? I'm not sure how long our conversation lasted, but I tried several times to sell myself to him as someone who had experience in the field, that I was worthy of an offer, to convince him that I could be an asset to his show. "Also," he said, getting up once the video finished playing, "tell your agent not to put his own name at the end of your show reel." I knew then that I hadn't gotten the job.

However, 2011 was a different year, and my confidence had grown significantly. The Jennings episode felt like a distant memory as I chatted with the media executive over dinner. I felt on top of the world: network bosses were now calling me, not the other way around. After dinner, I took a cab back to the apartment I had bought in the city's Adams Morgan neighborhood. For several years, I had been splitting my time between Washington and Atlanta, hoping CNN would allow me to move permanently to DC. I had been given the go-ahead to anchor from there for about a week a month, but maintaining a base in two cities became exhausting. Nurturing friendships in Washington, where part of my family still lived, was particularly challenging, as I was so often absent that I could rarely commit to plans. Still, taking the bus from Adams Morgan, down Connecticut Avenue, to the CNN Washington bureau near Union Station was a joy. I had always loved this city, and working there as an anchor was what I wanted to do, even though the bureau itself was not set up to accommodate CNN International shows. I used one of the small single-camera positions with a DC backdrop and kept the studio aspect of the show simple, with no standing shots and wide angles.

Either later that evening or the next day, the network executive reached out again. It did not take long for the messages to turn personal. And then, shortly after a few exchanges about journalism and art, small talk over instant messaging—the modern equivalent of banter—the media executive declared his love to me, like a childhood crush, without much warning, blurted out by a married man, still wearing his wedding ring, to me, a single woman who was both flattered by and wary of this unexpected overture.

For a man with a family, the media executive appeared unconcerned with proposing public meetings. He invited me to a few embassy events when he was in town and introduced me to people in the industry. We took walks together and stopped for coffee or hot tea on the way. The weather in Washington in the winter can be cold and biting.

On one of our last outings, I was bundled in a big coat and thick, knitted scarf. An unspoken bond had developed between us. I was single and made no secret of the fact that I wanted to find a life partner, but was firm with him that there was to be no relationship with him unless he was truly separated. I was old enough to know that married men rarely leave their wives for their mistresses, and I wasn't about to allow myself to become attached to a man who was still sharing a home with his spouse. When husbands talk of growing apart from their wives, I have found that it is often news to the wives. Most often, it's an excuse on the part of the man to initiate a flirtation or even an affair.

The professional offer I had hoped for never materialized. The media executive made vague allusions to mentioning my name at big meetings in New York. "They're fans of yours," he would say. "I brought your name up. They like you." The more time passed, the clearer it became that his interest in me had little to do with my reporting or anchoring abilities. In the pre-#MeToo era, executives weren't as careful about blurring the lines between the professional and the personal.

On New Year's Eve 2012, I received a message on my cell phone. He was thinking of me at midnight. I had not once even allowed him to hold my hand. I had kept my physical distance. On that evening, however, I wondered how we had gone from a professional dinner in a seafood restaurant to him proclaiming love, the kind that disrupts marriages, the kind that upends lives. It was time to end this—what would one even call it?—relationship. I had had enough. I issued a sort of ultimatum, but in the softest way possible. "I understand," "This must be tough," "These things aren't easy," I remember saying. Messages couched in comforting words, wrapped in gauze. After years of romantic disappointments, I had trained myself to push my feelings down; not to ask, only to suggest, that I wanted love, respect, and marriage.

I took a seat on the small balcony of my condo on Fourteenth Street in midtown Atlanta. From the eighteenth floor, I could see beyond some of the smaller residential units ahead and into Piedmont Park to the east, a beautiful open space built in the nineteenth and augmented in the early twentieth century based on plans by the sons of New York's Central Park designer. I had spent years in Atlanta, where CNN was headquartered at the time, after my first stint in London. I felt isolated and lonely there. It was a city that suited families with children well thanks to affordable homes and quality schools but offered very little for single women, especially those in their thirties and forties for whom finding a life partner can become increasingly difficult. I had made significant professional strides as an anchor and correspondent based in Atlanta, but I also felt stuck: the network had carved out a role for me there, and it was not making it easy for me to relocate elsewhere. I looked at my cell phone and felt anger rise up inside of me. A week had elapsed since the media executive called to say he had told his wife that their marriage was over, and I had heard nothing since. "I won't love you halfway. I just need to know this is true," he wrote in one of his last emails. "This world has conspired to bring us together—I will not give up."

I decided to call him. I wanted to let my anger take the lead. This time, I would be direct. "What do you mean you told her you were unhappy? Did you say the marriage was over?" I remember asking. There was silence at the other end of the line. I was tired of being understanding. "Hello?" I asked again. He replied in a low, exasperated voice; was he at work? I don't remember exactly how he phrased his answer, but it amounted to: *Stop asking me about my marriage.* "Have you had love interests outside your marriage before?" I had asked him when he first declared his feelings for me. He paused. "Not like this. Not in this way," he'd replied.

This wasn't a breakup; we had never dated, but it affected me deeply nonetheless. I let myself drift into a brief, profound depression. It wasn't that I loved him or even found him attractive; it's that I had spent months allowing myself to be used by a man in an unhappy relationship in need of emotional entertainment.

"No one will ever love me," I texted my friend Stephanie Halasz. I had been flooding her with messages about how lonely I felt in Atlanta and that the media executive debacle was proof, beyond any doubt that, at forty years old, I would never find a partner to share my life with. "Do you think you need to talk to someone?" she eventually responded, phrasing the suggestion as a question. Stephanie, a CNN producer I'd worked with and who'd become a close friend, was not someone who indulged in sentimentality easily. I knew, therefore, that her advice to visit a shrink was likely rooted in genuine concern for my mental health.

I never ended up seeing a therapist, because the media executive fiasco had flipped some sort of internal switch in me. Pretty soon after the no-breakup-breakup and for the first time, I felt fundamentally inspired to take control of my relationships. I made a decision to never allow anyone to lie to me, lead me on, or waste my time again. From Francesco to Tristan to Simon and a few others in between, I realized the only common denominator was me. Like a sort of religious epiphany, like seeing some sort of divine light pierce through the clouds and shine upon my face, I felt imbued by a strange power, a sudden realization that I would only accept the best kind of man going forward. If that man did not come, then I would have to be happy on my own.

Part 10

Beirut

The Thirty-Four-Day War

Imagine yourself on a country road drive on a sunny day. The windows are rolled down, and fresh air travels in and out of the car. You feel the breeze against your skin. There is a lovely tune coming from the radio, something soothing and uplifting like "What a Wonderful World." You are happy in the way happiness sometimes washes over you, for no other reason than because you are in no pain and nothing is troubling you and all around you is peaceful and clean and calm. Then you crash into a tree. The Lebanese finance minister Jihad Azour once used a similar analogy to describe what happened to his country on July 12, 2006. A war so explosive and unexpected that it took even veteran Middle East experts by surprise.

Following several days of cross-border attacks between the militant Shia group Hezbollah and the Israeli army, and the killing and abduction of Israeli soldiers, Israel launched a ground invasion into southern Lebanon and an attack on the country's infrastructure, including Beirut's international airport. There had been skirmishes and killings between the militant group and Israel before, so the explosion of all-out war seemed to come out of nowhere.

251

I was in Mykonos in Greece on vacation when hostilities broke out. I left a day early to fly to Damascus from Athens and drive from the Syrian capital to Lebanon, through the Bekaa Valley. It was, at the time, the only land route to Beirut, as the airport runways in Lebanon were dotted with bomb craters. I was heading into a war zone with only a few bikinis and summer beach clothing. I hoped I could borrow more appropriate attire on the ground. Once in Damascus, at the Sheraton, where foreign journalists often found themselves assigned the same few rooms, I was stuck with another crew reporting on the impact of the war on Syria. Tens of thousands of refugees from the Bekaa Valley had streamed into the country fleeing aerial bombing. My bosses in Atlanta told me to stay put until there was a need for me to travel to Beirut, which was already staffed for shows with another team.

It took a few days for me to be dispatched to Lebanon after the network sent the anchor on the ground back to base. "You've escaped," then CNN reporter Aneesh Raman, who'd also been assigned to Damascus, told me. "We'll miss you at the Sheraton pub." I set off alone from Damascus with my first driver, who dropped me off at the Syrian-Lebanese border. After I crossed, another driver and car took over on the Lebanese side, while a second vehicle followed us in case of a breakdown. It is common in war zones to travel with two cars, one for travel and the other one as a spare. Breaking down in the middle of a conflict could spell disaster. There is no emergency number to call, no roadside assistance to get you out of the danger zone.

As we approached Beirut, I saw several bombed-out gas stations and, closer to the city, the shells of buildings blackened by fire. I felt that familiar rush of excitement journalists experience when physically approaching a big story. I'm *there.* Inside Beirut, I was driven to the Markazia Monroe, a no-frills suites hotel on Riad al-Solh Square and also close to the Grand Serail, the prime minister's residence and offices. It was, at that point, one of the safest places to be in the Lebanese capital. The Israeli military, which had been pounding the

Shia stronghold of Dahiyeh in the south of the city day and night since the start of the war on July 12, was unlikely to hit any targets close to the administrative capital. Every few seconds, we could hear the bunker-busting bombs a few miles away in South Beirut, some close enough to shake the foundations of the building close to our position. At the hotel, I dropped off my suitcase full of vacation clothes, then headed to the CNN bureau across the square. "Ah, Miss Gorani!" Ingrid Formanek said, greeting me as I walked into the packed office. A producer with outsize charisma, Ingrid is heard before she is seen. Either her voice or the clank of her dozens of bangles and bracelets precedes her entry into a room. She is an industry legend who was played by Helena Bonham Carter in an HBO movie recounting her work for CNN during the first Gulf War in Baghdad. "How do you fancy interviewing May Chidiac?" she asked me. CNN wanted to profile the famous Lebanese television host who had narrowly survived a car bomb attack the previous year, losing a hand and part of a leg in the explosion. Syrian interests in the country had been blamed for the attempted assassination after she had vocally opposed meddling by the Assad regime in her country's affairs. Several other high-profile critics of Syria and its allies, particularly Hezbollah, had also been targeted and killed around that time.

On our way to May Chidiac's house and back, we heard the distant thuds of the relentless Israeli bombing campaign. Hezbollah, heavily armed and supported by Iran, was fighting back hard, launching rockets into northern Israel and engaging Israeli soldiers in guerrilla warfare on its own terrain. The Israeli military was taking significant losses. The war was not going well for a country unused to heavy casualties, while the other side signaled that it was willing to endure quite some pain. Every day, I would take my position on the balcony of a Markazia Monroe suite with the Beirut skyline behind me, interviewing Lebanese officials and their Israeli counterparts from across the border on live television. Central Beirut, relatively spared in comparison to the Hezbollah stronghold of Dahiyeh and south Lebanon, where the heavy fighting and bombardment were taking place, became a sort of broadcasting hub for television networks like CNN. Field anchoring combines both the structure and strict timing of a studio show with the unpredictability of an outdoor position. In this case, what we couldn't always predict was the occasional air strike landing within earshot of our setup.

I anchored on the Lebanese side, and a former colleague, Fionnuala Sweeney, anchored on the Israeli side. Every evening, we would dual host a show from both sides of the war. I was still wearing the flip-flops from my Mykonos wardrobe, unable to replace them with Beirut shopping completely shut down during the hostilities. A producer whose room I checked into the day I arrived had left her laundry behind, so I wore some of her blouses on air. "Enjoying my blue shirt, Hala?" she emailed when she saw me in it on television the next day.

By the standards of Baghdad, the Lebanon War of 2006 was not a particularly dangerous one to cover for the journalists, like me, who remained in central Beirut. Many of the stores and restaurants were closed, and it was a frightening period for the people of the city, but I could leave the hotel and cross the square to the CNN bureau without security or body armor. Every few days, I ventured out alone through Solidere, the downtown retail area renovated by the country's assassinated former prime minister Rafik Hariri, another Syria critic killed for expressing views that displeased Damascus. His assassination in 2005 led to massive protests that precipitated the Syrian military withdrawal from Lebanon but did not end its involvement in Lebanese affairs, particularly its close ties to Hezbollah.

Hotel staff went home at the end of their shifts. They were Christians, Muslims, both Sunni and Shia, and viewed us as the source of all information about the war, asking us questions no one really knew the answers to. "Will they bomb the bridge that I use to go visit my mother? It's the one right behind here," one of the night managers asked, pointing to an area at the front of our building. "No, I'm sure they won't," I would answer. I had no idea, of course, but what did it cost me to try to provide some reassurance? Thankfully, the overpass in question was never hit.

Every night, Lebanese ministers and analysts would come to our position at the Markazia Monroe, on the terrace overlooking Riad al-Solh. "Sneak me a cigarette, will you? Don't tell my wife," one of our regular cabinet minister guests asked after every appearance. "Just don't call it a bribe," I sometimes replied. CNN had dispatched reporters across the region in key locations in Lebanon and Israel, as well as Arab capitals throughout the Middle East. Ben Wedeman, Nic Robertson, Michael Ware, Brent Sadler, and many others reported on the hostilities while CNN and CNN International anchors hosted special shows from both countries around the clock. I was based in Atlanta then and, in my midthirties, had achieved what my younger self would not have imagined possible when I watched CNN cover the first Gulf War from my dorm room in Washington in 1991. I remember taking in the moment: I was coanchoring my own daily program and fronting the only story anyone was talking about from the field, alongside some of the most senior on-air talent in the world. The kind of programming CNN International produced on its own feed then is one that smaller international television budgets would most likely not allow today. I never took for granted how fortunate I was, even then.

The war lasted exactly thirty-four days, ending, as quickly as it had started, with a United Nations–brokered peace agreement. The day after the cease-fire went into effect, I went to Dahiyeh in South Beirut, the Hezbollah neighborhood that Israel had bombed ceaselessly for a month. Hezbollah's television channel Al-Manar had set up a makeshift studio atop the rubble of a bombed-out building, broadcasting live from the ruins, telling the world that nothing as trivial as a completely leveled office block would keep them from going to air. There was official Hezbollah tape surrounding some of the destruction, similar to police tape at a crime scene, inscribed with the words *divine victory*. The Arab world saw Hezbollah as an army victorious against Israel. Their leader, Hassan Nasrallah, became a sort of pan-regional folk hero, an Arab Che Guevara figure who had stood up to Israel. In Aleppo, around the same time, I saw posters of Nasrallah on walls and in storefronts and the yellow "Party of God" Hezbollah flag hoisted onto lampposts.

For a few years after the war, Hezbollah was seen, by some, as a fighting force that had defended Arab honor, until the Syrian uprising in 2011, when it entered the conflict firmly on the side of Bashar al-Assad and his protectors in Iran. It was clear then that it was sect over country and power over anything else.

The following day, I went to Paul's, a café at the entrance of Gemmayzeh, a trendy nightlife neighborhood in East Beirut. As quickly as it had been suspended, social life returned to the city in what seemed like a matter of hours. I could hear the conversation a couple of tables away from mine. A group of young Beirutis, speaking French, were discussing the war. "I wish the Israelis had finished the job," they said, expressing their desire to see Hezbollah annihilated. The notion that the militant group had fought in the name of all Lebanese or Arabs resonated only in certain milieux. Among some Christians, like those aligned with the Lebanese Forces party, for example, Hezbollah was guilty of running a state within a state with its own self-serving military force, and it, alone, was responsible for provoking this unnecessary war.

In Lebanon, a country that counts eighteen officially recognized sects, what group is aligned with which group shifts based on wartime alliances, peacetime accords, and foreign influences and power plays. There are the Sunnis, the Shias, and the Druze, the Maronites and the Protestants, the Armenian Apostolic Church, the Greek Orthodox Church, and the Melkite Greek Catholic Church, among other Christian and Muslim sects. Their division of power was reestablished in 1989 in an agreement designed to end the Lebanese civil war that had brought the country to its knees after fifteen years of conflict, where at one time or another, it seemed like every possible conflict permutation took shape. Muslims fought Muslims, who fought Christians, who, in turn, fought other Christians. The Taif Agreement sought to end the infighting by transferring some of the power from the Maronite Christians to other sects, after the Maronites had enjoyed decades of outsize power granted to them by the former French colonial rulers. All militias were meant to disarm (they didn't), and Hezbollah was allowed to keep its weapons in its role as a "resistance" group against Israel, though holding Western hostages no doubt helped its negotiation position.

The civil war ended, but the sectarian tensions remained. Modern-day Lebanon, created by French colonial powers in the 1920s, combines a majority Christian center with Sunnis in the north and Shia in the south, if one is allowed to oversimplify the sectarian spread. France, which saw itself as the protector and guardian of Eastern Christians, wanted the country the Christians ruled to have geographic girth. Just as Aleppo was looped into a nation-state called "Syria," again as the result of secret French and British handshakes, Lebanon became a country with a dizzying patchwork of competing interests. When these Western nation-state creations were conceived, Arabs had no say in what territory their countries would cover or how they would be ruled. Lebanon, whose capital was once the playground of the Middle East, became the battleground of the region's rival sects and warring countries. Its people, the primary victims, known for their resilience during the worst crises and conflicts, could not have imagined how much worse it would all become.

The Paris of the Middle East

Miss Austria, Miss Iceland, Miss France, and fourteen other Miss Europe contestants were the main attraction at the Hotel Saint Georges beach in the week preceding the main event. One of the most beautiful that day, thought my mother, Nour Gorani, was Anna Ranalli, who was representing Italy and would compete against the other beauty queens at the Casino du Liban on June 11. Nour, then seventeen years old, had traveled with the nuns of Aleppo's Franciscan school and convent to the Lebanese capital to sit the first part of her French baccalaureate degree exams. It was the first year she had worn makeup and dressed in adult clothing. Beirut in the early '60s was the place to be. The military dictatorships in Egypt and Syria had wrecked Alexandria's, Cairo's, and Damascus's status as cultural and social centers. Beirut had started to eclipse them all with its restaurants, shopping, and schools. The "Paris of the Middle East" attracted high-society visitors from across the region. It wasn't just partygoers who descended on the coastal city. Spies and bankers also came for their slice of the action.

In the years before the civil war brought the country to its knees in the mid-'70s, Lebanon had become a sort of playground for international visitors and its own elite. The sectarian tensions that exploded into open conflict were kept at bay. "You didn't feel it in Beirut," Nour says today. "You had the best shopping and the best hotels. Even Saudis escaped their country so they could watch a belly dancer and have a drink in peace." The Lebanese knew how to keep their visitors happy. Whereas the Syrian and Egyptians nationalized, the Lebanese deregulated. If you wanted to do business without the heavy hand of autocrats hovering over you, Beirut was the place to go.

When the nationalization drive in Syria following the creation of the United Arab Republic started reaching individual businessmen and landowners, some of those Syrians smuggled cash to Lebanon to keep their funds safe in Lebanese banks. The code word one family friend used to describe a thousand Syrian pounds was "one book." "I sent you ten books in a suitcase," he would tell his interlocutor in Beirut on the telephone, in case the Syrian secret police were listening in on the call. There was worry when, in one conversation, he announced sending "ten and a half books" to Lebanon. Would the secret police uncover the ploy? "Perhaps avoid announcing that you're sending only parts of books," he was later advised.

My mother was in Beirut because she could no longer take her high school exams in Aleppo. A crazed mob had tried to burn down the city's French high school during the Suez Canal crisis in 1956. The Arab attackers blamed France and the United Kingdom for trying to maintain colonial control of the canal and had taken aim at the Lycée Français in Aleppo to vent their anger. In the following years, students of French-affiliated institutions in Aleppo were forced to travel to Beirut, where France had continued to maintain an official academic presence, to sit exams and collect their diplomas. Though schools that taught the French curriculum remained, they were no longer official academic outposts accredited by the French government. Little by little, France was disengaging from its former colony, and, in the '60s, my mother's generation would be the last to be a direct product of the French schooling system.

The Ba'athist coup in 1963 delivered the final death blow to France's remaining cultural influence in Syria. The revolutionaries placed regime-approved administrators in France's former academic outposts, replacing envoys sent by the French government. The soft power of education and culture was erased so quickly that the children of those who spoke fluent French would learn only rudimentary phrases in elective French classes in Syrian state schools. The former occupiers' legacy disappeared, like a political enemy erased from a Stalin-era photo. The new rulers promised equality and the glorification of Arab culture but, instead, did nothing more than blow up what was there before. In their worldview, the rich, the cultured, the landowners, and the aristocrats: they all deserved contempt. The official Ba'athist ideology called for Arab enlightenment and equality. In practice, the ideological slogans were used as a cover to steal from ordinary Syrians and oppress those outside the party. The system was designed to promote and reward only members of the party. Doing business meant collaborating with those in charge and bribing officials. The entire country started running on corruption. From getting paperwork done to paying off judges: no one trusted Syria anymore. "A professor failed my niece at university twice, and when the family asked why, they were told that he expected a handout to give her a passing grade," a Syrian friend told me.

Beirut, during that time, was a refuge and an escape from what was happening at home. For those who could afford it, there was a shopping district downtown with upscale brands like the Italian knitwear designer Luisa Spagnoli for women and Sulka, a luxury clothing and accessories shop for men. Women would still buy fabrics to have clothing made by seamstresses and tailors back in Syria based on the latest Dior or Jacques Fath designs found in magazines sent from

Europe. A bride-to-be would travel to Lebanon for a few days to buy fine lingerie and dresses because import restrictions cut off the supply of Western clothing and accessories to the Syrian market. Until the civil war in 1975 in Beirut, money would buy you designer clothing, high-end dining, good schools, medical care, and freedom. Name your price and Beirut would oblige.

Lebanon in the '60s extended beyond Beirut, of course, and the seeds of what was to come had already been sown. The state the French unilaterally created by combining Mount Lebanon with the Sunni north and the Shia south after World War I was a complicated patchwork of sects and tribal fiefdoms. All the ingredients for the civil war that would devastate the country were already in place, ready to be stoked by outside interests across the region. Soon, the small island of luxury, calm, and easy living would explode too. Like the Syrians before them, the Lebanese who could afford to fled to stabler countries, returning for visits only when the violence decreased. Another generation of Arabs forced to pick up and leave when the bombs, kidnappings, and shortages made life in their home country unbearable.

A relative once told me that during the civil war, when he was on his way to class at university, his car was stopped by a man at a checkpoint. He did not know if the man with the AK-47 was Christian or Muslim and, therefore, did not know what sect or fighting force he was aligned with.

"He asked me for my ID. I said I didn't have one. So he asked for my name and then put a gun to my head," he told me. "He wanted to know what religion I was from based on my name, I guess. I thought about it and tried to figure out if I should give him a name that sounded obviously Muslim or obviously Christian, based on his appearance."

"What did you do?" I asked, imagining myself in a similar situation. A gun pressed against my temple. My relative's name was neither obviously Muslim nor unmistakably Christian.

"I told him my name was Mohammed," he said.

"But your name isn't Mohammed." I didn't understand why he had said that it was.

"Well, I thought if I'm going to get killed for who I am, let it be for who I really am," he answered.

The man at the checkpoint lowered the gun and let him go.

The Man of My Dreams

SEPTEMBER 1, 2012

Men live on a continuum. Women experience life in cycles and phases. Cycles, obviously, pertain to their biology. Phases, however, are more or less clearly defined chapters, imposed by social norms. There is childhood, when the expectations of female roles and relationships are signposted. There is adolescence, the years of raging hormones and inner chaos. There is, after that, a rather long period of fertility and desirability, which, in my experience, lasts until a woman reaches midlife. Beyond that, as women approach the tail end of their childbearing years, there is a gradual awakening to the reality that despite progress in gender equality over the past decades, middle-aged women are valued less than their younger selves, especially in industries like mine, where they are disproportionately judged on their looks and youthfulness. My first coanchoring role was with Richard Quest, who was eight years older than I was. My second major coanchoring role, in 2004, was with Jim Clancy, who was twenty-one years older. Women on television are almost never allowed to be overweight or gray-haired. Is there a female Wolf Blitzer in a prominent role? Female anchors are expected to change their on-air outfits regularly, while men face almost no scrutiny in that department. When Australian presenter Karl Stefanovic decided to wear the same suit on his morning show every day for a year in 2014, he said no one noticed, even though his female coanchor was routinely judged "harshly" on her fashion choices. Past a certain age, though it's not explicitly requested of them, women often feel pressure to get cosmetic procedures to appear more youthful if they are on air. There are exceptions, of course, and much of what I have felt about my own identity as a television anchor could be sexism I may have internalized over the decades. I hope the women now starting out in on-camera roles will not feel those pressures to the same extent and that the gender pay disparities in journalism, the lack of female heads of networks, and the ageism that affects females significantly more than their male counterparts will slowly give way to more equal treatment on both sides of the camera. Let's be honest, though, we still have a long way to go.

By the fall of 2012, at the age of forty-two, I was rarely being asked whether I wanted children. I hadn't heard back from the media executive, who had blocked my telephone number and unfollowed me from social media accounts. A few months later, I saw him in New York at a large embassy dinner he was attending with the wife he'd said he was divorcing and, after spotting me, he appeared to run out of the building. Apart from a few superficial and occasional flirtations, I had come to the conclusion that I would be one of the unlucky women who, despite their best efforts, or perhaps because of them, end up alone. I cried about my romantic frustrations often during those years. I wanted a partner, much more so than children. I wanted to build a home with a man and do the mundane and boring things couples do. "You're in your nesting phase," Simon had told me when we started dating, after I told him I had shopped for household necessities at Target. "I'd rather shoot myself than go there," he had added.

On Saturday, September 1, 2012, a sunny and warm late-summer day, at the National Evangelical Church across the street from the prime minister's palace in Beirut, sitting in one of the pews, I turned around, rather suddenly, for no particular reason. My eyes met his, and there was no doubt in my mind: he had been looking at me. I had never thought of him romantically, but, in that instant, like a revelation, I noticed him in a way I hadn't before. I had always found him attractive when I worked with him in the field. He was a six-foot-three, green-eyed, tanned war cameraman who had covered conflicts around the world, and I was sure I wasn't the only woman who found him appealing. We had met eight years before in Libya and had worked together a few times a year since. We crossed paths in Cairo during the revolution and in Amman, when terrorists attacked Western hotels. We had also worked together on assignments in Dubai, Beirut, and Tripoli for *Inside the Middle East*, the show I hosted for almost ten years on CNN International. During those years, he was married to a Lebanese woman he'd met in Beirut, and I knew him to be unavailable. My interactions with him, therefore, were purely professional and, unlike some other globe-trotting journalists, he always acted in the reserved way men do when they are clearly not the cheating kind.

But that day, as I was standing in a pew waiting for the bride to walk down the aisle, wearing an asymmetrical black Armani dress I had overpaid for after my suitcase was lost on my way to Lebanon, a lovely connection between two people invited to the same wedding materialized, leaping over wooden pews and remaining suspended over us, like an electrical charge, until the wedding party that evening in the mountains over Beirut.

I had flown from Atlanta to Beirut with my friend Ryan Cooper, a producer and later executive with CNN International, who was and still is one of my dearest friends and traveling companions. It was his first time in an Arab country, and I was relishing my role as a guide. Ryan is an American from the Midwest whose experience of the Arab world was a journalistic one, from afar, as the producer of international news shows that ran reporting from the region. Here, he could see and experience it all for himself on the ground. "This is where we anchored from during the war," I said, pointing to the Markazia Monroe building, which had since been bought by another hotel chain. We drove up to Byblos, and, in an especially daring escapade, I took him to the Hezbollah Resistance Museum on a guided tour of the old Israeli-Lebanese front line, on an outing that included the veteran correspondent Arwa Damon, based in Beirut at the time. "Can you guess where I'm from?" our guide asked us in American-accented English. "Iran?" I asked, realizing quickly that my suggestion was way off the mark. "New York?" ventured Ryan. "Brooklyn," our guide answered with what sounded like pride in his voice. Not for coming from the United States but for having ended up in that spot, giving tours of the Hezbollah tunnels twenty miles from the Israeli border, as if he had managed to escape America to embrace his true purpose in this shrine to Shia resistance, complete with destroyed Israeli tanks in a purpose-built open-air sunken garden. An unexpectedly modern glass-and-concrete building housed exhibits of captured Israeli gear, and mannequins dressed in militia uniforms were positioned in fighting stances in the tunnels.

I was happy during that trip. I had accepted that I would most probably not get married and that I was likely too old to have children naturally. For the first time in my adult life, that year, the idea that I could find fulfilment while living unattached to a man slowly grew inside of me until it occupied more space than my longing for a partner.

The groom, a CNN executive, had organized the wedding in his ancestral family home in the Chouf Mountains. Dozens of my friends and colleagues sat at long tables under fruit trees in the courtyard of an old stone house, lights in the trees and traditional Lebanese food on buffet tables, the stars and moon above, like constellations shining bright only for us. Perhaps the stars were responsible for my sentimental mood. More likely, it was the fact that I was sitting next to Christian, in the kind of mood that comes but a few times in one's life, of feeling transported by the first waves of romantic fancy. Some of my previous relationships had started similarly, and so I was ready for, even expectant of, a sentimental dead end. But, at an age where time had started passing with increasing speed, I decided that, for once, I would not wait to be approached. Instead, I would do the approaching myself.

On our way down from the Chouf Mountains in one of the buses the groom had hired to drive wedding guests back to Beirut, I reached over and held his hand. For the first time in my life, I made a first move, without the guarantee that it would be reciprocated. What did I have to lose? I had waited for men to act first my entire life, as if women making the first move was a sign of desperation. In reality, being at the mercy of someone else's will is the real helplessness. It led me to all the wrong places with all the wrong people. I had known Christian for almost a decade, and I knew he was decent and kind, generous and loyal. If he could be the man I was looking for, why not give it a try?

The Final Straw

Eight years later, Beirut was a city in crisis hosting tens of thousands of Syrian refugees, many of them from Aleppo. Almost a decade earlier, they had hoped to ride out the war but a year after the March 2011 revolution, months during which it appeared Aleppo would stay on the fringes of the revolution, the smaller protests had swelled and the rebel forces in the north had entered the war in earnest. The distant thuds of mortar fire in the Aleppo countryside would resonate across the city, from the poorer eastern neighborhoods where regime opponents started to organize, all the way to western Aleppo, where most of the Syrian-based Gorani family lived. Soon, the old city around the citadel became a front line. The old Aleppine houses of Jdaydeh, some refurbished into traditional restaurants and hotels, were set ablaze during some of the worst fighting between rebel forces and the regime's army. In 2007, almost one hundred years after the return of the Istanbul Goranis to Aleppo, a few hundred yards from their ancestral home, the Beit Kbeer, I had signed the Sissi House restaurant guest book after a meal there. I imagine it burned now, along with everything else. What went first at the Sissi? The tables and chairs?

The menus? The wooden window frames in the central courtyard? At what point did the words I inscribed on the page burn and turn to ash? My name Gorani, set ablaze, erased forever from Aleppo.

"We left Aleppo for a few months," a relative said to me after traveling to Beirut in 2012, "until things calmed down. No one predicted that it would last as long as it did." Those who could afford to travel out of the country packed enough for a season, perhaps two. Aleppo International Airport was closed, and the only escape route involved driving to Beirut in taxis that would track rebel and regime battles on a daily basis to avoid getting caught up in the fighting. At the height of the war, a cramped back seat fare cost several hundred US dollars. A more comfortable passenger seat sometimes several thousand. Drivers took parallel roads and backstreets in journeys that could last up to twelve hours. In addition to a stray mortar or a lone bullet flying through the air, there was always the risk of kidnapping on the way. Some of the Islamist groups had splintered into a constellation of criminal gangs that kidnapped and robbed those foolhardy enough to venture out in vehicles for hire, huddled together for protection, quietly praying that the journey would end safely.

In Beirut, the Syrians who had kept their money in Lebanese banks were part of a small group of privileged refugees who could afford to rent apartments in the city. The luckiest among them owned property in Lebanon and could escape the fighting. The less fortunate lived in shelters and tents, relying on handouts, sending their children to plow the fields of Lebanese farmers or to sell plastic flowers to drivers stuck in Beirut traffic. Hunger will strip the proudest among us of our scruples.

Slowly, the Aleppo residents with connections abroad left, one family after the other, replicating in exile their former social lives in the city. Among my remaining Aleppo family members, a few aunts and uncles, their cousins and children, most migrated to Lebanon. Others left for Europe or America. In Beirut, Aleppo social club bridge games appeared, Aleppo ladies' lunches, Aleppo coffee visits: an Aleppo replica within Beirut came together while the original one burned.

Back home, apartments were ransacked and occupied by regime forces, houses were burglarized or trashed by vandals. The housekeepers and drivers often continued to live in the mansions of their employers. Sometimes, they were hunted down by the secret police for taking part in anti-Assad demonstrations, when it seemed the regime had only weeks left. "Ahmed, leave now," a text to the doorman of a family friend read in 2012, "they are looking for you." Someone had seen the *mukhabarat* officers in a house not far away, asking for him. They had knocked on the wrong door, which had given Ahmed time to flee. When the officers arrived, the remaining residents said Ahmed had gone back to his village and that they had not seen him in months, though he had left only minutes before. In Aleppo, police visits rarely ended in near misses like the one that saved Ahmed. More often, they came unannounced and, after a bang of the door, snatched those they suspected of anti-regime activities. Many were never heard from again.

After years in exile, the Syrians of Beirut became a permanent fixture in the city. I would visit the cousins and aunts and uncles I would normally have seen on my trips to Syria in Lebanon instead. There was both a feeling of familiarity and of alienation during those reunions, as if I were writing with my left hand, struggling to form letters with a pen, even though I knew how to spell the words. My aunt Aida, my cousin Mazen, my uncle Hisham, the more distant relatives: we should all have been in one place but landed in another, looking out onto the Mediterranean Sea, eating a mezze spread on Zaitunay Bay, the banter and the jokes, the gossip, the "How is your mother? How is work?" questions but never "There is a war, our lives are demolished, what do we do now?"

In the end, it's all about luck. Where you are born, what passport you carry, where a war breaks out, what criminal gang decides it will run your life into the ground. It is all happenstance, like a wheel turning and stopping on the word *refugee*. My uncle Hisham died in Beirut, and I wondered what his last thought was, this brilliant surgeon from Aleppo who had spent his life and career tending to the sick and injured in Syria, as he took his own last breath in a city he had never intended to live in. My uncle should not have died in Beirut.

As if the ignominy of exile wasn't enough, the Lebanese banking system collapsed in 2019. What was revealed was an elaborate Ponzi scheme, and the country's banks could not honor their customers' withdrawals. The Lebanese economy, which relied heavily on dollar inflows, first started struggling in 2015 when the amount of foreign money pouring into the country slowed for the first time in over a decade. The central bank started concealing the liquidity crisis by taking on more debt while financial institutions continued to benefit. The subterfuge wouldn't last long; in 2018, some banks began limiting how much of their own money depositors could access. Soon after, desperate account holders were given a few hundred dollars a month to live on. Some branches closed their doors altogether. Cash machines ran out of bills. "The bank told him he could have eighty thousand of the five hundred thousand dollars he had in his account if he promised to never ask for more," I was told about one family friend's deal. "I get four hundred fifty dollars a month from my lifelong savings if I promise to never sue," another Lebanese-based Syrian told me. Depositors were so worried they would end up with nothing that they accepted offers they wouldn't have considered only a few months before.

The extent of the grift by the country's political and financial leaders soon became painfully apparent. Desperation drove some to extremes. In September 2022, an interior designer named Sali Hafez burst into a BLOM Bank branch and, with the help of activists live streaming the operation on Facebook, doused the floor with gasoline and threatened to burn the building down if the tellers refused to pull cash from her account. "I had begged the branch manager before for my money, and I told him my sister was dying, didn't have much time left," she later explained. "I had nothing left to lose." In video of the incident, Hafez climbs on the bank manager's desk, wearing all black, dressed like a bank robber, except that she was robbing herself. Hafez ended up leaving with $13,000 and was hailed as a hero on social media. Lebanon became the country where people are forced to steal their own money back from the criminals who govern them.

Sometimes when the happenstance wheel spins, it falls on a catastrophe that no one had even conceived of, as if a scriptwriter had run out of disasters to inflict on their characters and so imagined something so obscenely tragic that it would seem an unlikely turn of events even to those willing to suspend their disbelief. In August 2020, as if the worsening financial collapse wasn't calamitous enough, ammonium nitrate stored at the Beirut port exploded. The equivalent of more than a kiloton of TNT detonated, causing a blast so powerful it was felt in Turkey, Syria, Palestine, Israel, and Jordan. It was heard in Cyprus, 180 miles away. The explosion generated a magnitude 3.3 seismic event. "She was sitting in her living room and a shard of glass sliced through her," a friend told me about her sister-in-law's death. Another 217 people died that day. Hundreds of thousands lost their homes. Lebanon had managed to endure a civil war, several wars with Israel, a Syrian occupation, millions of refugees, the COVID pandemic, and enduring tribal and ethnic tensions, but the port explosion proved, for some, to be one tragedy too many. Buildings were reduced to rubble and the windows of seafront properties burst inward, shards of glass and shrapnel killing and maiming those inside: a child playing on the floor, a woman reading a book on her balcony, a man watching television on his sofa. The burnt shell of the grain silos that were next to the warehouse that stored the ammonium nitrate and the massive four-hundred-foot crater the explosion caused became a symbol of the corruption and criminality that had led to the moment Beirut fell to its knees, and its residents wondered if they were simply cursed. Who had allowed fireworks, believed to have been the spark that ignited the explosives, to be stored next to a confiscated shipment of ammonium nitrate? Tarek Bitar, the judge tasked with the investigation, was blocked for a year from doing his work by judicial and political officials. When he resumed his probe and brought charges against top prosecutors for obstructing justice, the suspects detained in the blast were all released. The victims, revictimized, know there will likely be no justice. "There's no life even though we're still alive, but we're dead inside. They killed us from the inside. They slaughtered us from the inside," said Mirna Habboush, who lost an eye when the blast ripped through the car she was driving near the port. Human rights organizations were gathering victim testimonials so that, even if justice wasn't served in the courts, there would be a record for future generations of the criminality that paved the way for the port explosion to happen.

Syrians who had fled the war in their country felt like no matter where they went, disaster followed. Just when it seemed things couldn't get worse, after the initial displacement, the banking system collapse and the port explosion in Lebanon, a massive earthquake hit Turkey and northern Syria in February 2023, where already uprooted refugees were made homeless again. Some, unable to accept this triple curse, returned to the homes they fled in Syria, unsure of what they would find there and risking arrest or imprisonment. Anything was better than living in the muddy craters the earthquake had left behind.

Syrian president Bashar al-Assad, who had been written off by many Western observers and leaders during the first few years of the uprising, was by then firmly back in power. His army, with the help of Russia and Iran, had taken back large parts of the country except for a sliver of land in the north controlled by rebel groups and areas of Kurdish control in the northeast. His representatives were once again invited on news networks to discuss aid shipments to the thousands of earthquake victims on the Syrian side of the border. Watching regime officials give interviews on mainstream networks felt, in some ways, like pre-2011, almost as if the previous twelve years hadn't happened.

A few weeks after the disaster, Assad and his glamorous wife, Asma, once pariahs even in the Arab world, made an official state visit to Abu Dhabi in the United Arab Emirates. Asma emerged from a plane wearing a crisp white pantsuit and a Chanel necklace. In her left hand, a rectangular clutch with interlocking nacre ball clasps. She emerged at the airport in Abu Dhabi onto an azure carpet and was later hosted by the Emirati First Lady, Sheikha Fatima bint Mubarak, at her palace. Bashar and Asma al-Assad felt confident enough to travel abroad together for the first time since the uprisings began. The smiles and handshakes, the reintroduction of the Syrian First Couple on the world stage, flying on an official visit far from the country they had helped to destroy. There was something grotesque about the spectacle, as there always is when a country overlooks abuses in favor of strategic self-interest. As a journalist, I have always tried to remind viewers of the hypocrisy of the leaders of every country, including the United States when it appears to lecture the world on democracy yet sells weapons and rolls out the red carpet for the leaders of countries with abject human rights records.

When I watched Bashar and Asma deplane in Abu Dhabi, I wanted desperately to believe the last twelve tragic years in Syria and the region had not been for nothing and that those who suffered had not done so in vain. That one day, justice would be served. My friends sent WhatsApps with vomit emojis accompanying articles on the visit. A few days after the Assad visit, Saudi Arabia's foreign minister traveled to Damascus in another first since the uprisings. Soon after, Syria was readmitted into the Arab League, from which it had been ejected in 2011. The US and other Western nations stayed mum. The sanctions against Damascus remain, and there is an inquiry into the death of a US citizen in government hands, but journalists who cover the State Department told me that American officials have privately acknowledged that isolating Syria has failed and that engagement through regional allies like Saudi Arabia and the UAE was worth a try. The regime was slowly being reinstated, inch by inch. At least for now, there would be no real accountability.

The Jungle

The camp had no electricity and only a single, narrow pipe connected to the mains supplying running water. The hundreds of refugees gathered there lived under flimsy tents and tarps, surrounded by bags of rubbish, empty bottles, tin cans, diapers, and discarded food. The trash wasn't just all around them; it was, quite literally, under their feet. The city had moved the undocumented migrants to a parcel of land below a highway overpass and above a former municipal dump. A few feet under the tents and tarps were layers of decades-old buried litter, pressed into a solid mass and covered by earth.

Residents of "the Jungle," as it was nicknamed, on the outskirts of Calais in northern France, slept sometimes twenty-five to a tent. The Eritreans and Ethiopians had built a church out of tarp and two-by-fours and had nailed a wooden cross on the fragile structure's highest point. The Sudanese, Afghans, and North Africans had isolated an area to pray, with a daily schedule pinned to a timber pole to remind the Jungle's Muslims when it was time to face Mecca, to the southeast, and worship Allah. The whole settlement was so unsound that a vigorous gust of wind would have uprooted the entire place in seconds.

279

On the overpass above, a few bored police officers looked at the mass of human misery under their feet. Every night, a dance between the migrants and the authorities unfolded: some of the refugees would try to sneak inside a van or hold on to the chassis of a truck to hitch a ride across the channel to England, and the gendarmes would run after them, pry them off the bumper of a moving vehicle, or catch them before they could scale a wall at a border crossing. Most told me they had relatives and communities already in Britain and wanted to join them there. There was nothing keeping them in France, they said. They were young and physically robust, and they were willing to risk their lives to get there.

I followed a young Eritrean man named Abraham into his tent. He told me he had boarded a migrant boat bound for Italy, that he had set off from the Libyan coast in North Africa and had walked or hitch-hiked the entire length of Western Europe, only to end up sleeping under a highway in France, his goal just one successful channel crossing away.

"In every refugee camp abroad, the conditions are better," a Doctors of the World representative visiting the camp told me. "France is not respecting the minimum humanitarian standards." Behind us, there was a man, crouching so that he could rinse soap off his face with water from the pipe the city had installed, bizarrely, only a few inches above ground level. There was no way to access water while standing, so activities like shaving required particular corporal bendability. I noticed a pregnant woman eying our camera crew nervously, disappearing into a tent. The Jungle's migrants in Calais had become a hot topic on both sides of the channel. In France and in Britain, populist politicians on the Far Right called them invaders. The Jungle itself was dismantled in October 2016, but that has not stopped the migrants from trying to reach the UK. In 2022, the Conservative governments of Boris Johnson and, later, Rishi Sunak, promised to send refugees who crossed the channel on boats to Rwanda, in eastern Africa. Even those fleeing persecution or conflicts in their homeland would be denied the right to claim asylum. Illegal entrants would be put on a plane with a one-way ticket to Kigali.

I had traveled with my crew to Calais on the Eurostar, the high-speed train that connects London to France, Brussels in Belgium, and Amsterdam in the Netherlands. I had covered many refugee stories before in the Middle East. The millions of Syrians fleeing Assad's bombs or ISIS, the Afghans desperate for a better life, the economic migrants from poorer parts of Africa and Asia, all in search of safety and opportunity. This was my first story on refugees in a country where I'd once lived. How were their stories any different from the ones that forced anyone else's ancestors into leaving their homes in search of a safer, better life? By 1920, a famine and poverty in Greater Syria had pushed hundreds of thousands of refugees to immigrate to the Americas, including Selim and Salha Hosni, Jews from Aleppo, who settled in New York in 1910 and whose grandson Jerry Seinfeld became one of America's most successful comedic entertainers.

Had there not been an exit for them, or regular migration routes for my parents, or the warm welcome extended to Ukrainians after the Russian invasion in 2022, how many of them would have attempted dangerous crossings, ended up stuck in camps, waiting for paperwork that never arrived, and been called *invaders* by Western tabloid newspapers?

I don't know what happened to Abraham from Eritrea. Did he make it to Britain, or did he drown trying? The next day, I boarded a Eurostar back to London. On the train from Calais, I ate a meal served to me on a tray. I may have had a glass of wine with my supper. At the same time, Abraham was sleeping in shifts under a tent in northern France. Apart from the police, he had told me, the biggest problem was that this was "a very dirty life." The notion that luck can play such a large role in determining who among us ends up living on top of a decommissioned garbage dump—and who doesn't—is never clearer than during these assignments. What separates the migrants from those who live in rich and stable countries is a simple accident of birth. My two-hour train journey might take Abraham months and involve multiple attempts of trying to cross into Britain in a variety of ways. The same distance separates our starting and end points. I follow a straight line; he follows a circuitous road with barbed wire and armed guards, like a character in one of those video games in which players fend off rivals and jump over obstacles to score points. A few months after my visit to the Jungle, a twenty-two-year-old Sudanese man, Husham Osman Alzubair, boarded a freight train near Calais bound for Britain. He was found dead of head injuries on the train's rear wagon. He wanted to join family members already in the UK and study civil engineering there.

In the Mediterranean, there is an invisible graveyard on the seafloor, where over twenty-six thousand migrants have died on dangerous trips from North Africa to Europe since 2014. Those not recovered have remained in the deep waters while, over their corpses on the surface above, thousands of overpacked dinghies continue to attempt the crossing each year.

Part 11

Somewhere over the Atlantic

Just the Two (and a Half) of Us

There was a break in the heat wave the week Christian and I got married in Marrakech. We had chosen a hotel in the city's Palmeraie, just outside the bustling medina, where palm trees and lush gardens offer space for larger gatherings. We booked the entire venue for close friends and family, a large compound with individual tented bungalows decorated in the traditional Moroccan style with four-poster beds and handmade-tile bathrooms. The main building, a villa shaped in a semicircle overlooking a round pool with white columns and an indoor fountain, looked like something out of *The Thousand and One Nights*, with high, domed ceilings and grand orientalist paintings hanging on color-washed walls.

We chose to have a large wedding party, the kind an older couple might find over the top; but it was my first—and hopefully last—wedding, and I wanted to make an event of it. We had gotten married in a civil ceremony two weeks prior in London with a few friends and the family members who were able to attend. The Marrakech celebration would be for a much wider group of people, though by Middle Eastern wedding standards, ours was little more than a backyard get-together.

We agreed on a list of about 120 guests, including friends, family, and some of the network executives I felt obliged to invite. I expected them all to decline the invitation, but, to my surprise, most of the bosses came. I often hear stories of brides stressed because of problems with flowers or wedding bands or food, but I had seldom been calmer than on my wedding day. We had used the hotel's in-house planner and, as long as we had wads of cash to settle our bill and tip generously, everything was done for us. "Flowers for the centerpieces: white, pink, or white and pink?" Nadia would ask. "Hmm...White?" Next question: "Candelabras or small candles on the table?" I liked the idea of dramatic candelabras. And so on, until we had ticked all the boxes for food, wine, the style of chairs on either side of the aisle, and every other detail a wedding planner is responsible for. I didn't really care about those things, anyway. The location was dreamlike, and we had flown in a DJ—who happened to be a boy I'd gone to school with in Neuilly-sur-Seine and had exchanged little love missives with in class at age eleven—and I was confident that the celebration would be a success.

Something about this wedding healed lifelong wounds. I had not enjoyed a close relationship with my father, Ficrat, after my parents' divorce. We were not estranged, per se, but we remained out of touch for many years at a time. He had wed again in the early '80s, around the same time my mother married my stepfather, Amr. My father and his wife, Leigh, had four children, which made them my half siblings, and neither of us made any real effort to reconnect during that time. I invited them all to the wedding. I had found love with Christian, and I wanted to leave whatever old family wounds had been present in the past well behind us. Rather unexpectedly, I eventually developed close relationships with my two half sisters, Alexandra and Gabriella. Though they were much younger than I was, sixteen and eighteen years my junior, respectively, a sort of genetic familiarity seemed to draw us together in ways that felt natural. In the beginning, calling anyone my "sister" felt awkward. I would occasionally try the appellation on for size with people outside my family, but it took some time to overcome the sense that our relationship hadn't matured to the level of full siblinghood. In the first few years following my wedding, I would look for physical similarities in our faces. I could see in Gabriella our father's mouth and jawline and in Alexandra a similar nose to mine. We've never discussed this late-in-life rapprochement explicitly, but with each meeting, it became obvious that new bonds grew, in the way I imagine nerve endings reattach after an injury.

By the time Christian and I got married, the question of why we didn't have children had receded, but not disappeared completely. Like a muted soundtrack continuously playing in the background, the fact that we were a childless couple, in a world where most people choose to have children, was something that continued to occupy a space in our relationship. Sometimes, friends and family tried to delicately bring up the subject; occasionally, Christian and I also talked about whether remaining childless was something we could happily live with. It was clear by the time we got married, however, that we would not have kids of our own. I was forty-five, too late to become pregnant naturally, and so I knew that my identity as a woman would likely not include motherhood. I would never become the mother of another human being, a status so elevated that it is often said, even to childless women, that one only learns what true love is when they become a parent. Almost daily, women without children are told they will never experience that unique love or selflessness or fulfillment. That they are, by virtue of not having procreated, not quite women. They have not mothered and so they are not worthy of the same esteem. *If you were a mom, you'd understand.*

I would probably have been able to have children at the very beginning of my relationship with Christian with a few drugs and some medical wizardry. I had a few tests done, which determined that I was medically fine and able to carry children, but stopped short of embarking on a fertility journey. In my most private moments, I wonder if that was a mistake. But the regret I feel at not having tried dissolves so quickly that I must come to the conclusion that my desire for children of my own was always rather weak. I never felt an urge for children when I was single, and so whatever maternal curiosity I had developed came later, only when Christian and I became romantically involved.

It is a curious space to occupy: wanting a child but only with a person we meet too late in life. I have come to accept that this is my reality. It doesn't make me sad, even though a part of me will always mourn the children Christian and I never had. I sometimes look in the faces of teenagers I cross paths with whose features could be a combination of our two faces and wonder: Would my daughter look like her? Would our son have been as tall as that boy?

Then we got a dog. He had floppy ears, and we named him Louis. "We have each other, you, me, and him," Christian said one day when I was crying over feeling frustrated at work, pointing to a bewildered-looking spaniel. "The three of us." I wiped a tear. "The two and a half of us, you mean." "Sure," Christian said. "We're a team."

Lights, Camera, Action

"THREE MINUTES!" my producer Laura McMillan said. She was holding not one, not two, but three phones to her (two) ears, something that made no sense, except that nothing was making any sense that night on the terrace of CNN's Paris bureau, a few crucial minutes before the announcement at 8:00 p.m. sharp of which two candidates had made it to the second round of France's presidential election. Producers are hardwired to handle stress. They count the number of seconds in a show. They interrupt regularly scheduled broadcasts with breaking news, speaking in a calm and measured voice to the anchor on set through an earpiece, aware that the smallest timing mistake could cause a disastrous domino effect, all the while making sure that no editorial errors slip through, ruining the reputation of the show, the credibility of their anchor, and their own careers. Good producers can take a punch. Occasionally, or rather once in a lifetime, a technical meltdown so great and so unusual happens that we cannot overcome it in time for the live show. On the night of April 23, 2017, in a series of unlikely events that I still don't understand to this day, my audio in Paris was not syncing with my mouth, and no one in Atlanta, where the control room was located at CNN Center, could understand why.

"COUNT TO TEN!" the control room ordered.

"TEN, NINE, EIGHT, SEVEN, HELLO, HELLO, I'M HALA GORANI IN PARIS," I said, tapping my microphone.

"COUNT AGAIN!" the director shrieked.

"ONE, TWO, THREE, FOUR," I counted, enunciating each word as if speaking like a kindergarten teacher would help solve the problem faster.

I tried to remain calm and not add my own anxieties to the complete collapse of our live output, but about ninety seconds before the top of the hour, seated on a stool with the Arc de Triomphe and the Champs-Élysées in the background, the city lights scintillating as they only do in Paris, I asked, "Are we gonna make it?" suddenly in a small voice I didn't recognize. "COUNT TO TEN AGAIN," the control room ordered me for what felt like the one hundredth time. "HELLO, HELLO, HELLO, HELLO, ONE, TWO, THREE, ONE, TWO, THREE," I repeated, sounding, at that point, like a madwoman. My mouth and voice were still out of sync. Laura looked at me with frustration I've never seen on a human being, the kind of look that combined desperation and what appeared to be a desire to physically assault whoever was responsible for putting her in this situation.

Missing the 8:00 p.m. announcement on Election Day in France is a capital crime: the entire country is watching, waiting for the faces of the two finalists to appear on their television screens. No one is late. Ever. It doesn't happen. But on that one Sunday night in April 2017, it almost did. A few minutes to the top of the hour, still unable to go out live from Paris in the lead-up to the announcement, an anchor in Atlanta had to take over for me. As I sat, helpless, on the Paris bureau terrace, someone in the US state of Georgia was about to tell the world which two candidates would face off in the second round of the presidential election.

"COUNT AGAIN!" I was told.

Behind the scenes, cameramen, engineers, producers, and production assistants were all trying to resolve the issue, which I still didn't understand.

"THIRTY-THREE, THIRTY-FOUR, THIRTY-FIVE!" I screeched. I had never counted that high for a sound check before. I looked down at the return screen to check the time: 7:58 p.m. Two more minutes.

"KEEP COUNTING!"

"FIFTY-TWO, FIFTY-THREE," I continued, breathless.

Suddenly, a glimmer of hope: "I think we're good. Are we good? I think we're good," Laura said, with only seconds to spare. Her features softened.

"We see you and we hear you," the control room director anchor in Atlanta told me in my earpiece. My voice and lips were synchronized again. I could take over from Paris, just in time to see the faces of the two finalists, Emmanuel Macron and Marine Le Pen, appear on the screen of our affiliate network in France. "You couldn't tell you had just had a heart attack," one of my colleagues messaged me.

That part of my job, the big moments, the technical difficulties only we are aware of, all the moving parts that somehow come together thanks to us; all of that is what gave me joy as an anchor. The third phone Laura was holding up to her face during the cataclysm that knocked us off air was eventually put away. Once on live television, we all breathed out again. There was a carousel of guests booked to join me on the terrace to comment on Marine Le Pen's Far Right's electoral successes in France and the brand-new party Emmanuel Macron had manage to create out of thin air. The young, not-even-forty-year-old political whiz had beaten the candidates representing the traditional parties to his left and to his right. He would eventually become president and later gain a majority in parliament.

I had covered every French presidential race since 2002, when Marine Le Pen's father, the Far Right, openly anti-immigrant leader

Jean-Marie Le Pen, had advanced to the second round of the election against Jacques Chirac, a center-right incumbent who personified the political mainstream. But in 2022, twenty years after I first hosted a French election special, CNN International decided to not send an anchor to Paris. The race, once again pitting Macron against Marine Le Pen, was covered with a couple of correspondents in the French capital and a presenter in London.

International news networks, for several years, had been losing ad revenue as new digital platforms emerged, eating away at their audiences. As a young anchor, I was one of a handful of presenters fronting prime-time news shows, but, in the span of a couple of decades, the linear television model was visibly flailing. Younger viewers sometimes didn't own televisions at all. Streaming made appointment viewing obsolete. International viewership was difficult to measure, as there were no ratings similar to the ones that measure audience levels in national and local markets. Even the CNN domestic network was having trouble increasing its ratings. Apart from breaking news stories like the Russian invasion of Ukraine, the chaotic US withdrawal from Afghanistan, or a big live event like Election Night, when viewers tune in en masse, it was often a struggle to keep viewership numbers up during regular programming. Although highly publicized ratings wars made it seem like cable news viewership was massive, these channels were, in fact, competing for a tiny slice of the viewing population. Prime-time shows on cable news channels barely registered more than a few hundred thousand viewers in the key, younger, demographic coveted by advertisers. Dayside programming registered even weaker ratings.

Established networks had built their business model around linear offerings, meaning programming that follows a traditional beginning, middle, and end structure, airing content in a way that is noninteractive. It assumes that people will watch a show chronologically and, ideally, in one sitting. Adapting to the digital world, where many people get their news from social media and apps, felt like retrofitting underfloor heating to a concrete basement. It required breaking long-established cable and satellite deals to stream fully; it meant creating a brand-new product, a sort of hybrid of digital, streaming, and live news. Cable news without the cable. News for the cell phone generation.

After a stint covering the Russian invasion of Ukraine in the spring of 2022 as both an anchor and correspondent, I headed back to the studio in London. I wondered whether a big, expensive production like our French election coverage would ever happen again. We had engineers and satellite trucks and two control rooms and three cameramen: the glorious business of live television. Over the previous decade, I had started noticing an increasing number of reporters filming live reports on their iPhones, streaming their shots on a dinky tripod, without anyone to produce or film the content. I worried that the fragmentation of the audience into a constellation of smaller viewership clusters would continue to affect international television coverage. I yearned to report on the US conventions again, which I had not been sent to do in 2020 for the first time in twenty years, or travel to present special shows on France, Syria, or Russia. As a result, I was spending more time at base and reporting in the field less often. I still loved anchoring, which demands a particular set of journalistic skills, especially during interviews and breaking news, but I yearned for more opportunities to report from the field. Without varied programming and capable anchors, a network's output can sometimes become a boring string of news reports without the necessary analysis and context. Part of what attracted me to the role, the ability to occasionally spend time experiencing a story from within, however, was gradually becoming a rare occurrence. I missed that part of my career.

I was in London during the 2022 French presidential election, exactly twenty years after I'd first anchored a live election night special from Paris. In September 2021, CNN International had decided to cover the German elections from London, a show I anchored from the network's new studios in the city's East End. It was an odd exercise and not one I found pleasant: talking to the correspondents in Berlin and experts elsewhere about the news in Germany from afar, in a studio with robotic cameras. From a sensory perspective, it felt like reporting while wearing a virtual reality headset: I could experience the story through video and audio on a screen, even though I was not physically there, but I could not touch or smell it. After our election coverage was over and Olaf Scholz's Social Democrats emerged from the German federal election race as the largest party in the Bundestag, signaling a big shift from Angela Merkel's sixteen-year chancellorship, I took public transportation back to my home in northwest London.

Anchoring in 2021, when COVID restrictions remained in place and most of the world was still working from home, was like an out-of-body experience. I commuted daily to an empty building where my producer, Laura, and I and a skeleton crew bounced around a deserted newsroom. It was so quiet that when someone made a coffee, the gurgle of the boiling water from the machine could be heard from several rows of desks away. The automated lights in the hallways, almost always off, would suddenly switch themselves on when someone walked by, as if spooked by an unexpected visitor. The cleaning staff were the loneliest I've ever seen anyone. They came to work every day for a total of twelve people on our floor, running after us every time we used the bathrooms to wipe down a doorknob or spray the counter after we were done washing our hands. Most of the time, they huddled in small groups, talking in hushed whispers, waiting for the next opportunity to pounce. I almost felt like apologizing that I wasn't making more of a mess.

Being an anchor had been such a large part of my identity that it took me some time to accept that not being *there* was a crucial missing piece; the *there* of the Egyptian revolution, the *there* of the French election, the US conventions, the Haiti earthquake, the Iraq invasion, and all the other stories that shaped who I became as a journalist. I had achieved so much in my career, anchoring shows from London, Atlanta, and Washington and fronting some of history's most defining stories on location, and something gradually started shifting within me, slowly in the beginning, but eventually occupying enough space in my consciousness that it was impossible to ignore. I needed to go to the important stories again and not just let stories come to me, in the lonely, air-conditioned bubble of a television studio.

When the COVID lockdowns eased in Britain and people started coming back into the office a few days a week, the excitement I thought I would feel did not materialize. It was a stint anchoring and reporting from Ukraine a few weeks after the Russian invasion in 2022 that served as a reminder of what had made me run back home the day I wrote my first wire copy at Agence France-Presse in 1992: the love, pure and sincere, of a story well told.

The Clock

My brother, Zaf, sent me a photo of Hikmat-Hanim's brass travel clock on the desk of his Washington home. "Broken pivot," he wrote, "one of the hardest repairs." The clock, still stopped at 3:06 p.m., stared back at me over WhatsApp. My mother, Nour, had given it to Zaf years earlier, and he had never bothered to have it repaired. The ornate timepiece from Berine Gorani's apartment in Aleppo, where it had lived in my grandfather's study since Hikmat-Hanim's death in 1961, had traveled from Istanbul in 1909 to Aleppo, to Paris, and, finally, to Washington, DC, was one of the only links Zaf and I had to our great-grandmother Hikmat-Hanim. I had hoped that my brother, who collects and writes about rare watches, would be able to fix it. We could reestablish a link to Aleppo and to our ancestors in Istanbul, I imagined, romantically. "The problem is that my watchmaker has retired and all he does now is smoke weed," Zaf wrote back.

A few days later, Zaf messaged me. "Technically, it ran," he captioned a video of the clock's hour and minute hands spinning, but at ultrahigh speed. "The part that slows it down is broken," he wrote. "It's got all the right parts, it just doesn't work. Kind of like the Middle East."

The clock's journey hadn't started in Istanbul. It was an unbranded brass travel timepiece manufactured somewhere in Europe in the nineteenth century, either in France or in England. It featured a white enamel face inscribed with roman numerals in an ornate golden case enhanced by flower carvings and flanked, on either side, by Doric columns. The aesthetic preferences of refined Ottomans in the latter half of the 1800s had very perceptibly shifted toward a European standard of taste. The ruling class, whose empire was flailing and losing huge chunks of territory in Europe, was keen to model itself after its dominant Western rivals. The empire pushed major reform initiatives of its administration and judicial system, and the sultan's architects built palaces like Dolmabahçe, inspired by the design aesthetics of French chateaux, with gilded ceilings and manicured gardens. Hikmat-Hanim's clock was one of many small items imported from Europe that reflected this new taste for European bibelots. It wasn't an expensive piece—there are thousands like it on the market even today—but it was by her side for most of her life; the first thing she saw in the morning and the last item she glanced at while lying in bed at night. She would have lifted it up from its small brass handle many times. After the death of her husband, Behjat Gorani, in 1916, Hikmat-Hanim took the travel clock with her to Istanbul on summer visits every year. Her excitement was such that she would pack many weeks before her trip, a long multiple-leg train journey back to the only city she considered to be her real home. Hikmat-Hanim would wind the carriage clock manually every twenty-four hours or so, so that it kept time, its hands marking every minute from the moment she returned to Aleppo from Istanbul to the exact time of her death in 1961.

In that sense, the clock that my brother held in his hands in Washington, DC, had come full circle. It had traveled from the west to the east and back to the west again, in a sort of loop across generations and continents, broken but still ticking, albeit too fast. It had shadowed my family's travels through the decades. It had remained with us throughout, following a path of displacement that mirrored our own, a mini-monument to the roads and highways we'd navigated, the trains and the planes we'd boarded—reluctantly or enthusiastically—a visual, tangible symbol of how far from home we had all ended up.

The Saturday Lunch

My mother's eldest sister, Neimat, Berine and Assad Gorani's first-born, has her Neuilly-sur-Seine apartment painted every two years so that the surface of each wall, in a precise tone of rich beige, is never discolored by the sun, and so that there is no opportunity for a crack or a chip to appear. The clothing in Aunt Neimat's closet is arranged by color and by season. All her hangers match. Winter outfits are covered in the summer, and summer dresses are carefully wrapped in the winter. Her taste for luxury and quality extends to the kitchen, where food is always prepared with the finest organic ingredients. Aunt Neimat is the most elegant woman I know. I'll confess to having benefited from the fact she has three sons and no daughters and would sometimes pass down a designer dress or piece of jewelry to me. A little something that had stopped fitting into her collection.

Every Saturday when she is in Paris, Aunt Neimat prepares a lunch to which cousins, nieces, nephews, and the occasional out-of-town guests are invited. Her late husband, Wassel, who died at ninety-five years old in 2015, shared Neimat's taste for the best ingredients and the most refined cuisine. Their cook, Saddiqa, a Lebanese woman who

301

works for several Levantine families in the Paris area, learned over the years the precise way in which Wassel and Neimat like their Syrian dishes prepared.

Food is not just food in the Middle East, particularly when served in the home. It's a reflection of culture, taste, sophistication, and even status. In Syria, especially in Aleppo, which is renowned for its cuisine, food is a multilayered mix of overlapping cultures. Kibbeh, the ground lamb meatball usually filled with pine nuts and bulgur, comes in an astonishing number of varieties, including one version stuffed with tangy cherries. The sweet-and-sour combination is due to the Armenian influence in the city, which saw a massive influx of Armenian immigrants and refugees in the decade following the 1915 genocide. There are also Ottoman influences, due to Aleppo's proximity to Turkey's southern border. Just as importantly, the land around Aleppo is known for how fertile and plentiful its crops are. This gives vegetables and fruit grown in the region a richness unique to that part of Syria. How you prepare a dish is, therefore, about the cook's identity as much as it is about taste. Kibbeh in Aleppo does not equal kibbeh in Damascus or Beirut. There are small but crucial differences in content, spice, and texture.

At Aunt Neimat's weekly Saturday lunches, there are always at least two main dishes—sometimes three—and a selection of accompanying sides. The salads—tabbouleh, fattoush, or endives with avocado and tomato—are presented in circular plates alongside at least two varieties of kibbeh. Kibbeh labanieh (meatballs in yogurt sauce) is a dish found in most of the Levant and is regularly served at Aunt Neimat's Saturday lunch. Distinctive Aleppo dishes like kibbeh sajeeyeh (so named because it is shaped like a *saj*, the concave cooking grill used to make Arabic bread) and kibbeh seeneeyah (meaning kibbeh cooked in a pan in the oven, served and cut from the serving dish directly) are often on the menu as well. The Saturday feast usually also involves lamb or chicken dishes with rice, pine nuts, and crispy onion with a side of garlic yogurt, followed by French cheeses and at least two desserts from Le Notre, a renowned Parisian boulangerie.

The Saturday lunch has been one of the only constants of my life; the closest to a base; a place where I know I will find family. Aunt Neimat has lived in the same apartment since the 1970s, when we first moved to France, and so her home is the one I've known the longest. I've lived in a dozen cities since, but it's in this small corner of a Paris suburb that I feel more at home. I am still close to Aunt Neimat's three sons: Nabil, who's my age and has moved to Peru; Mouss, who became an orthopedic surgeon and who one day made me sign a piece of paper acknowledging that he is God on earth (he kept it until we were well into our forties); and the eldest, Samer, who is now a dentist, the quietest of the three siblings. All are married with children. More distant cousins occasionally join the lunch, with their spouses and children, if they are passing through Paris from a trip abroad. The wider extended family, now scattered all around the world and growing as new generations come in, is less able to find time to come together as a group. Summer vacations used to be an opportunity for us all to unite, but my many cousins now have families and vacation plans of their own. In recent years, we've only crossed paths when there is a wedding or another event that brings the wider family together. Once again, the Goranis and their descendents have scattered, this time not through migration but as new generations have children of their own, taking us farther from the small group of immigrants who first came to Paris in the 1970s.

It's difficult to imagine a world without the Saturday lunch, but one day—hopefully not for many years—we will lose this gathering place. I'm not sure anyone from the younger generation will take Aunt Neimat's place. When that day comes, we will truly feel adrift.

BA Flight 217

LONDON HEATHROW TO WASHINGTON DULLES,
NOVEMBER 14, 2022

I don't know how other people experience religious conversions, or revelations, or divine suggestions to go one way rather than another when there is a fork in the road, but for me, it happened unexpectedly, on an airplane over the Atlantic, one random November Monday. For exactly ten years, since November 2012 when I experienced a panic attack on a flight from Atlanta to Berlin, I had suffered from an extreme form of fear of flying. Like many people with similar phobias, I often took antianxiety medication that I washed down with a glass of wine or two. I did not care in the slightest that this was not medically advisable, as it was the only way for me to get through turbulence on long-haul flights without experiencing an overwhelming fear of death by plane crash. "Take half a pill," my mother, Nour, who suffered from similarly debilitating panic attacks on planes, would often tell me before a trip. For years, Nour had her routine down to the minute, taking a pill about two hours before the flight and then, right before boarding, pulling out a mini bottle of whiskey from her handbag and drinking it in one swig. On a few occasions while traveling with my mother, I noticed some sideways glances from people who, I assumed, wondered if she had a tragic substance abuse problem. "HE IS VERY HANDSOME," she once said a bit too loudly as we were waiting to board, pointing at a middle-aged man standing by the ticket scanner. "DON'T YOU THINK?" she asked, insisting on the point as I tried to change the subject. My brother, Zaf, and I have endlessly joked about Nour's preflight rituals, especially since she ordinarily barely drinks alcohol at all.

On this particular flight to Washington, DC, I decided to experience turbulence without antianxiety medication. I had tablets with me in case I wasn't able to handle the stress and felt a panic attack coming, but planned on doing my best to avoid taking anything. When I spoke to a therapist about why I'd suddenly developed a fear of flying after traveling on airplanes for decades without any issues, he asked me what was different about November 2012. "What was happening in your life when you had that first panic attack?" he asked. "Nothing, really. I was happy, in fact. I had just started dating my future husband, and I was going to Berlin to meet him. I was happy. For the first time in a long time," I remember telling him. He jotted something down in a notebook. I went back to him a handful of times, but sitting across from a stranger whose job it is to analyze my phobias and anxieties didn't appeal to me. My next few flights were just as harrowing as the ones I had taken before, so I canceled my next session. Many years later, I realized that November 2012, the first time I felt secure in a relationship, was also the first time I felt like I had something precious to lose. I wondered if my fear of dying was a fear of losing what it had taken me my entire adult life to find: the love and respect of a man that I loved and respected back. I had told Christian early in our relationship that I wanted a life partner, something women are generally warned not to do. *Don't scare men off,* is the advice women hear throughout their lives. Younger women are, thankfully, starting to behave differently, but waiting for men to act is something women of previous generations have learned to do, even the most accomplished and independent among us. I was exasperated by that approach, which had brought me nothing but frustration and heartache. "If you don't want the same thing, I will accept it. But I won't wait for something that won't happen, either." Christian was not a demonstrative partner. He was a war cameraman who barely flinched when filming a getaway drive out of Tikrit in Iraq while insurgents sprayed the car he was riding in with bullets. The attack, during which his team's security detail shot back, was broadcast live on CNN. He once fell asleep in an armored personnel carrier while others around him were on high alert. He was quiet for a few seconds. "I want the same thing," he replied.

The day I flew to Washington in November 2022, when the plane started shaking, I closed my eyes and breathed through the turbulence, in the same way I breathe through the moment a needle enters my vein when blood is drawn while I watch the first drop appear until enough pull is applied to fill several vials. It's just a moment, after all, and soon, this moment will pass. It will become a memory. I was on my way to Missouri to visit our old house in Crestwood, and I was looking forward to the trip, so I tried to focus on the destination. One deep breath. And another.

If it's my time, it's my time, I thought. I was not sure why this particular thought occurred to me. Something lifted.

"If it's my time, it's my time," I repeated, this time in an imperceptible whisper.

My heart rate dropped. I let go of the armrests, my fists unclenching. I imagined the plane in midair, suspended to nothing, over the Atlantic Ocean where there is no chance of survival in case of a crash. Thoughts that would ordinarily terrify me, what-ifs that would send me into a nervous spin, this time hovered over me for an instant and quickly evaporated. The captain turned off the seat belt sign. I had experienced turbulence for the first time in ten years without any fear. After trying therapy, meditation apps, self-help books, and medication, the notion that I would give up control of what might happen to me on a plane was, in the end, the only thing that seemed to work. It must be what being religious feels like. I could certainly understand the appeal of letting go, of submitting to the will of a higher power. The "everything happens for a reason" approach to life shifts the burden of control from the individual onto something greater than we are: God or chance.

I had flown since birth, when Nour and Ficrat took my brother and me on a plane in 1970 from Seattle, where I was born, to Crestwood, Missouri. I was sent back and forth over the Atlantic dozens of times, alone, with a plastic document holder around my neck, after my parents divorced in the late 1970s. I had traveled in and out of war zones aboard jetliners and military aircraft, on helicopters and on propeller planes over disaster zones all without fear, imbued with a sense of mission and purpose. I wanted to go back to feeling this way. Intrepid.

My family story of migration and displacement had brought me here, delivered me into this moment, on this plane, BA flight 217, seat 14A: from Aleppo, to a mountain village in Abkhazia, to Dolmabahçe Palace in Istanbul, to the Beit Kbeer near the citadel, to London, to America and France and back in a multitude of ways and for a multitude of different reasons. All the while, my search for who I am and where I belong continues.

Perhaps this desire to never stop moving and to always search for a home is why journalism became my life's passion. Whether in a studio or on the road, transporting myself into the worlds and lives of others was the natural end point of the long road that many generations before me have walked, pushed into movement, forced into change. I will find a bit of myself in every story I tell, whether it is my own or someone else's.

Perhaps home, this entire time, was always the journey itself.

Select Bibliography

Bell, Gertrude. *The Desert and the Sown.* London: Heinemann, 1907.

Burns, Ross. *Aleppo: A History.* New York: Routledge, 2016.

Gorani, Assad. *Memoirs.* Beirut: Riad El Rayyes Books, 2000.

Hajjar, Abboud. "« Alep-Est » et « Alep-Ouest », territoires marqués par des divisions socio-économiques, puis espaces de guerre." *Les Cahiers d'EMAM* 30, 2018.

Mansel, Philip. *Aleppo: The Rise and Fall of Syria's Great Merchant City.* London: I. B. Tauris, 2016.

Mouradian, Khatchig. *The Resistance Network.* East Lansing: Michigan State University Press, 2021.

Rogan, Eugene. *The Fall of the Ottomans.* New York: Basic Books, 2015.

Watenpaugh, Keith David. *Being Modern in the Middle East.* Princeton, NJ: Princeton University Press, 2006.

Video/Images

Bundesarchiv. https://www.bundesarchiv.de.

"How Did the French Use a 'Divide and Rule' Policy in Their Mandate of Syria?" YouTube video, 2:30. Posted by Choices Program, August 10, 2021.

Institut National de l'Audiovisuel (INA). https://www.ina.fr/.

Acknowledgments

This book would not have been possible without the help, encouragement, and guidance of many people, some of whom may not even be aware of how much their generosity and time have meant to me.

First and foremost, I want to thank my wonderful husband, Christian Streib, for his unwavering love and support. He carefully read the book twice himself and then patiently listened to me read almost the entire manuscript to him out loud. I simply would not have been able to do this without him.

I want to express deep gratitude to my mother, Nour Gorani, whose side of the family I write about in this book and who provided invaluable help as I researched the history of our Gorani ancestors. Those who've read the book will know that entire chapters are based on her recollections and insights and could not have been written without her input.

My older brother, Zaf, was also a tremendous help, from recounting childhood memories in France and in the US to traveling with me to Missouri on a research trip. Thank you, as well, to my stepfather, Amr, who read an early draft of this memoir in one sitting, for his interest in my work. To Carmel, Gena, and Maya, thanks for cheering me on as I worked on this memoir. My father, Ficrat, his wife, Leigh, and my four wonderful half siblings, Alexandra, Gabriella, Zachary, and Dallas, have been an important source of support and encouragement.

I am also deeply indebted to my editor, Lauren Marino, and the team at Hachette Book Group for their support and professionalism. Lauren gave this first-time book writer a chance and the space and creative guidance to produce my best work. Thank you also to Niyati Patel and Fred Francis at Hachette for walking me through the publishing process.

To my agent, Jennifer Lyons, who has encouraged me from day one: thank you from the bottom of my heart. You gave me the confidence I needed to make this book a reality. To Fawaz Gerges, who told me when I hadn't written a word yet that he believed in my project, I will never forget your support during those early days.

Thank you, as well, to my extraordinarily caring friends for their support and feedback. Ryan Cooper, one of the best journalists and editors I know, always found time to look at my work, and his feedback was consistently invaluable. Dima Wannous, who read the very first version of the manuscript, was an immense source of confidence throughout the process. I am also extremely grateful to my dear friend Stephanie Halasz, who understood from reading a short essay I wrote previewing this book what this memoir was all about and, though she may not know it, helped me cross the finish line.

I want to acknowledge the wonderful women whose advice on how to navigate the publishing world helped me regain my footing when I felt insecure about working on such an ambitious project: Anushay Hossain, Clarissa Ward, and Lauren Collins, your tips and words of comfort helped me greatly.

To my rock star female journalism buddies and our awesome WhatsApp group: no one can fact-check Middle East history (or on occasion transliterate Arabic words to English) like Joyce Karam, Kim Ghattas, Deb Amos, Emma Beals, Laura Rozen, Liz Sly, and Louisa Loveluck.

To my former CNN colleagues Schams Elwazer, Laura McMillan, Mohammed Tawfeeq, Richard Quest, Anderson Cooper, Michael

Holmes, Chris Cuomo, Michael Ware, Jomana Karadsheh, Arwa Damon, Ingrid Formanek, Nick Paton Walsh, Ben Wedeman, Christiane Amanpour, and the many others whose stories are not all recounted in this memoir, it was a blast working with you. You made these crazy years of traveling the world reporting on the best and worst of humanity all worth it, and I'm so grateful that our paths crossed when they did.

So much of what we call *professional success* comes down to chance meetings and the kindness of people who make a call, write a recommendation letter, or simply pass on information at the right time. Among those who took a chance on me, I want to thank Jean-Louis Prevost, who helped me get my first internship at Agence France-Presse right out of college; Eithne Treanor, who told me about a job opening at CNN in London in 1998; Katherine Green, my onetime boss at CNN International in Atlanta, for sending me to cover some of the biggest news stories of my career; and David Lindsay, my *Inside the Middle East* executive producer, for his steadfast support and guidance during one of the most professionally fulfilling periods of my life as a journalist.

I want to also express my deepest gratitude to the men and women who have trusted me with their stories over the years, sometimes during the most difficult times of their lives. I think often of the people trying to survive in conflict zones or adrift in refugee camps, always with the sincere hope that they were able to find their way out and are now living peaceful lives.

Finally, I want to thank my wider family. My aunts, uncles, and cousins, as well as my dear departed grandparents, whose presence I felt throughout the writing of this book. Our family's story is unique, but it is universal. There is no family like it, yet in its reflection, many might find their own stories of displacement and their search for belonging. Thank you to the Goranis, the Ibrahim Bashas, the Katabis, the Sbais, and to my newest family, the Streibs. I will always feel at home when I am with you.